IMAGES
of America

WORTH

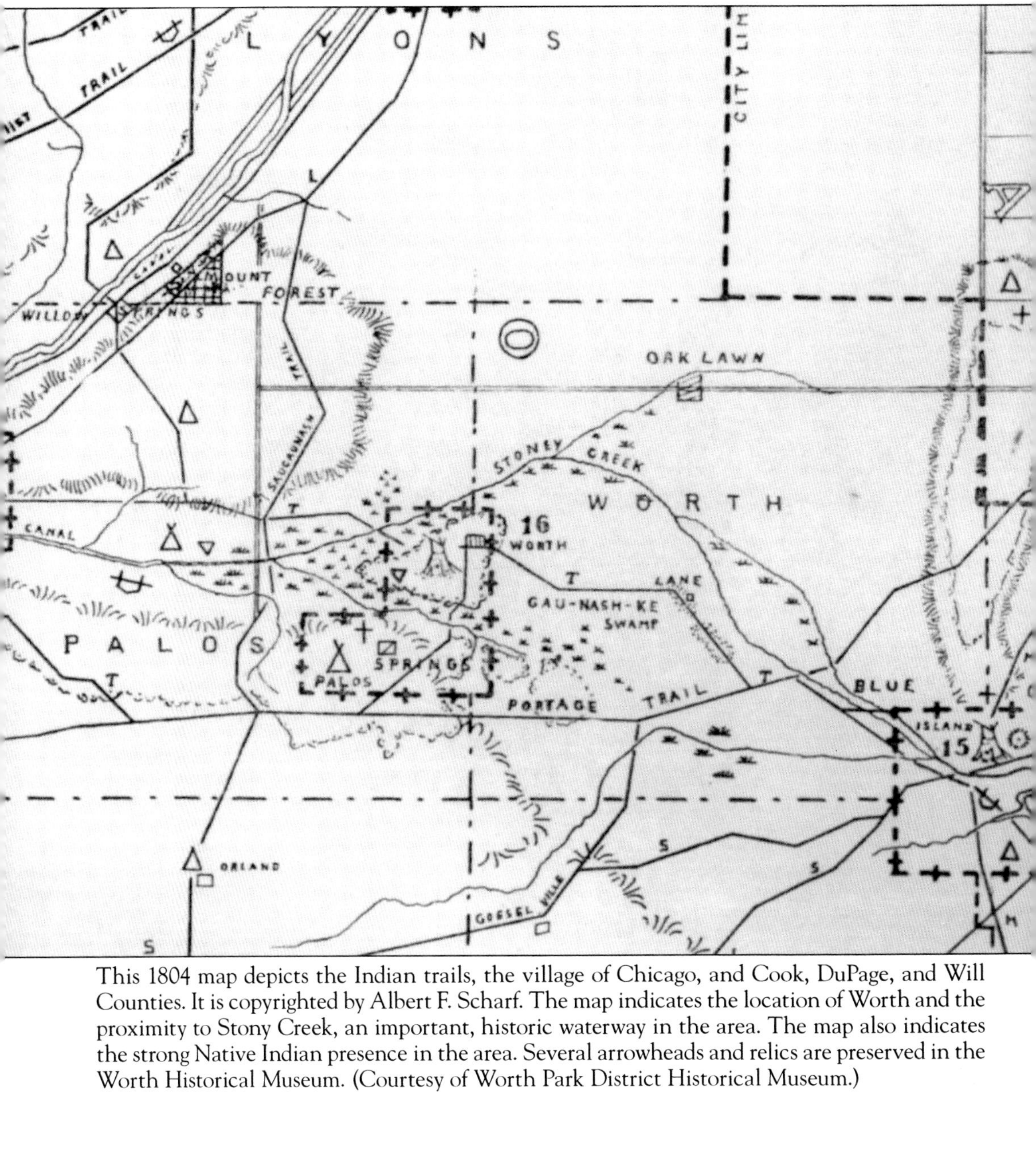

This 1804 map depicts the Indian trails, the village of Chicago, and Cook, DuPage, and Will Counties. It is copyrighted by Albert F. Scharf. The map indicates the location of Worth and the proximity to Stony Creek, an important, historic waterway in the area. The map also indicates the strong Native Indian presence in the area. Several arrowheads and relics are preserved in the Worth Historical Museum. (Courtesy of Worth Park District Historical Museum.)

On the Cover: Worthonians gather annually to celebrate Worth Day, or Worth Days as it is now called. This celebration happens at the end of summer to commemorate the early beginnings of the village of Worth. The annual parade moves west down 111th Street from Natchez Avenue to Harlem Avenue and includes many local social groups and businesses. Pictured here is the 1956 boys' Little League team riding in a decorated truck for the parade. The Little League team was started in town by Herb Stewart and Don "Lefty" Hanski. (Courtesy of Worth Park District Historical Museum.)

IMAGES
of America

WORTH

Colleen McElroy and the
Worth Park District Historical Museum

ARCADIA
PUBLISHING

ISBN 978-0-7385-9368-5

Published by Arcadia Publishing
Charleston, South Carolina

Printed in the United States of America

Library of Congress Control Number: 2011940629

For all general information, please contact Arcadia Publishing:
Telephone 843-853-2070
Fax 843-853-0044
E-mail sales@arcadiapublishing.com
For customer service and orders:
Toll-Free 1-888-313-2665

Visit us on the Internet at www.arcadiapublishing.com

This book is dedicated to the pioneers of Worth who have left a legacy of generations in "the Friendly Village," to those who are firmly planted, and to future residents who have yet to see why many have chosen to call Worth home.

Contents

ACKNOWLEDGMENTS

Since the dedication of the Worth Park District Historical Museum on April 23, 1995, countless numbers of residents have contributed their time, artifacts, and family stories to preserve the history of Worth. While it is impossible to name all the volunteers, it must be acknowledged that their love of local history and of the village of Worth made this collaboration of the history of Worth possible. The Worth Park District Historical Museum's archives, library, and photograph and artifact collections offer not only a look into the past of the village but also hold space for the future memories of Worth residents to come. With that, it is important to acknowledge the Worth Park District Board of Commissioners for providing the space and support to the museum throughout the years. By having the insight to provide valuable space proves their strong values in preserving the heritage of the village. Unless otherwise noted, all images appearing in this book belong to and are located at the Worth Park District Historical Museum.

Special thanks must be given to the families of Aggie Daniels, Chuck Templin, Dan Kumingo, Adele Benck, Helen Goy, Susan Lucas, Frank Homerding, Marvin Christensen, Tiina Russ, Christine Brooks, James Kennelly, John Schiera, Joyce Gallagher, Dave McNamara, and Elsie McNaughton; the members of the Worth Park District Historical Society; and the staff of the Worth Park District. Many thanks go to my forgiving editor, Jeff Ruetsche, and to my husband, Mike, and children, for without you I would not be where I am today.

INTRODUCTION

The tale of Worth is a journey that leads one from a Paleolithic time of underwater formations through mucky swampland to an island that became a booming town of the 1950s. Remnants of the stages of progression can still be seen in the town of Worth today. This book recalls the many civic-minded organizations and families that have shaped the community to become known as "the Friendly Village."

Nestled between ancient waterways and swamps, the geographical area of Worth has always been historically significant. Worth is bordered to the north by Stoney Creek, which is a 14,000-year-old waterway and known as the "Big Feeder." The southern border is the Calumet-Saganashkee (Cal-Sag) Channel, so called for the Calumet Saganashkee marsh that saturated the area. Cal-Sag was completed in 1922 and is an intricate part of the Illinois Waterway System.

The area underwent several name changes based on the state in which it was found by settlers. Home to Calumet Beach over 10,000 years ago, Worth was one of Lake Michigan's ancient beaches, rising 40 feet over the present-day lake. The area later became known as "Lane's Island" after one of Worth's first land purchasers, DeWitt Lane. Lane purchased land in the 1830s, as the land in modern-day "Worth" was being sold at government land sales and given away in federal land grants to veterans of the Indian Wars. One of the first recorded land purchases was made by John Blackstone, who purchased two 72-acre tracts located east of Harlem Avenue between 107th Street and 115th Street. Blackstone obtained each of the 72-acre parcels for $91.20 on June 26, 1835. In October of the same year, DeWitt Lane purchased two 72-acre tracts of land adjacent to Blackstone's property for $91.20 each. Not long after Blackstone had purchased the land, he quickly sold it to Lane for $250, as he had no intention of moving out of the Chicago area. Lane's property extended as far north as Stoney Creek to the Sag Swamp to the south, and the area became known as "Lane's Island." The high point of his property is located at the modern-day Worth Public Library along 111th Street. Although the government tried to spur settlement by offering land incentives, it was not until the late 1840s that the population began to grow. The building of the Illinois and Michigan (I&M) Canal and Calumet Feeder Canal increased population, and people began to take notice of the possibilities of life on the prairie.

Worth was home to the Kickapoo, Pottawatomie, Fox, and Sauk Indians prior to settlers in the 1850s. The last group to leave the area was the Pottawatomie in 1833 due to the Treaty of Chicago. Original homes in the area were not permanent structures, as the land was swampy and workers that first lived here followed the building of the I&M Canal. Canal construction spurred settlement more than the land incentives offered by the government, but it was not settled until 1858, when Worth's first permanent settlers John and Jane (McKenzie) Crandall came from Bremen in Tinley Park to build a home. The Crandalls decided to subdivide their land to encourage settlement and sold land to the Wabash Railroad in the 1880s to encourage commerce.

By the 1880s, Ed Bishop opened the first general store and post office in Worth. Locals could purchase everything from chewing tobacco to nails. It quickly became the center for menfolk to discuss politics, crops, and the weather around the infamous potbellied stove. Christian Rust opened the first blacksmith shop, and resident Wales Tobey donated land for the building of the Methodist Episcopal church. By 1883, there were approximately 100 people living in Worth. The Crandall family donated land for the construction of a new brick school, which still stands and is being used today.

Although progress was unmistakable, the Worth area remained a quiet farm community until the turn of the 20th century with the opening of the Worth Racetrack. The racetrack brought in new commerce; a hotel, which was opened by George Hildebrand; and other business opportunities that many saw as intrusive to the quaint charm of the town. In 1914, the federal government began construction of the Cal-Sag Channel to assist with the reversal of the flow of the Calumet River, just as the Chicago Sanitary Ship Canal did to preserve the cleanliness of the Chicago River. Workers would follow the construction of the canal, but many families chose to remain in the area. In order to meet the needs of some 300 residents by 1914, an organized system of government was created. On August 29, 1914, Harry P. Woods was voted president, and the newly elected officials planned streets, sidewalks, streetlights, and telephone service for the village. Dan Crandall, a descendant of the original Crandall family, was Worth's first police magistrate and was designated in 1921.

While the village was surely on its way to modernization, the real population growth was seen in the 1950s. After World War II, veterans made their way to suburbia, and over 900 homes were built between 1953 and 1954. According to a special assessment in 1956, the population went from 400 inhabitants in 1930 to close to 9,000 by 1960. It was during this time that many civic organizations began to form. The Lions Club, American Legion, Women's Forest Club, and Boy and Girl Scouts all saw their beginnings in the early 1950s. As the community saw the need to establish a central organization to handle recreation in the community, the Worth-Palos Park District was established by referendum in 1965. With this establishment came an organized system for residents to further the recreational needs of the residents. This book will explore the history of the spirit of camaraderie and teach the reader about the true spirit of the meaning behind Friendly Village.

Every day, thousands of travelers have contact with the legacy of the village of Worth as they pass it along the Interstate 294 tollway. Worth exclaims its pride of being "the Friendly Village" on its 135-foot-tall water tower. Worth has a history that extends before the settlement of Indians, explorers, farmers, entrepreneurs, veterans, and railroad men and still manages to live up to the motto inscribed on the tower. This book will attempt to explain the journey of this tiny village, nestled in the southwest suburb of Chicago. It will tell the story of the people, businesses, schools, and social organizations that have shaped this friendly community. As a curator, I have seen many walk through the doors of the museum excited to reminisce about growing up in a community where everyone knew something about everyone and where every family member had a hand in building the community. Many stories that are told are not of great importance as far as historical standards are concerned, but the minute details of everyday life are what make them important to the local history of Worth. They are the tales of the everyday activities and duties of citizens that are performed that have helped shape the community to what it is today. While it is impossible to report on every citizen that has shaped the history of the village of Worth in this publication, the museum has proudly preserved hundreds of newspaper articles and photographs that are available in the archives. I am honored to be a part of a community that cherishes its past and looks forward to the future.

One

The Island Village

Worth in the 1830s was not much different geographically than it is today. Despite major sewage improvements and advancements in infrastructure, the features of the land have remained the same. Originally called Lane's Island after DeWitt Lane purchased land from John Blackstone in the 1830s, this mucky swampy land was among the first inhabitable areas on the southwest side of Chicago. The Lane family settled near 116th Street and Cicero Avenue, which is modern-day Alsip. The name Worth Township was acquired in 1849 as the first post office was established in the area, yet the village of Worth was established in a general election held on August 29, 1914. The township of Worth extended from Eighty-seventh Street to the north, 135th Street to the south, Harlem Avenue to the west, and Torrence to the east. The namesake of the town originated from the US government. As areas were settled and the railroad came through small towns in the 1880s, post offices and train depots were named after famous Americans. Gen. William Jenkins Worth, the namesake, was a famous general. Like many of the pioneers that settled here, General Worth was known for his ability to maintain and achieve high standards and for his fierce bravery throughout challenging and unknown situations. This chapter introduces the early pioneers, like General Worth, who endured and survived the trials and tribulations of establishing a small town within arm's reach of a rapidly expanding city.

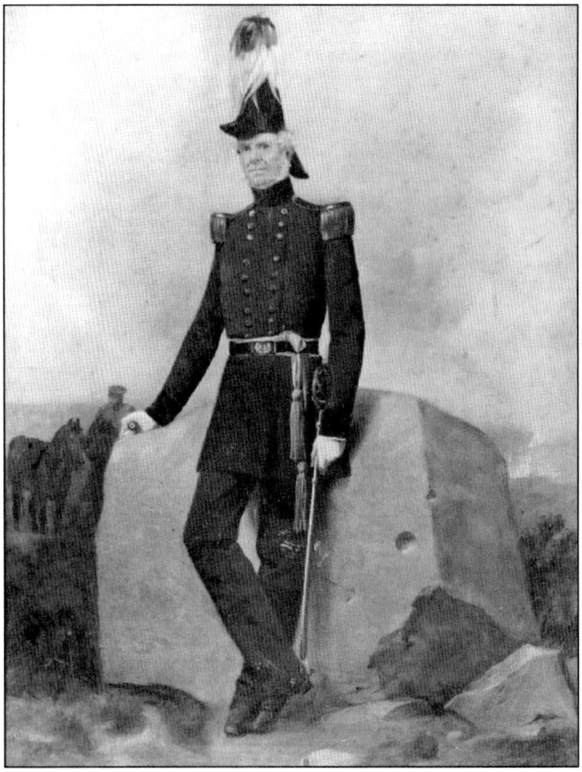

William Jenkins Worth was born in New York in 1794. He enlisted and fought in the War of 1812 and was an instructor at West Point, where he taught Robert E. Lee. He left West Point in 1820 and became a lieutenant colonel due to various achievements in the Black Hawk Wars. Worth acquired the rank of colonel by 1840 and, after a long and costly war in Florida against the Seminoles, was given the title of brigadier general by President Tyler. Due to his successful campaign in the war against Mexico, he was titled major general by 1847. General Worth died in 1847 of cholera and is buried in New York City. It is interesting to note that General Worth never set foot in Worth Township or the village of Worth. (Courtesy of the Chicago Historical Society.)

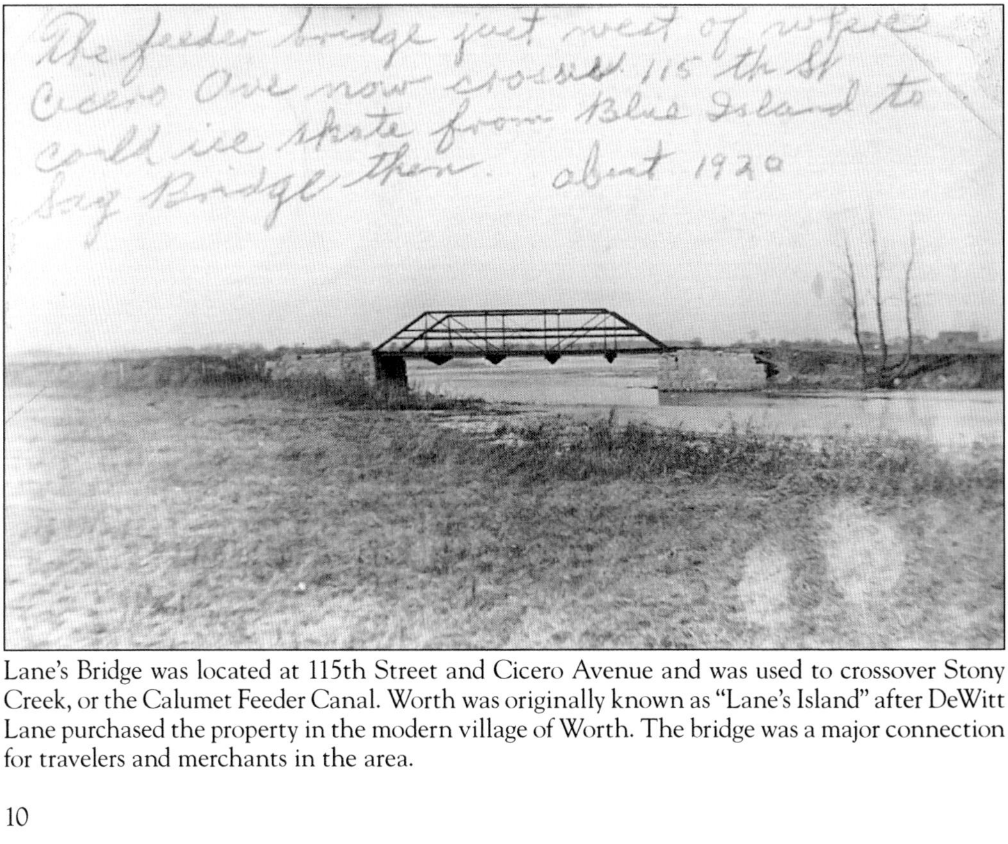

Lane's Bridge was located at 115th Street and Cicero Avenue and was used to crossover Stony Creek, or the Calumet Feeder Canal. Worth was originally known as "Lane's Island" after DeWitt Lane purchased the property in the modern village of Worth. The bridge was a major connection for travelers and merchants in the area.

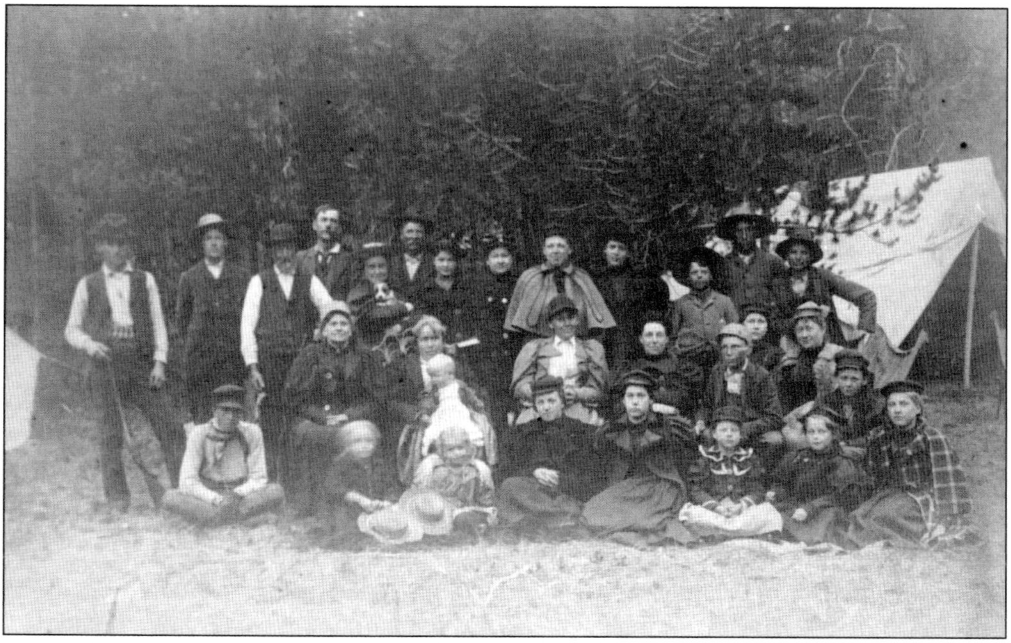

Although some new settlers came to Lane's Island as they followed the construction of the Illinois and Michigan Canal, continuing financial troubles created work lapses. These lapses caused fluctuation in area land sales. Seen here are some of the first temporary settlers, who lived along the banks of Stoney Creek. I&M construction lasted from 1836 to 1848.

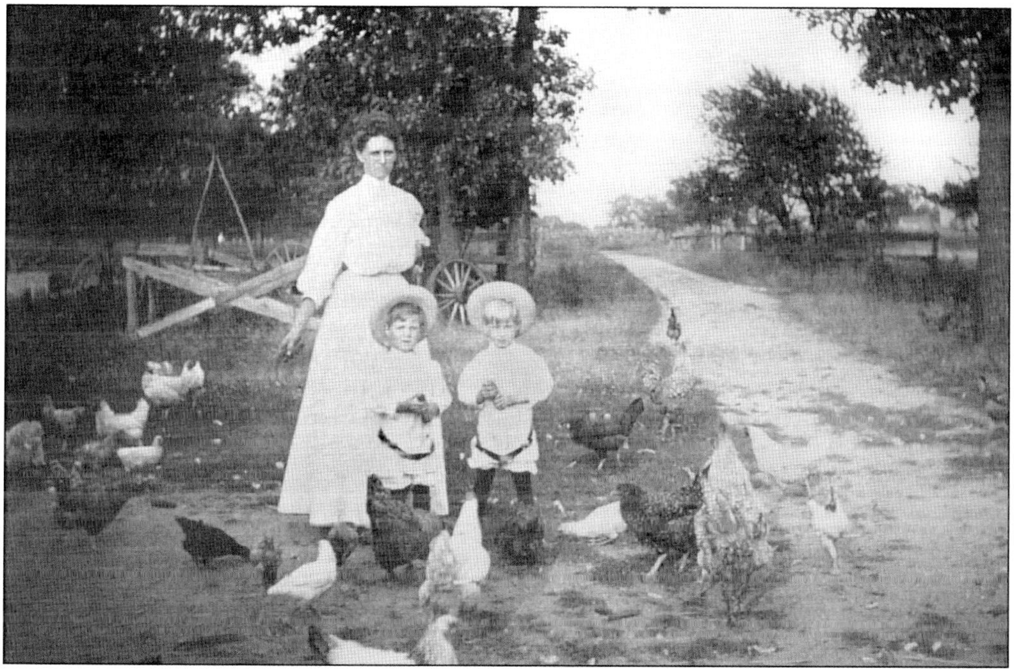

The Bidenkopf family moved to Worth in 1873. Clara Bidenkopf Rolfe is seen here with her twin sons Edwin and Erwin in 1902. Clara's husband, Benjamin, was a trustee on the first village board. Her son Edwin became the mayor of Worth from 1941 to 1943 until he was called to serve in the Army during World War II.

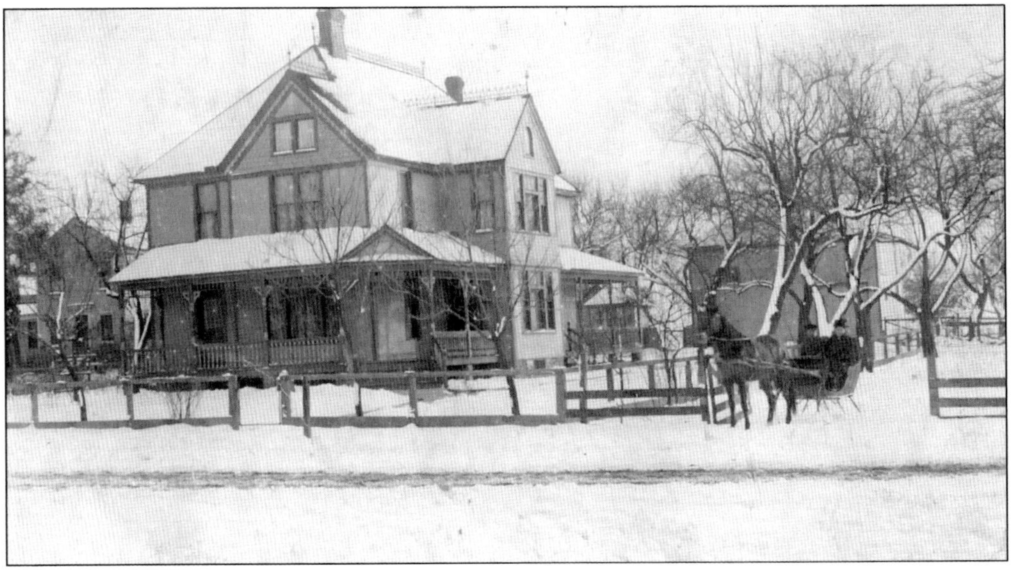

During the 1870s, Worth expanded rapidly as increasing numbers of settlers came to farm the fertile land. The Bidenkopf family came to the community in 1893. Pictured here are their orchard and home, located along 111th Street. Benjamin Bidenkopf purchased land for $19 an acre. He was the first veterinarian in the area.

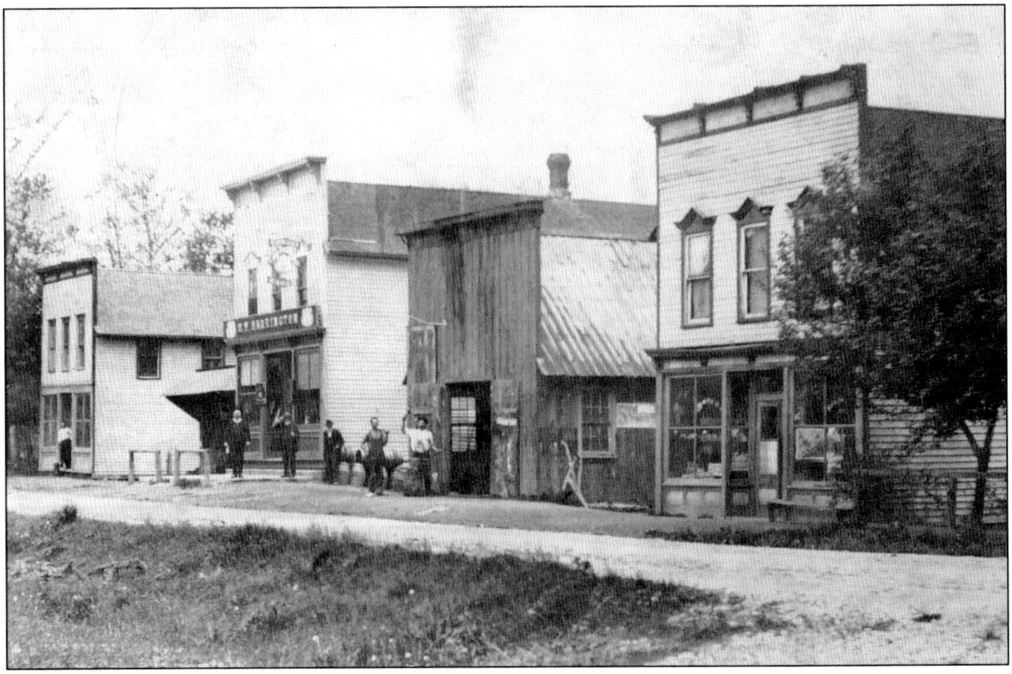

The commercial center of the community was on 111th Street and boasted a tavern, general store, and Christian Rust's blacksmith shop. The area to the east and north was little more than prairie and marshland as well as a hunting ground. Hitching racks can be seen in front of Harrington's Tavern, the second building from the left.

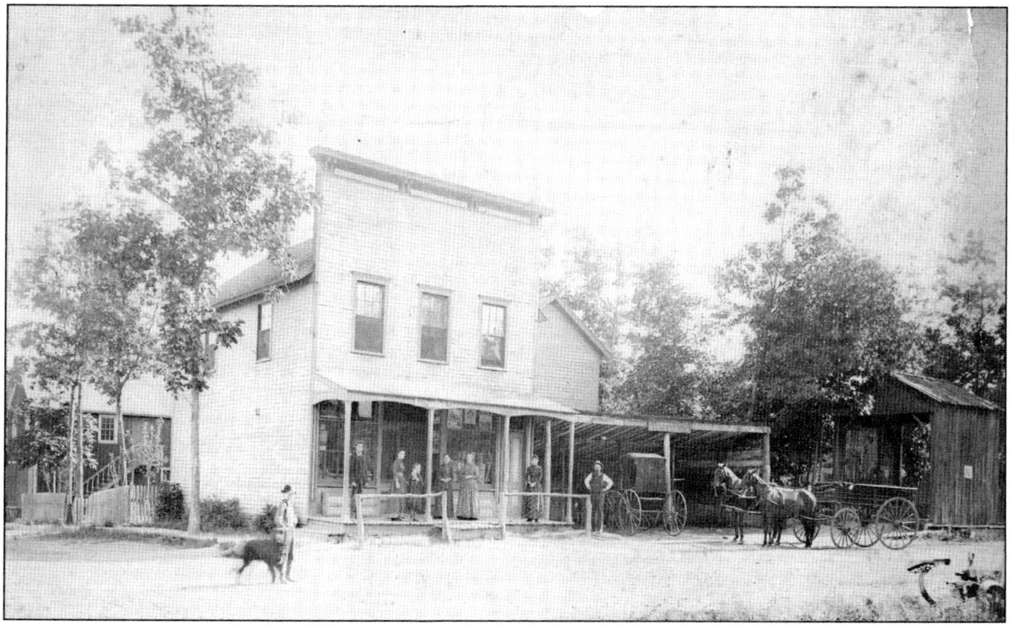

Edward P. Bishop built the first general store in the community in 1881. It was located at the northeast corner of 111th Street and Depot Avenue. Members of the Bishop family pictured here are, from left to right, Perry, Carl, Ida, Ethel, Lizzie, Elizabeth, Minnie, and Edward. Edward sold his Alsip farm to the Alsip Brick Company and moved to Worth as he saw the economic opportunity that the railroad brought to the area. He became the first postmaster in 1883 as well as the first justice of the peace. (Courtesy of Chuck Templin.)

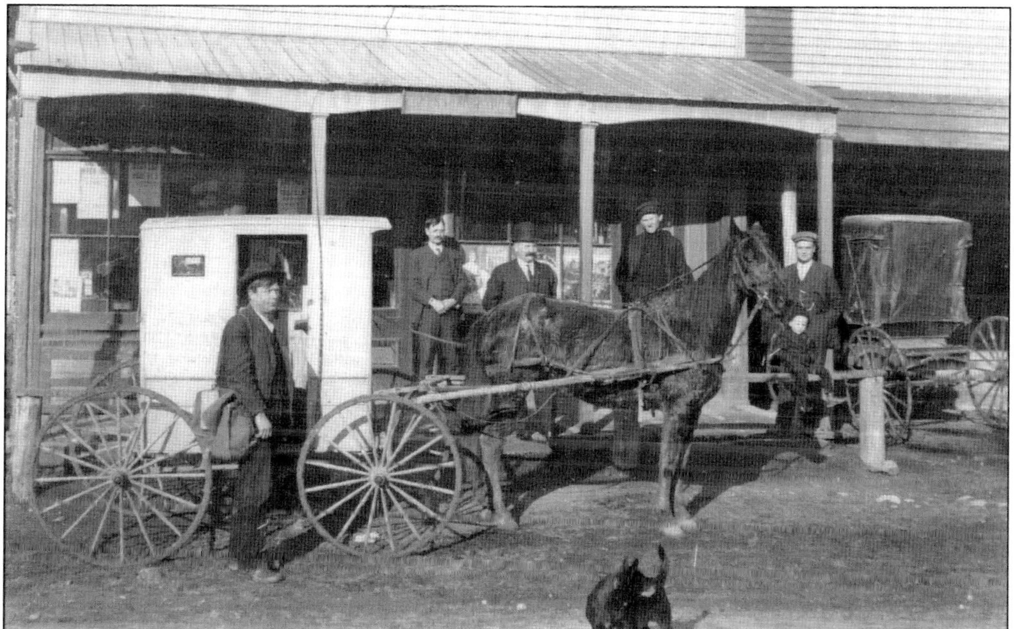

Shown about 1889, locals would congregate on the porch of Bishop's store and discuss the weather, crops, and activities around town. In this case, they were waiting for the mail to arrive from local carrier Louis Auburn. Henry Benck is standing on the porch, second from the right.

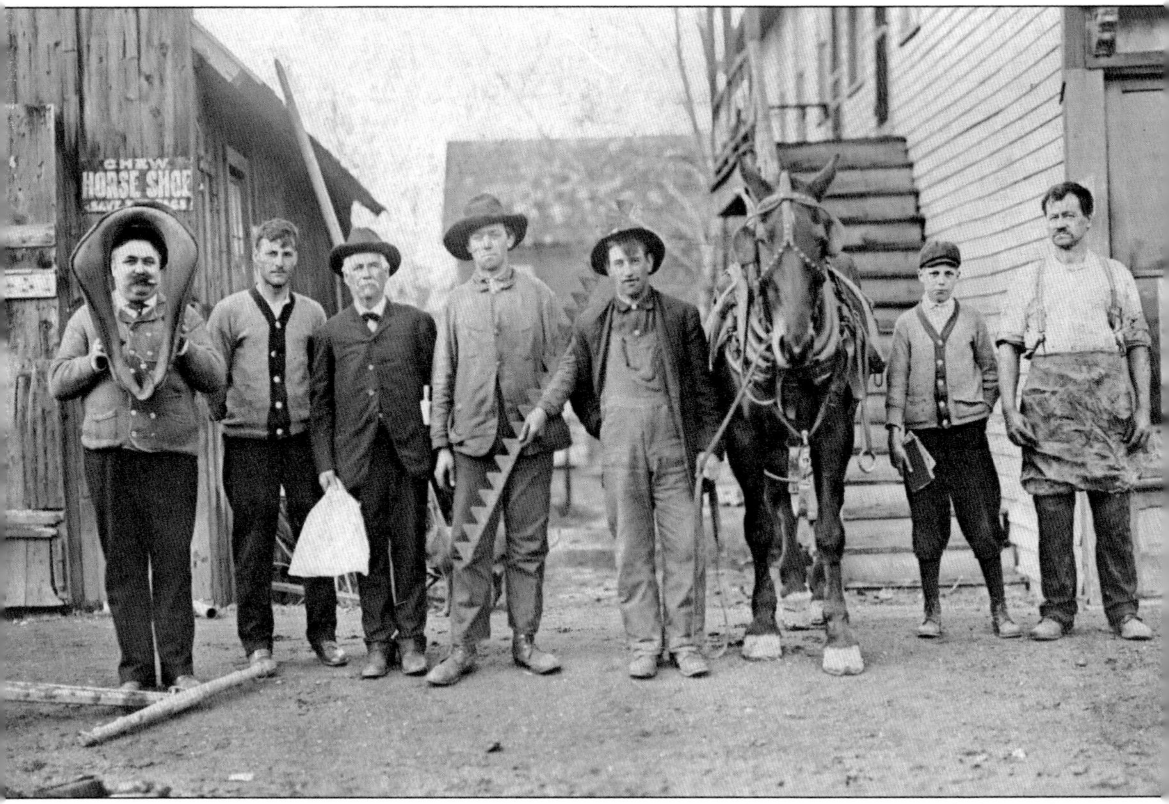

Pictured here are friendly villagers and local shop owners in the late 1880s. From left to right are H.W. Harrington, who operated a tavern at 7010 West 111th Street; medical school student Edward Rust; Michael McMann; an unidentified farmer; Mike Poorman; Alvin Dart; and Christian Rust, who owned the blacksmith shop seen at the left of the photograph. Rust became one of the first trustees in the village of Worth.

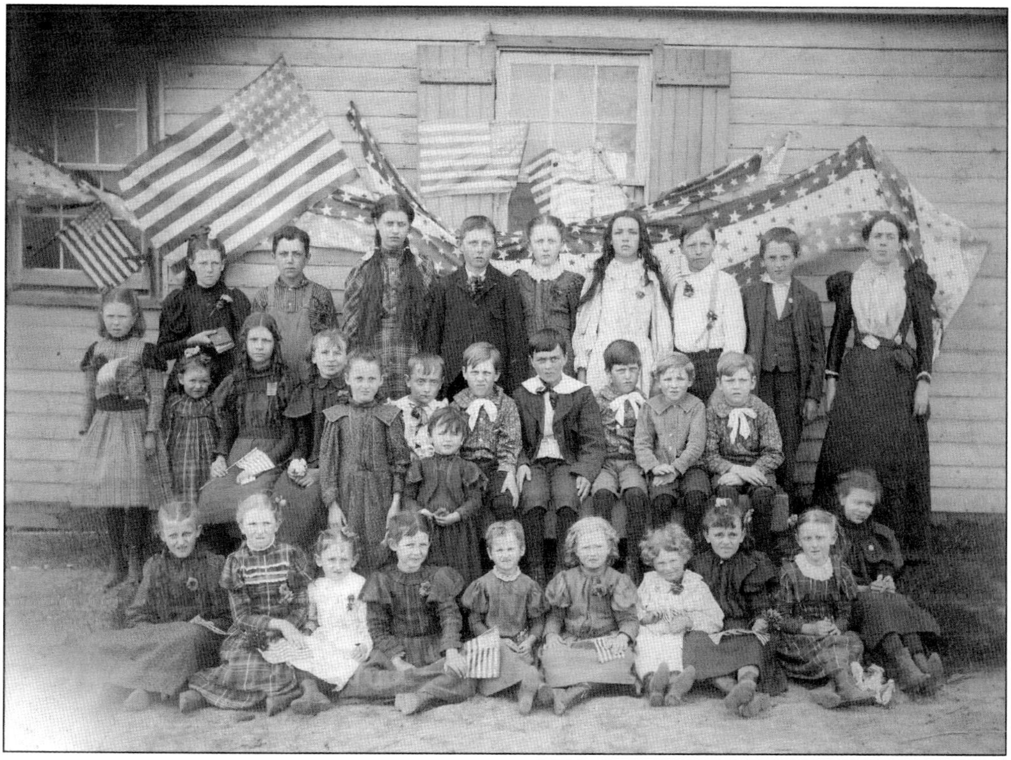

Showing their patriotism, 29 students proudly display their flags for a school photograph, taken around 1865. Worth Township sent over 250 men to the Civil War. This one-room, wood-frame schoolhouse served families in Worth and Palos Township. This school, known in early records as Lane School, was used as a recruiting station during the Civil War.

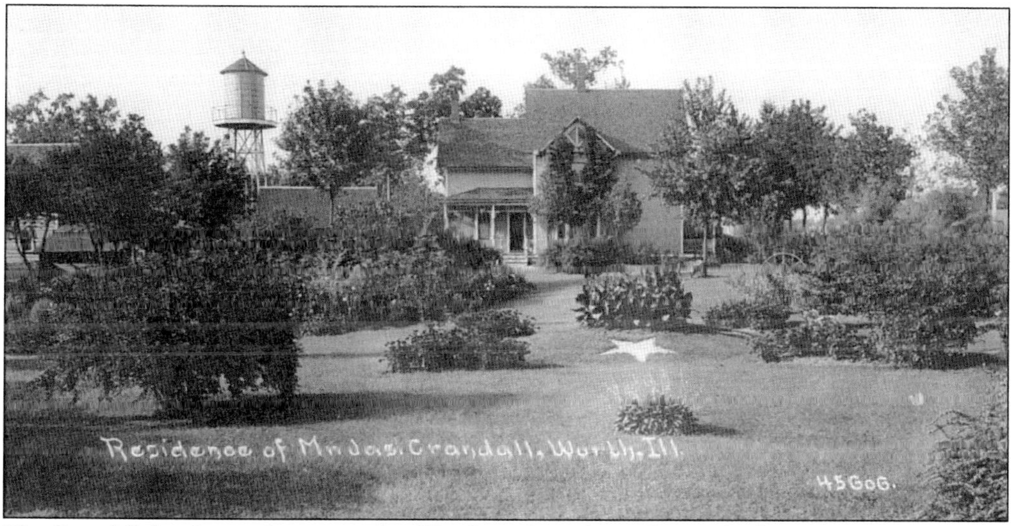

The Crandall family members arrived in Worth in the 1850s and were the first permanent residents. The property seen in this photograph was located at 6917 West 111th Street. They donated a portion of their land to the school district for the construction of a brick schoolhouse. Students were often caught picking Jane Crandall's prized roses and apples from her yard and presenting them to their teacher.

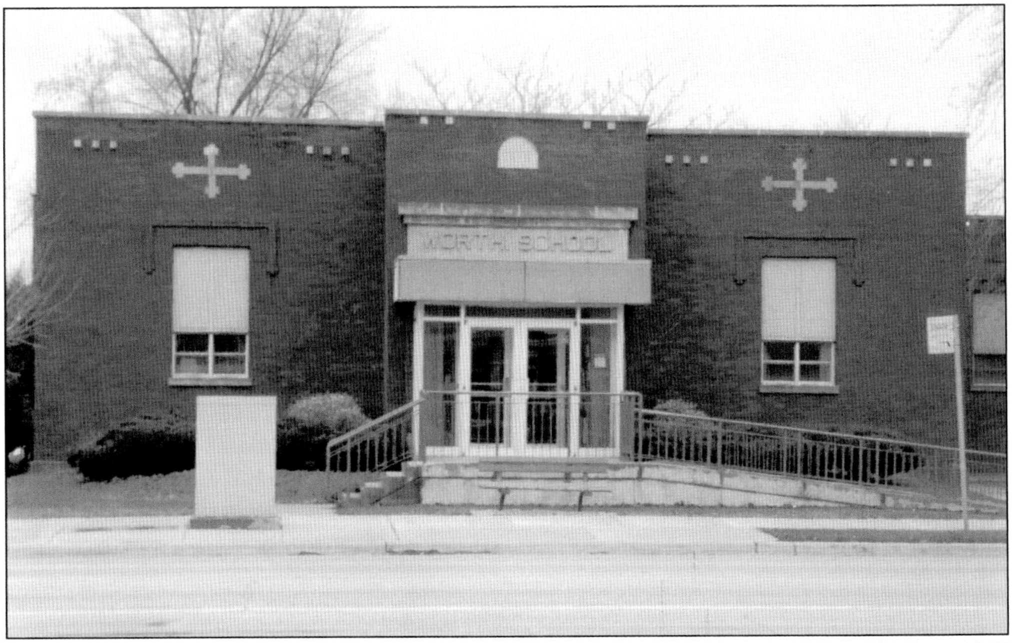

The brick schoolhouse seen here was the first two-room school in the area. It was built in 1915 and is still used as a portion of the Worth Elementary School. Several additions were added on in the 1940s, 1950s, and 1960s due to a population surge.

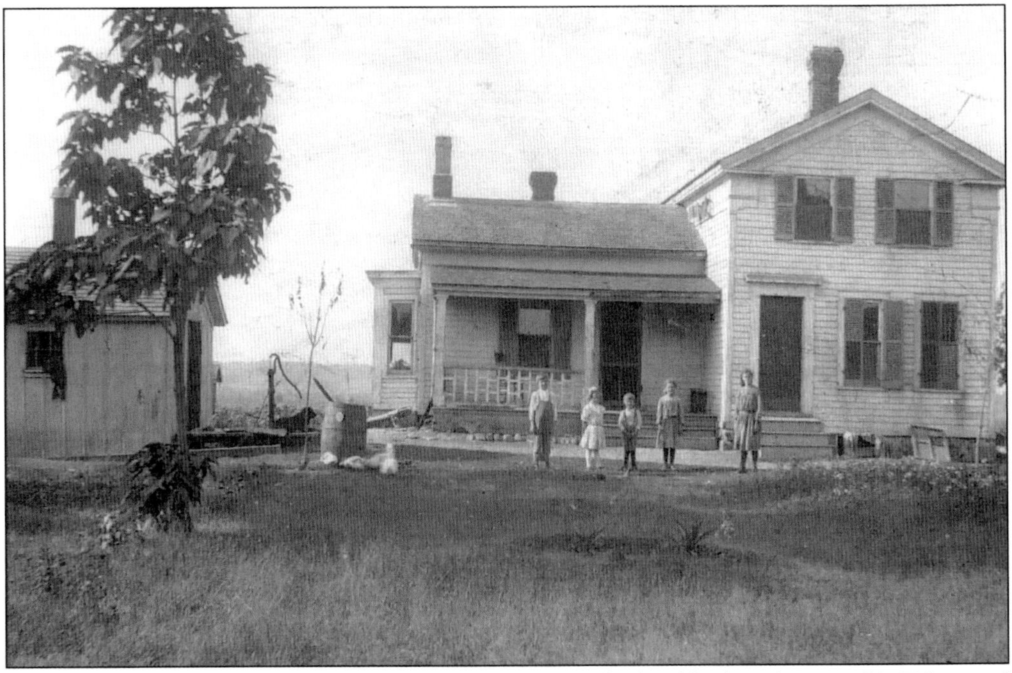

In 1874, Wales Tobey and his wife, Elizabeth, improved the land he bought in 1856. Tobey and family planted crops and constructed a farmhouse on their land, which was east of Harlem Avenue from 113th Street to the canal. This home is located at 7011 West 113th Street. Wales Tobey is remembered by the village for contributing land on 111th Street to the Methodist church in 1883. Son Clifford became Worth's postmaster.

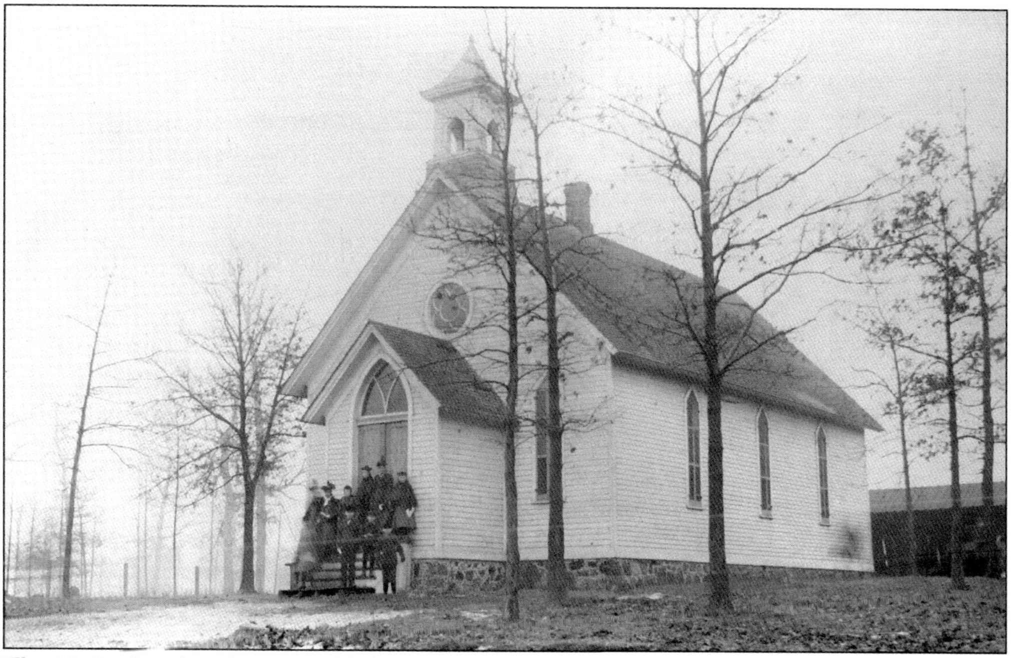

The Methodist church was established in October 1883 on land donated by the Tobey family. Pictured here are the Tobey, Crandall, Hildebrand, Bishop, and Ruth families. All were instrumental in providing financial and spiritual support. In 1946, the church was damaged by a fire and rebuilt at 113th Street and Depot Avenue.

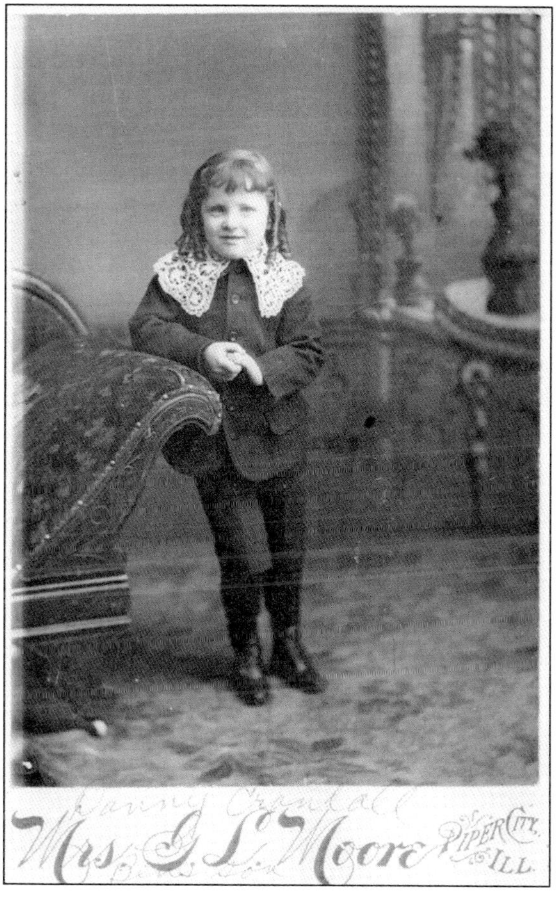

The Crandall family members were the first permanent settlers to live in the Worth area. Pictured here is Danny Crandall, son of Ben Crandall. Danny lived a hardworking life on the range and in hard labor in the cattle industry but returned to Worth in the early 1900s. Danny became Worth's first police chief in 1921.

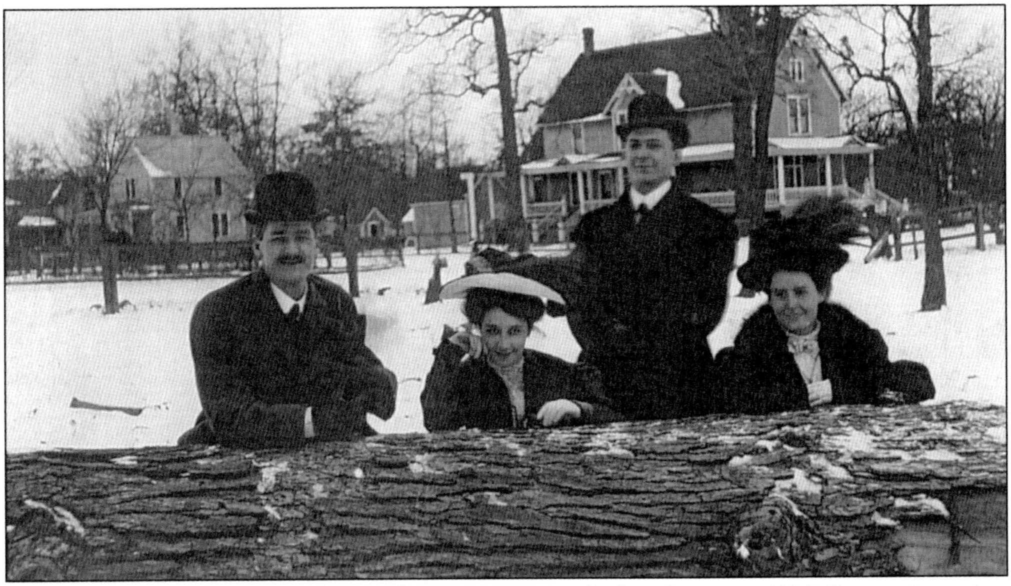

Members of the Crandall family pose for a portrait outside their home on 111th Street. A portion of their land was donated to the government to allow for the Wabash train station to be built. Pictured are, from left to right, Albert and Dollie Crandall and Lindon and Mabel Perry.

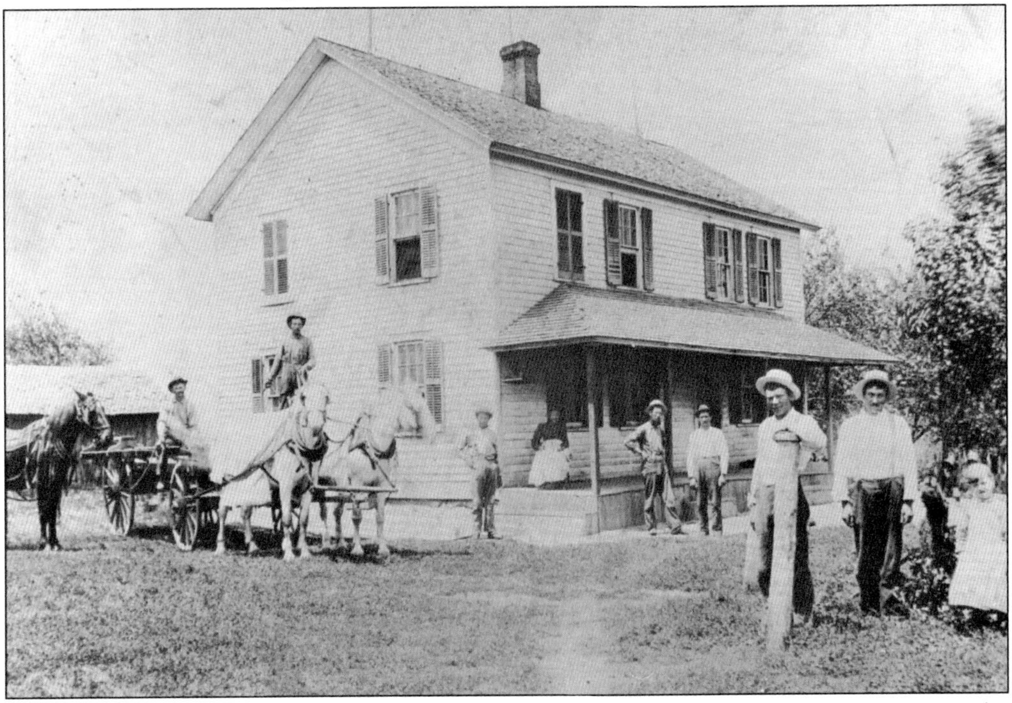

This is the home of John and Mary Leipstorff. The Leipstorffs emigrated from Germany in the 1850s. John worked for Cap McClaugry, operating a barge bulled by mules along the Calumet Feeder Canal, also known as Stoney Creek. He hauled supplies between the Sag and Blue Island. John bought the land between Harlem and Oak Park Avenues and 107th and 109th Streets from Wales Tobey on December 30, 1868. John and Mary worked the land and raised seven children. Their son Henry became Worth's first rural mail carrier.

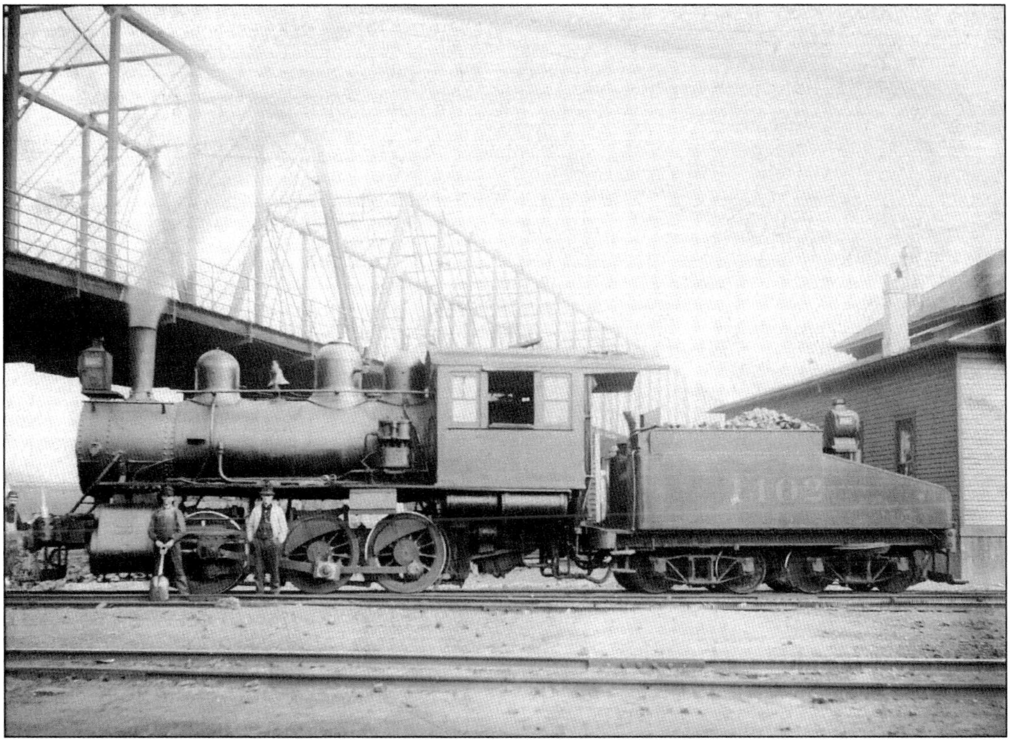

New Commerce came to Worth along with the Wabash Railroad Station in 1880. The railroad also marked the beginning of a new era in Worth, allowing men to come and go out of town for work. Markets and mail soon came to town. Many astute businessmen recognized the opportunities the railroad offered the settlement and established services in the vicinity of the railroad station. The government opened the first Worth Post Office in the station, which was later moved to the Bishop General Store. This home is located on 110th Street in Worth and was used as the first railroad and post office. Tickets were sold out of the front window. It is because of this establishment that Lane's Island became known as "Worth Crossing," as it was at the crossroads of Worth and Palos Township.

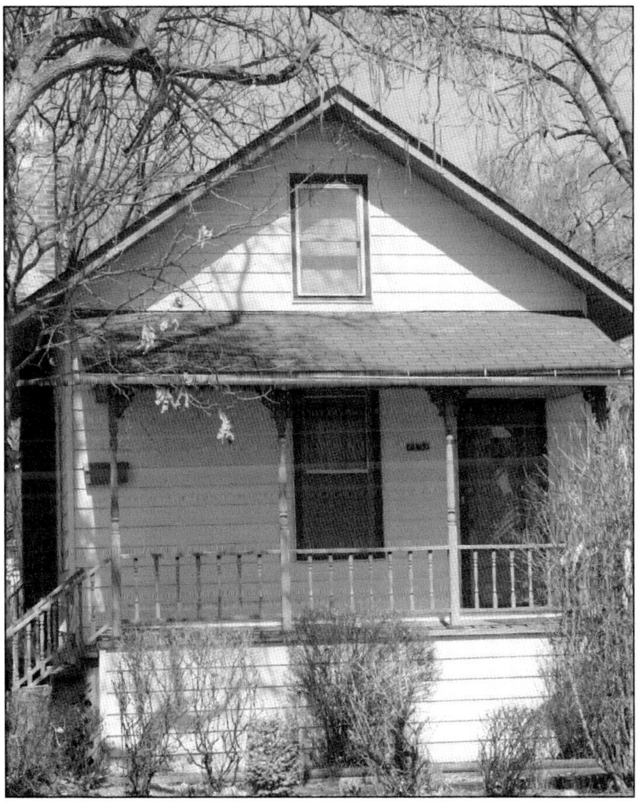

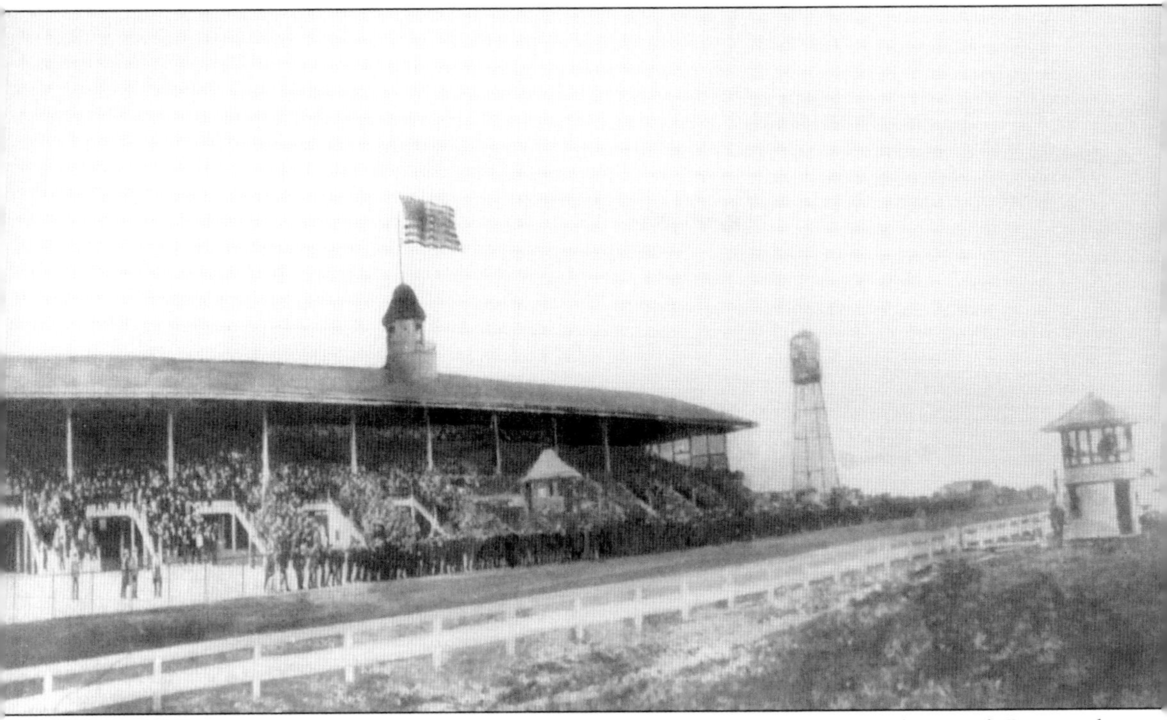

Worth remained a quiet farm community until the turn of the 20th century. The Worth Racetrack opened in 1900, and the Illinois State Gaming Board closed it in 1905. It was built between Ridgeland and Central Avenues and drew folks from miles around. Racing enthusiasts would arrive via the Wabash Railroad to partake in the activities. The property was used as a training ground for the Illinois home front during World War I and then sold and turned into Holy Sepulcher Cemetery. (Courtesy of Maurice Moore.)

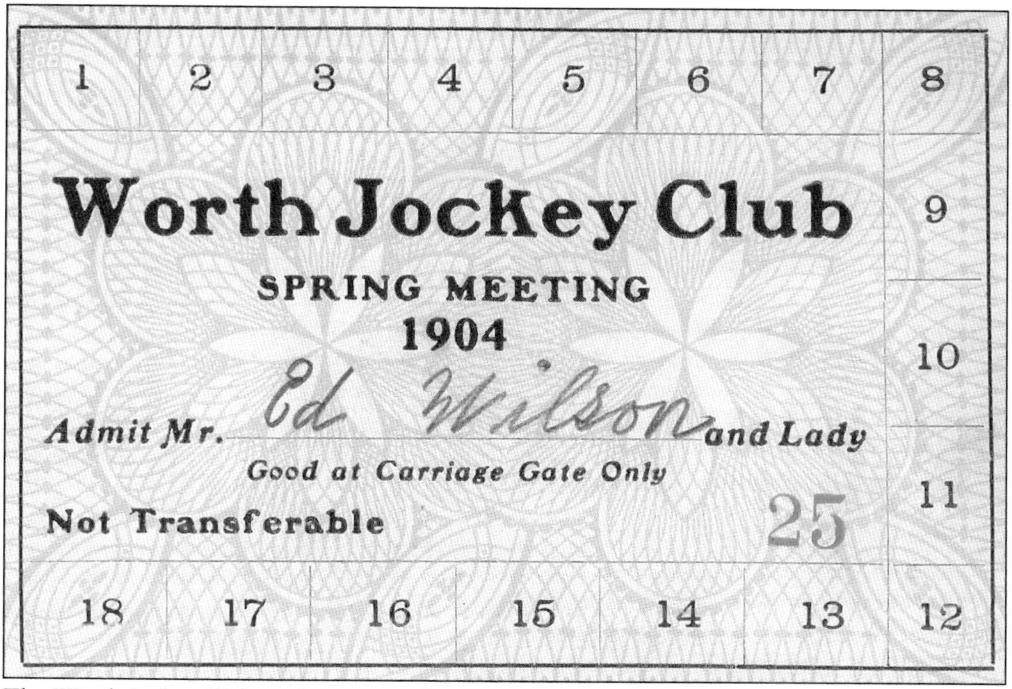

1 2 3 4 5 6 7 8

Worth Jockey Club

9

SPRING MEETING
1904

10

Admit Mr. Ed Wilson *and Lady*

Good at Carriage Gate Only

11

Not Transferable 25

18 17 16 15 14 13 12

The Worth Jockey Club card was owned by member and resident Edward Wilson of Worth. Card club members had their own special entrance and were given deals once inside the racetrack. Edward Wilson was a township road commissioner and collector in the early days of South Cook County. Edward Wilson, seen in the photograph at right at the turn of the 20th century, came to Worth in 1863. He was a successful auctioneer, township road commissioner, and collector. His brother Robert J. Wilson was a member of the first village board in Worth.

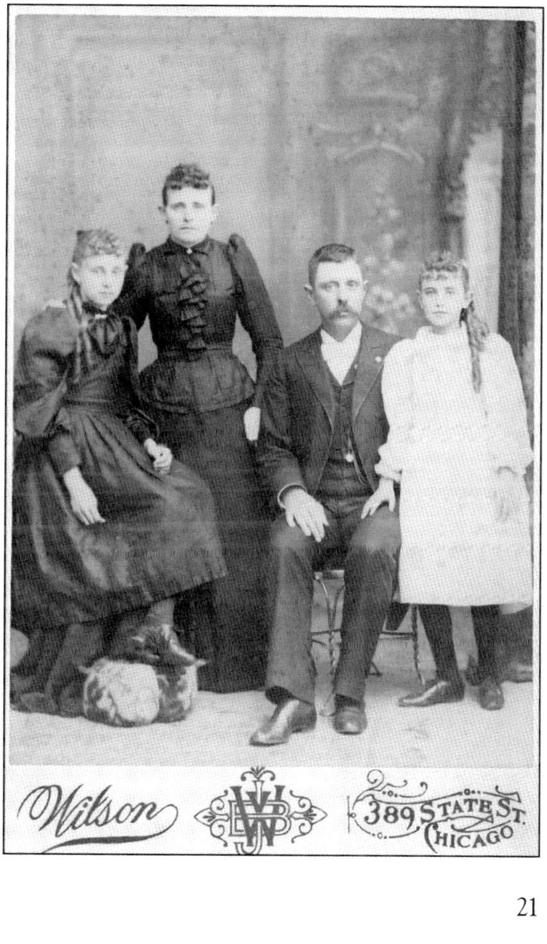

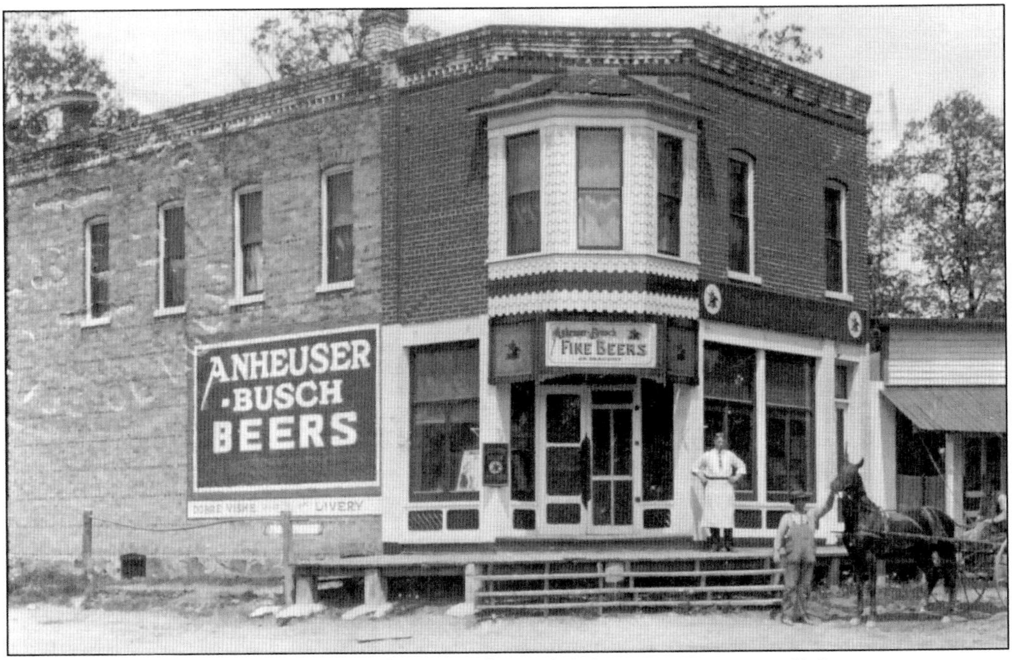

As the population grew and changed in Worth, so did the entertainment. Saloons, restaurants, and even a hotel popped up along 111th Street. This building sat at the corner of 111th Street and Depot Avenue and was a saloon and hotel. Fred Hildebrand and his wife, Emma, lived in a sister building two blocks away but managed this hotel. Rooms were rented to jockeys, trainers, and transient workers when the racetrack was operational. When the hotel closed, the building was used as a general store and contained a dance hall, which was where the first village board would meet.

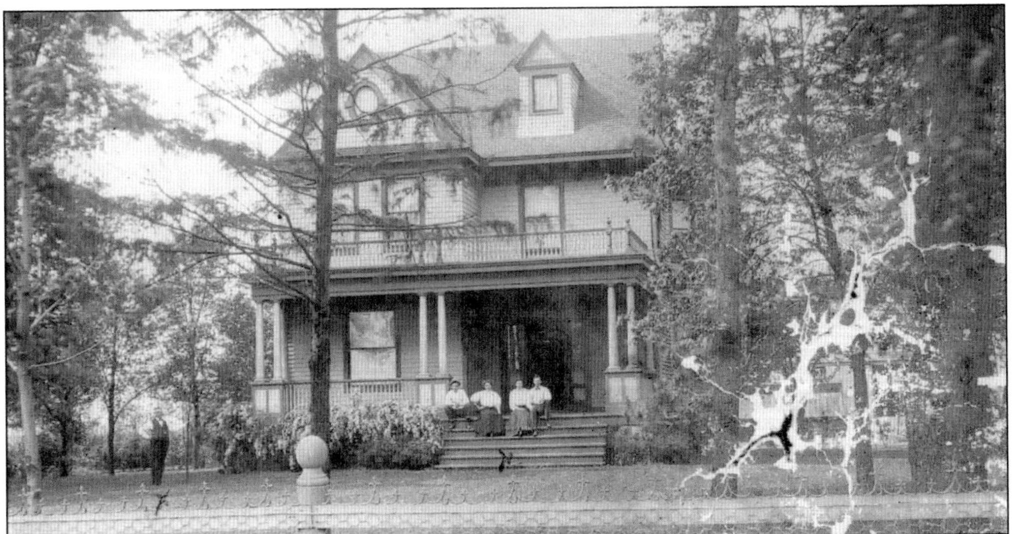

Henry Stuckert was the treasurer for the City of Chicago at the time of the opening of the racetrack. The Stuckert family had a home on the north side of 111th Street and Ridgeland Avenue in close proximity of the racetrack. Pictured are, from left to right, Henry Stuckert, Henry Streinreuter, Viola Stuckert Streinreuter, and twin sister Elsie Stuckert Tobey with husband Clifford Tobey. Cliff Tobey was postmaster of Worth for 27 years.

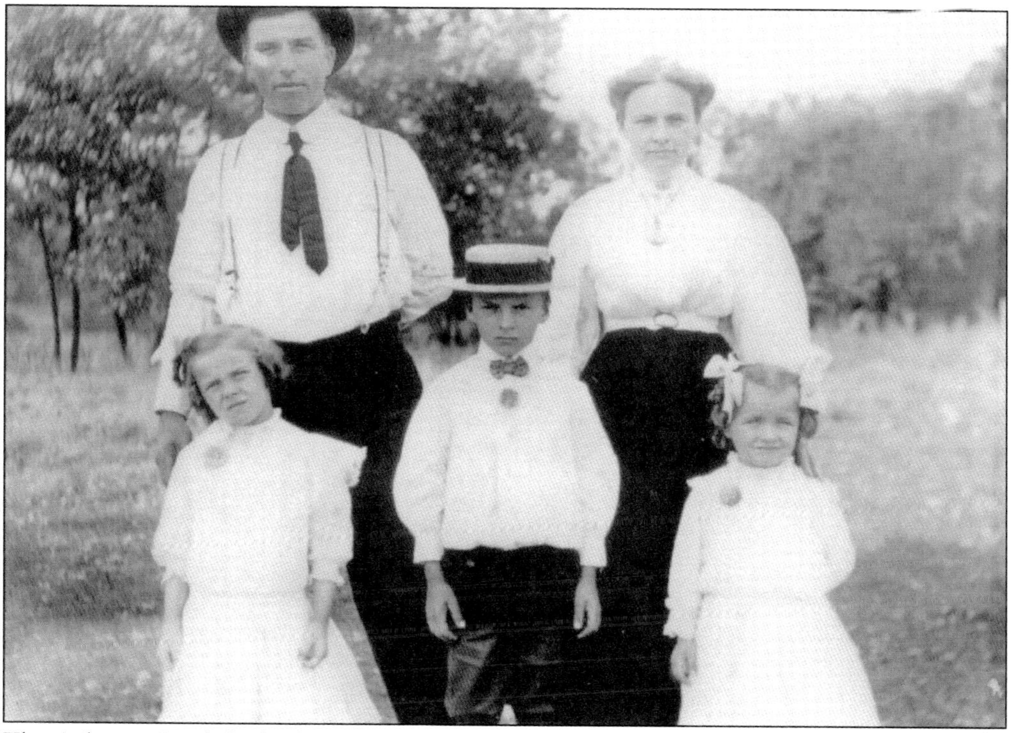

The Aubourn family had a farm located at 111th Street and Ridgeland Avenue. Louis Aubourn was the first rural carrier in the area. The Aubourn home was seen as the western gateway to this small town. When the racetrack came in to town, it was not uncommon for families to take in boarders and rent out farm space for horses.

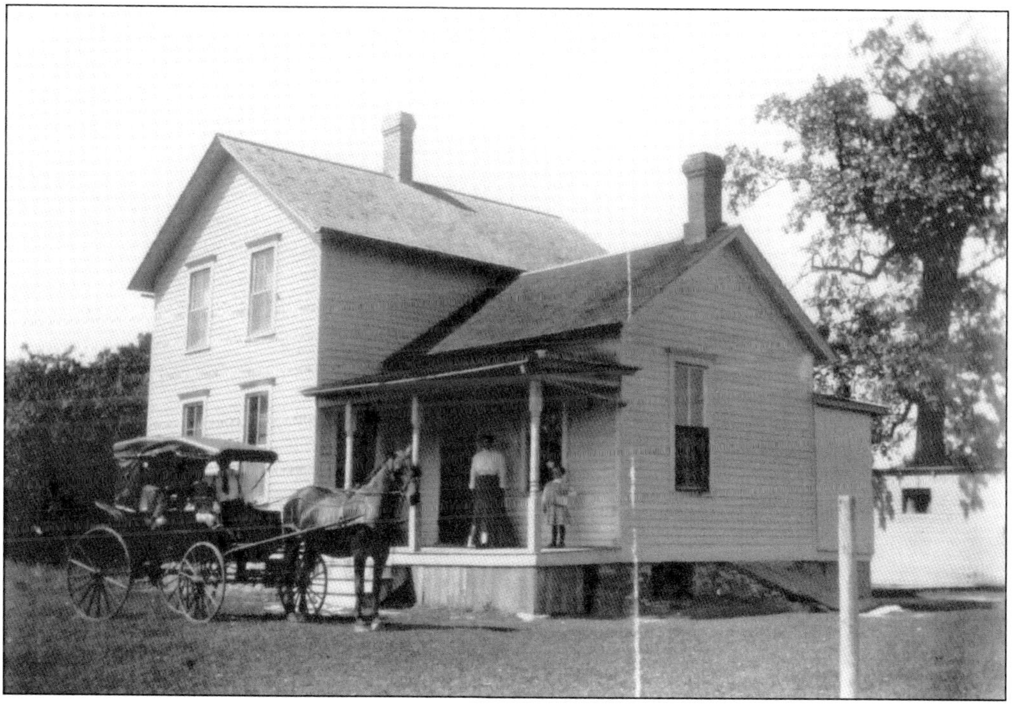

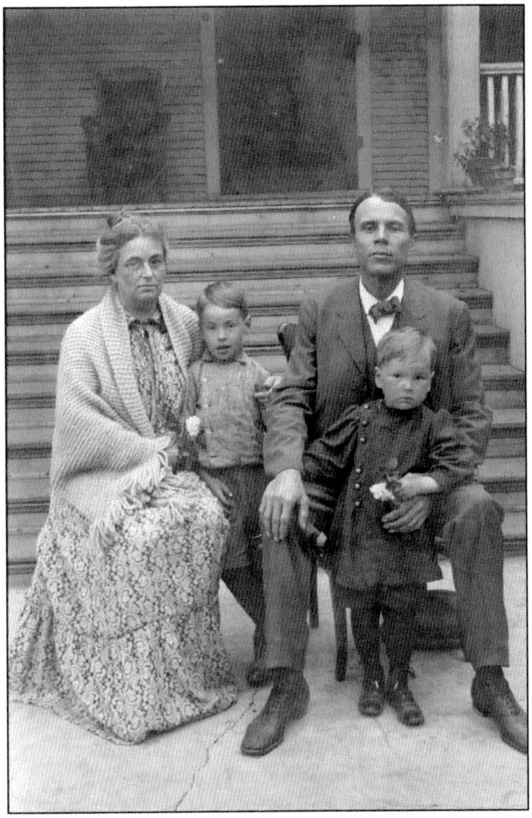

Robert Lucas and his wife, Ida (Bishop), were children of pioneer families. They are pictured here on their front porch with sons George and Bruce. Robert worked for the Yale Light Manufacturing Company and was the editor of Worth's first handwritten newspaper, the *Moral Advocate*. The family was very involved with civic organizations in town. Thanks to Robert's innovative practices, their home was the first to have indoor gas lighting and plumbing. This photograph was taken in 1908, several months before his untimely death. Robert's funeral was attended by over 100 friends and family members in 1908. Ida was pregnant with son Kenneth Lucas at the time of this photograph. Ida remained in Worth with Kenneth and George and taught piano and held odd jobs to keep her home. Bruce eventually moved to Chicago, George became a portrait photographer, and Ken became Worth Township supervisor and married Mildred "Sis" Roulo Lucas. The family was involved in the formation of the Methodist church in Worth and remained very dedicated to the community.

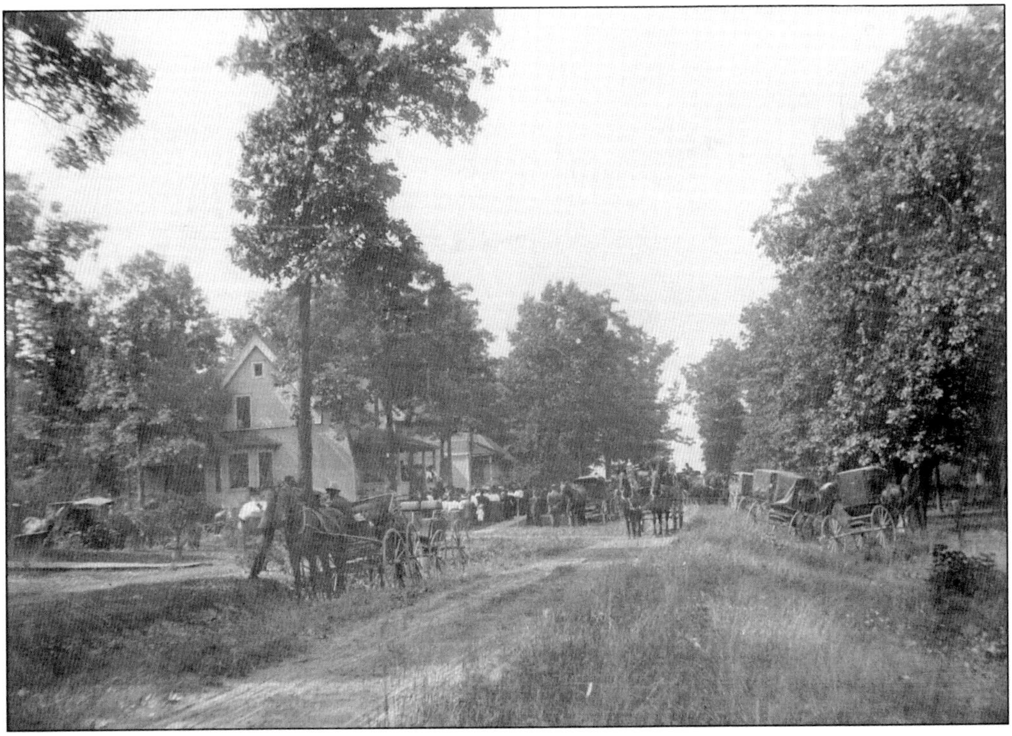

The railroad and establishment of the Bishop Country Store brought luxuries to town that were often found in the city of Chicago. Five-year-old twins Erwin and Edwin Rolf were often seen riding through town. Edwin (right) grew up to become the third mayor of Worth.

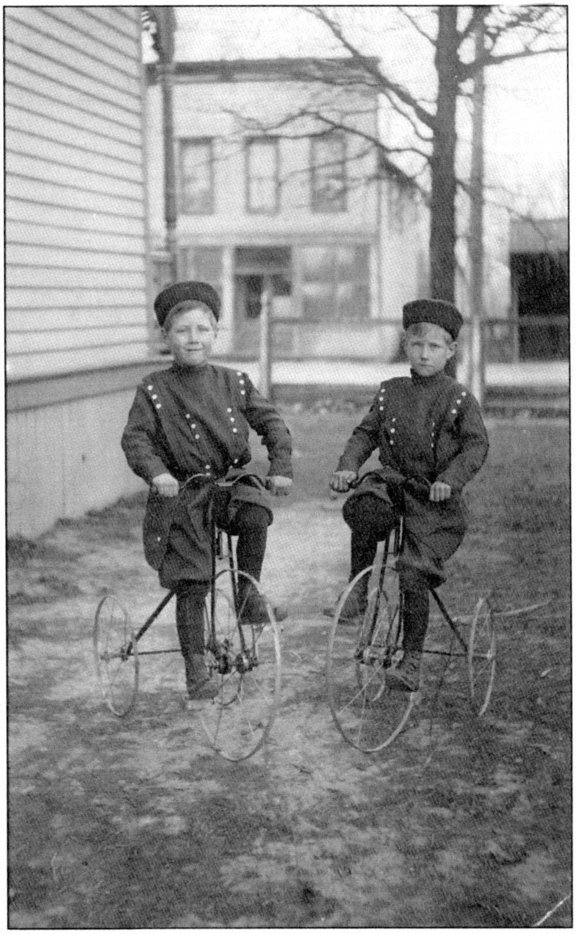

With the establishment of the post office in 1880, Bishop's store quickly became the center of town. The post office was moved into the store around 1883, and the first postmaster was Wales Tobey, another local landowner. This photograph was taken in 1912. Bishop's store was enjoying over 20 years of being in business, and one can only notice the strong presence of the crossroads that were established at the intersection of Depot Avenue and 111th Street. In the distance, the railroad boxcars are seen passing through town, a true sign of progress.

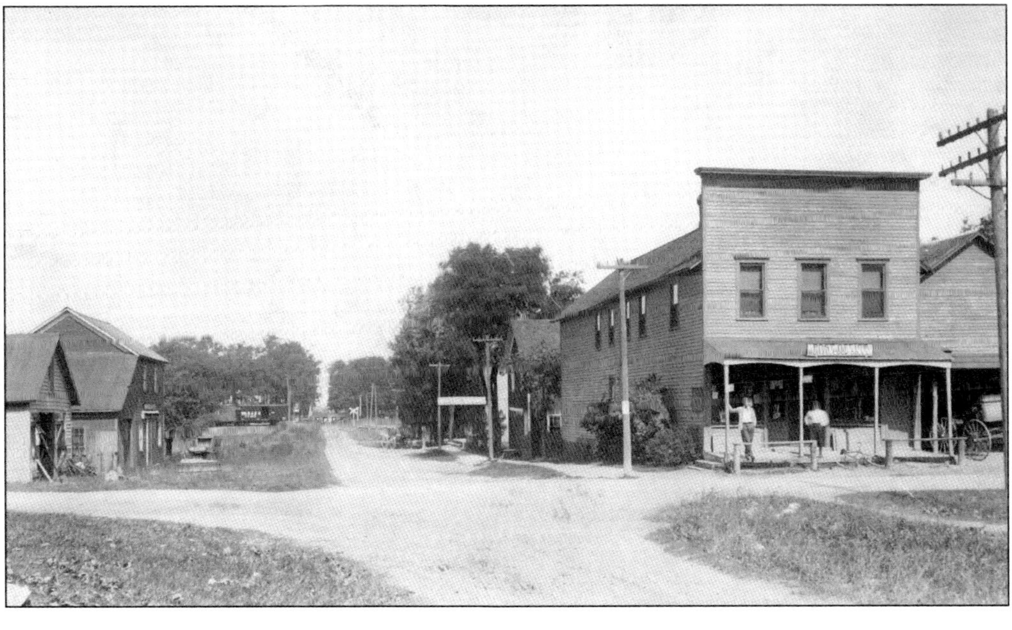

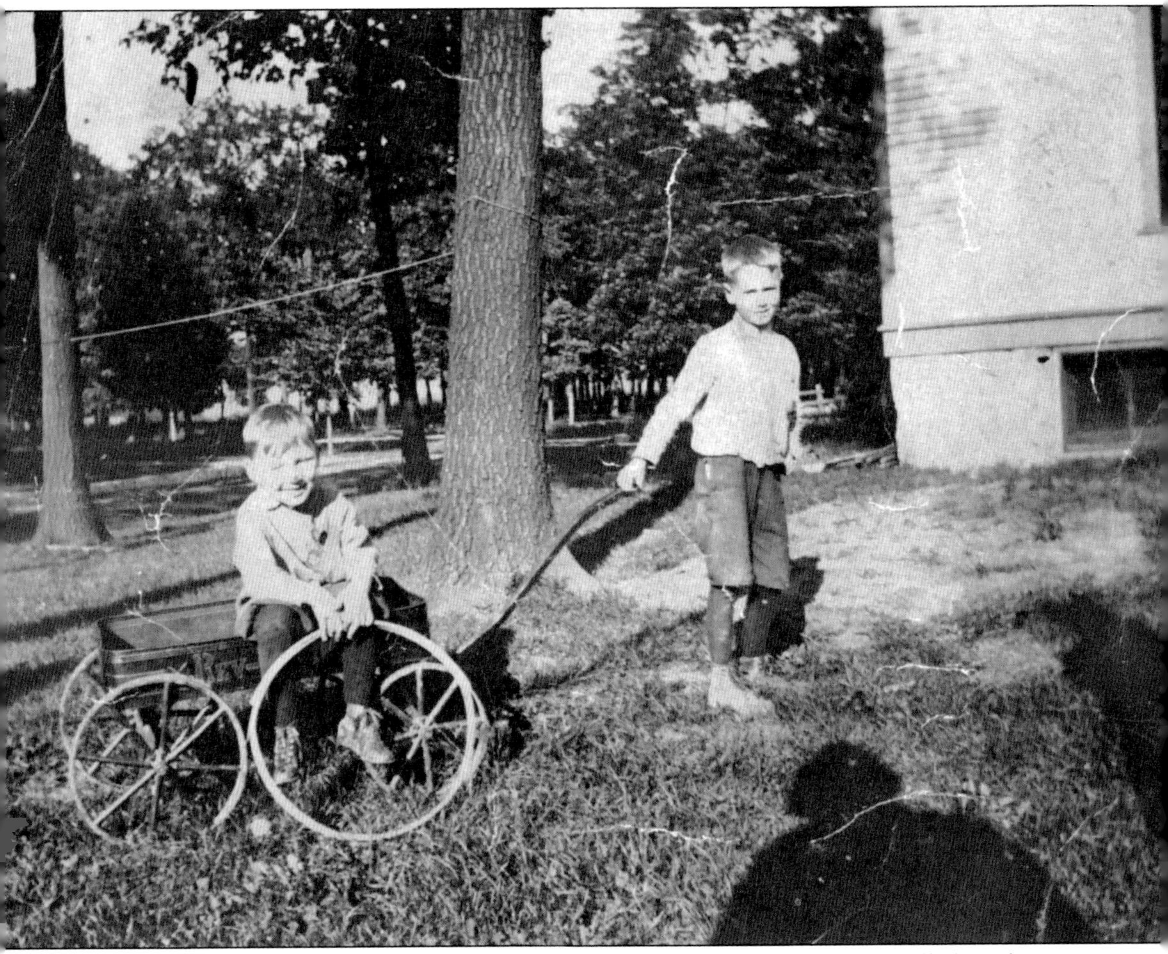

Generations of families have grown up in Worth. Ed Chapman is being pulled in the wagon by Ken Lucas. Ken grew up to become Worth Township supervisor. His wife, "Sis" Lucas, was a humanitarian, and both were extremely involved in the community.

Two

Incorporation and Transition

The year 1914 was a milestone for the village of Worth. The railroad and the building of a general store, post office, racetrack, and other amenities assisted in the growth of the town. The population of this tiny village reached 300. The construction of the Calumet-Saganashkee Channel increased the number of the townspeople by several hundred permanent residents. The Cal-Sag project began in 1922 by the Metropolitan Sewage District of Chicago and runs 16 miles long. It connects the Little Calumet River on the eastern border and runs west through Worth past the Saganashkee Slough, connecting up on the west with the Chicago Sanitary and Ship Canal. The channel was dug for the purpose of changing the flow of the Calumet River to prevent contamination of Lake Michigan, the source of fresh drinking water.

Technological advances were introduced in town with Worth's first installation of a telephone in 1902 at the home of J. Van Cleve Jeffers. A magneto switchboard served 15 phones in Worth by the end of the year. By 1910, there were 39 phones. As the population began to grow and the Worth Racetrack opened, a change was seen in the surrounding Chicago Ridge and Alsip communities. The need for order and municipal services in the township of Worth was much needed as the climate began to shift from a quaint farming community to one that drew many outsiders and racing enthusiasts. A referendum was held on August 29, 1914, which led to the incorporation of the village of Worth. A charter was issued by the state on October 8, 1914.

Among the first bit of business in Worth was to address citizen complaints of barking dogs, which ordered all fowl and "man's best friend" to be contained. The racetrack and railroad began to open the doors of this tiny town to a new era. In the first quarter of the 20th century, this tiny community was challenged to adapt to new and transient residents and technologies.

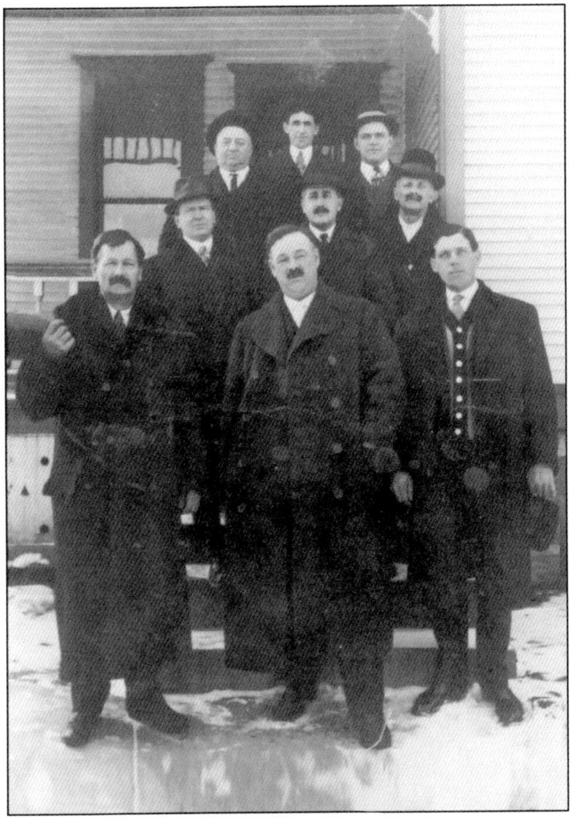

Members of the first village board are, from left to right, (first row) trustee Christ Rust, Pres. Harry Woods, and trustee Edward Lange; (second row) trustees B.F. Rolfe and Robert Wilson and treasurer Peter Cure; (third row) trustee George Piper, clerk George Monroe Peterson, and trustee Roy Shackleton.

Peter Markiewicz, a local deliveryman, is pictured here in front of the Foyle home. Bert Foyle was a well contractor who started his own business, Foyle & Sons, in 1910. Bert and his wife, Gertrude Markiewicz, moved into this home in the early 1920s, along with their seven children. Peter was the father-in-law to Edward Conway. Edward was the village blacksmith in 1920 and went on to become Worth's second mayor from 1930 to 1941. He was also fire chief of the volunteer fire department, and his wife, Gertrude, was the first president of the Parent-Teacher Association (PTA).

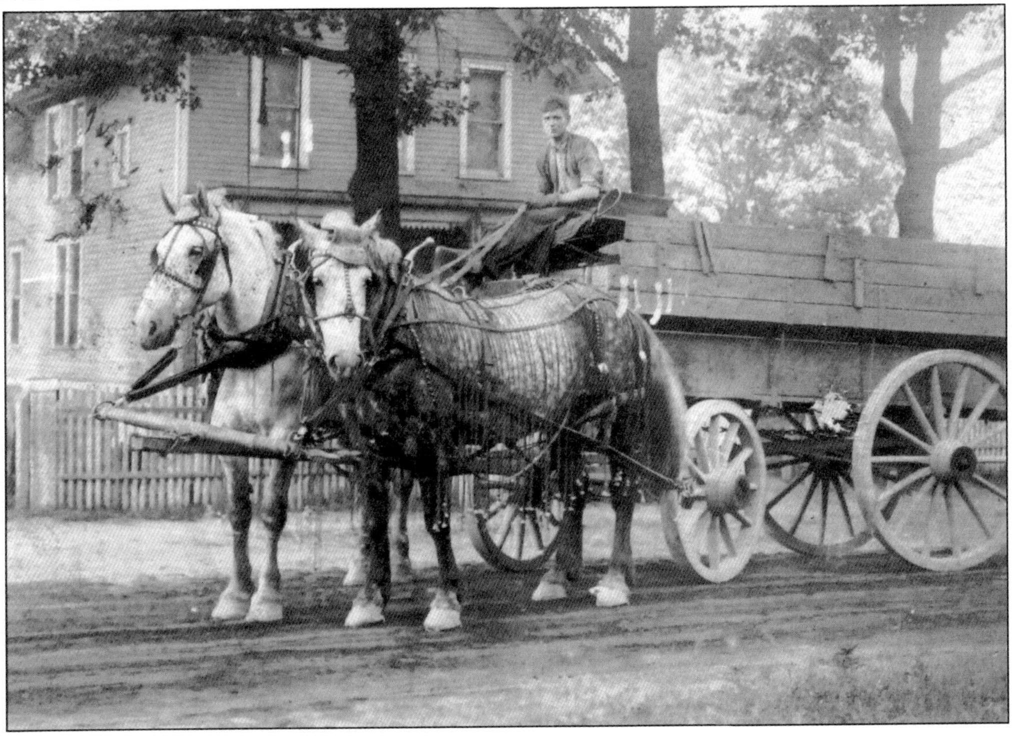

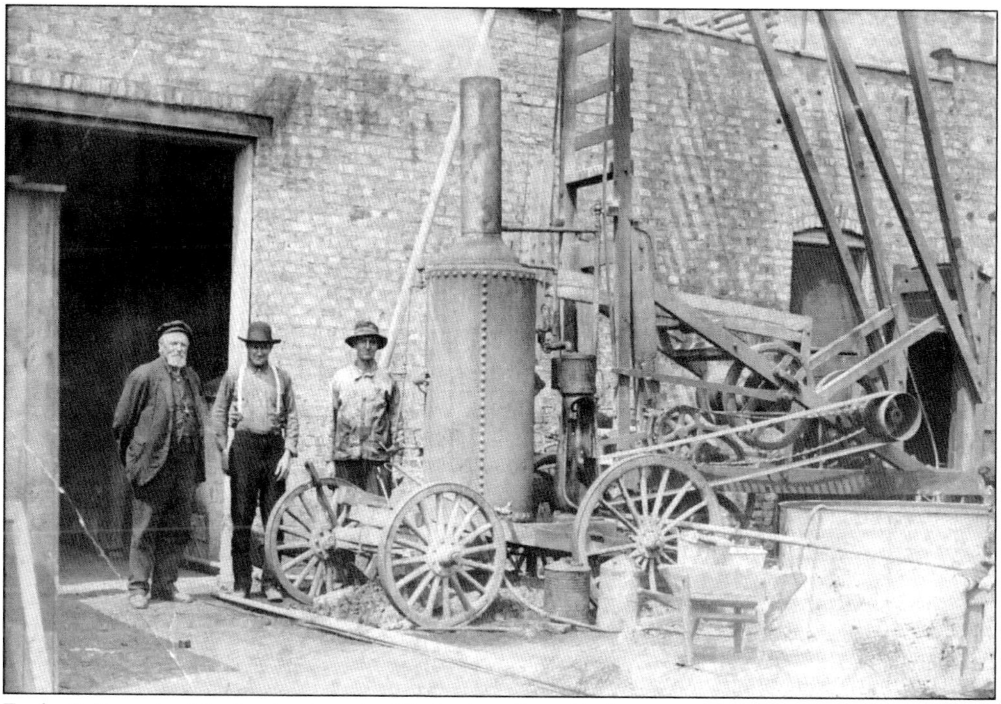

Foyle & Sons had its beginnings in 1906 when Bert Foyle operated one steam-powered well-drilling machine and used a horse and buggy as a means of transportation. Pictured here is the Foyle Pump Company located on 111th and New England Streets. Well drilling was common in the village through the late 1950s.

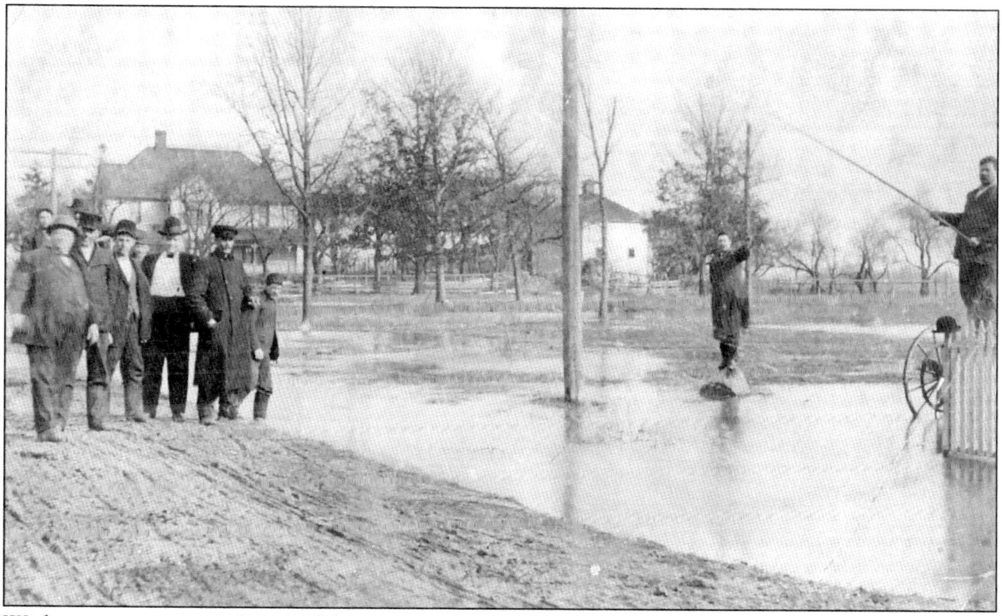

With progress comes the need for improvements. Drainage and infrastructure were among the top priorities of the village. Pioneer and blacksmith Christ Rust is seen holding his fishing pole at 6997 West 111th Street. He is showing his sense of humor after a big rain. Other locals stop to admire his fishing skills.

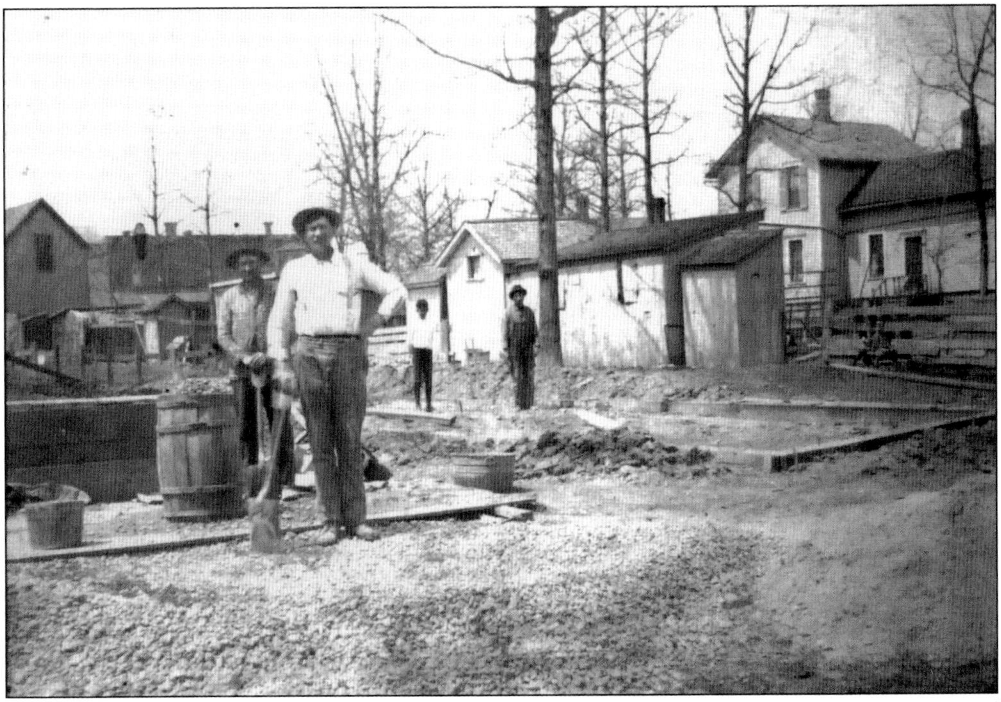

Benjamin Crandall, brother of the first pioneer John Crandall, is seen here implementing one of the village's first ordinances. Building a chicken coop and penning the animals was top order for the new village board. Seen behind the workers is 111th Street.

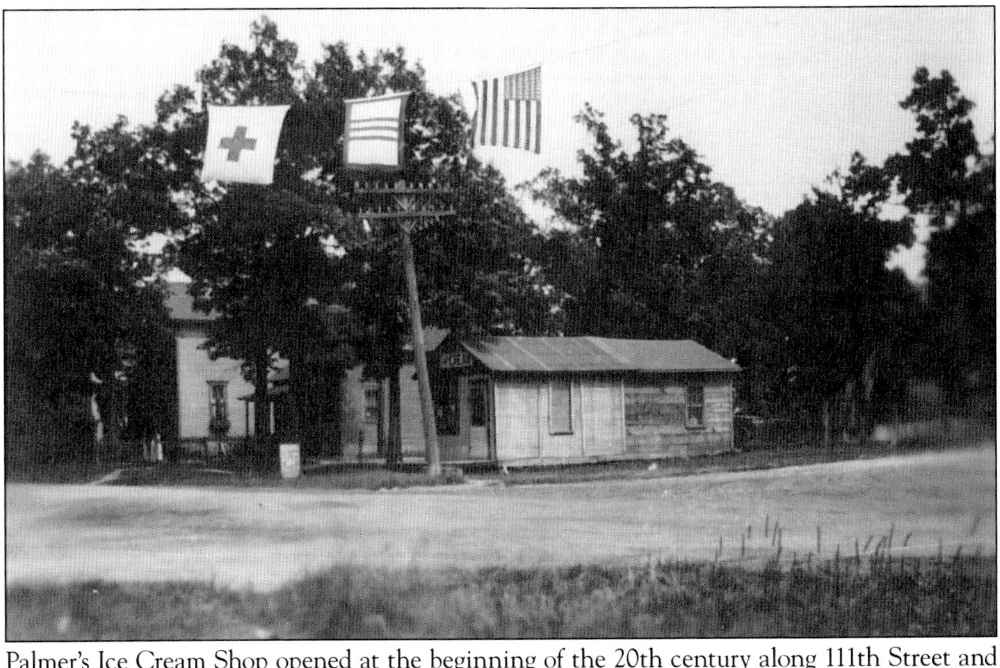

Palmer's Ice Cream Shop opened at the beginning of the 20th century along 111th Street and Depot Avenue. It was the gateway to the soon-to-be business district in town. The ice cream shop was open for over 10 years and sitting directly across from the old school made it popular with schoolchildren. This photograph was taken in 1915.

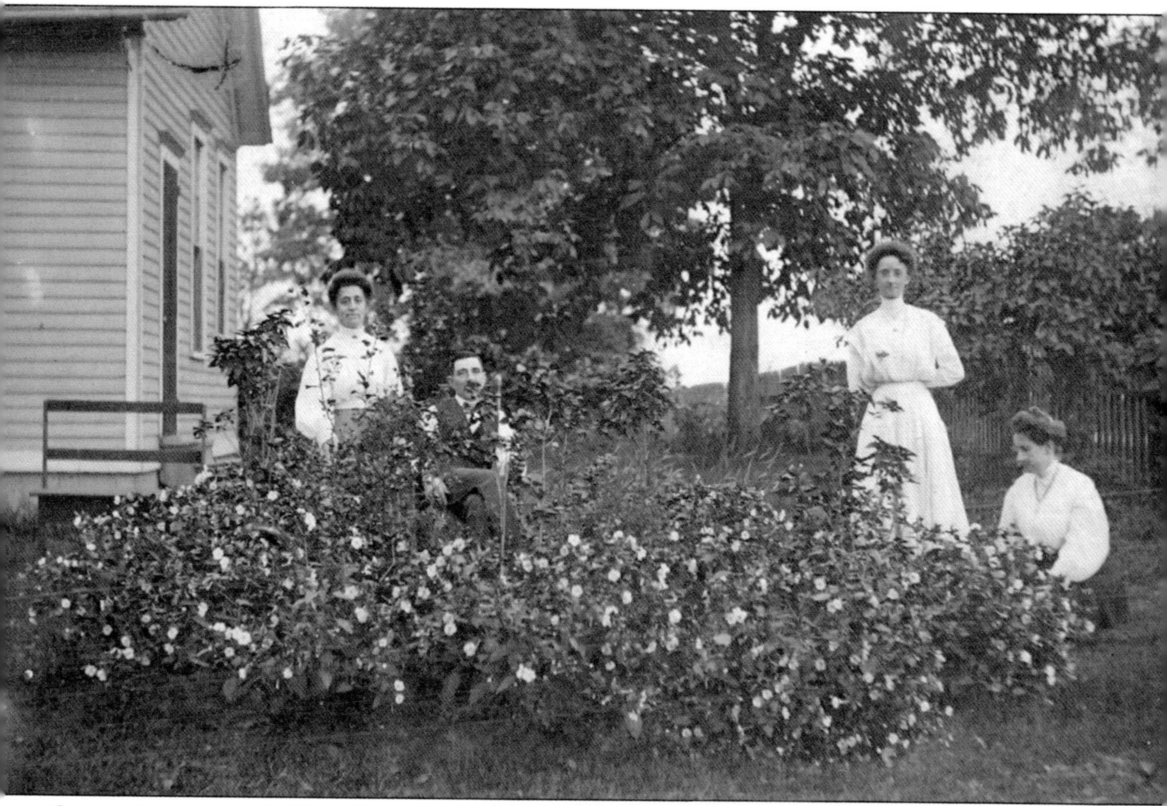

Seen enjoying a typical Sunday activity, these residents are having a garden party at a home in the heart of Worth. Located at 111th Street and Worth Avenue, the Heiser home hosted many luncheons after church.

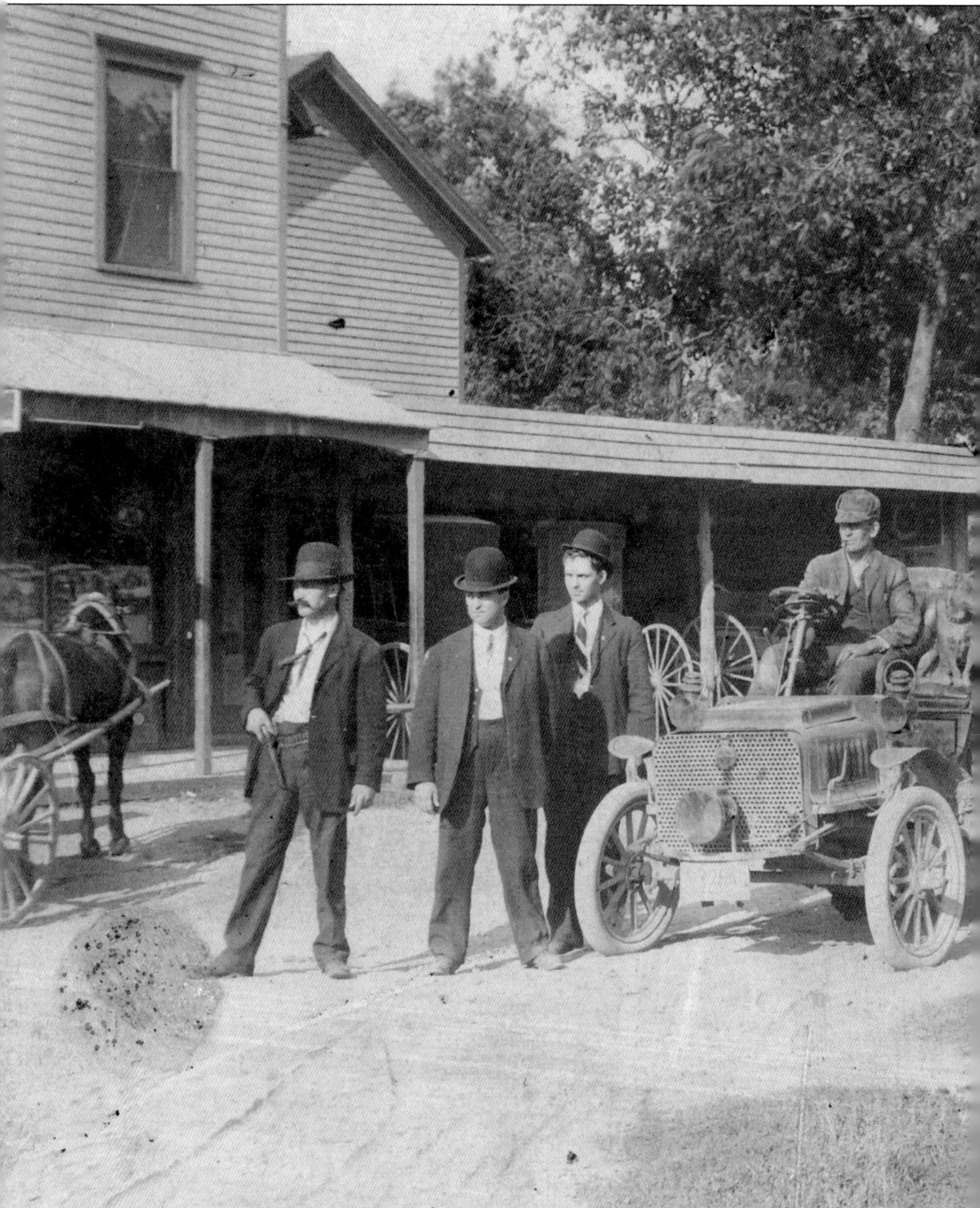

When some convicts escaped from the Illinois State Penitentiary in 1906, a posse of citizens was formed, led by officers, to hunt them down. Since it was felt they were probably hiding in the dense woods in the area, the posse headquartered in Worth on September 6, 7, and 8, 1906.

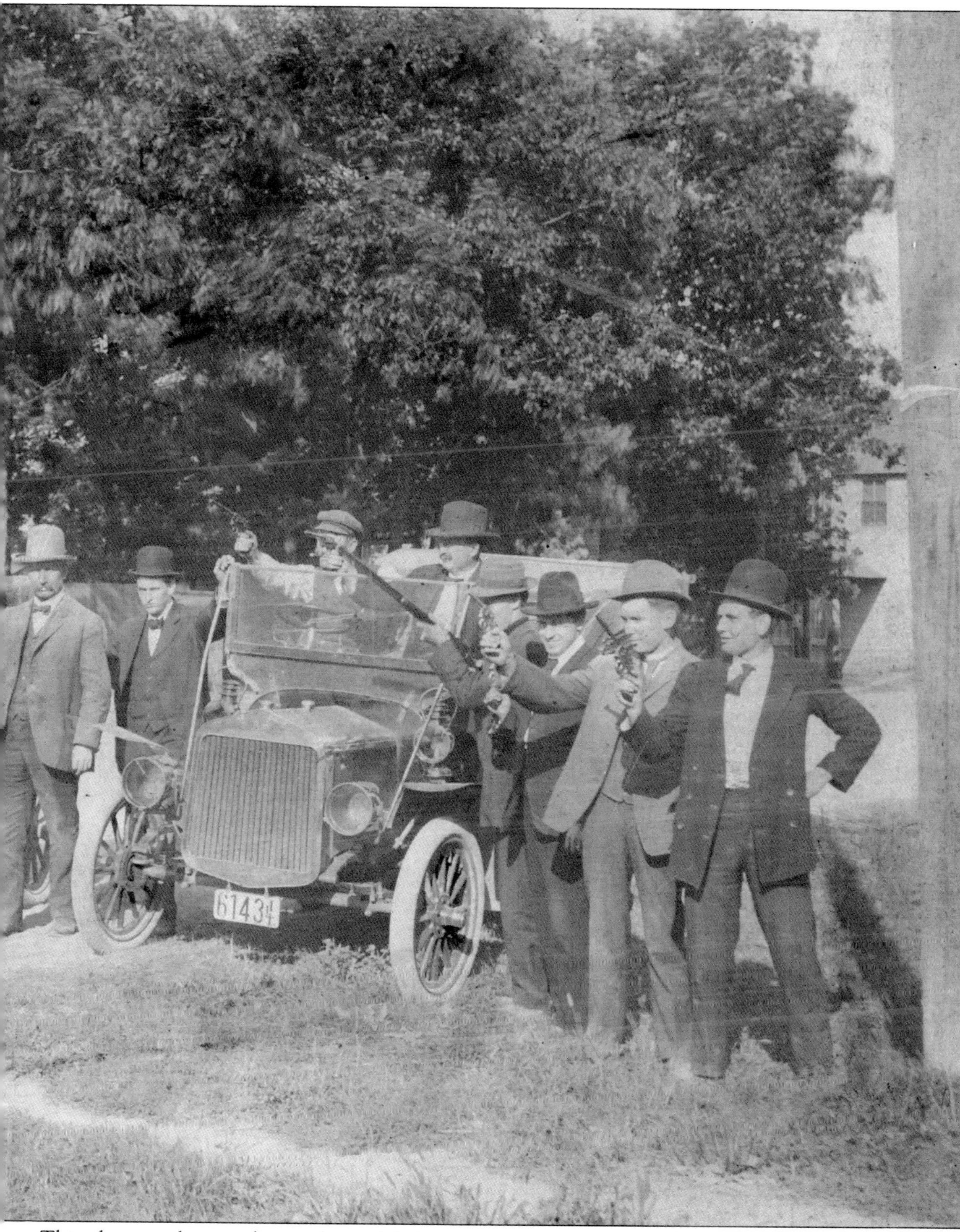

This photograph was taken in front of Bishop's store on 111th Street. The police department in Worth was not yet established, and services were relied on by volunteers and from Cook County, Illinois.

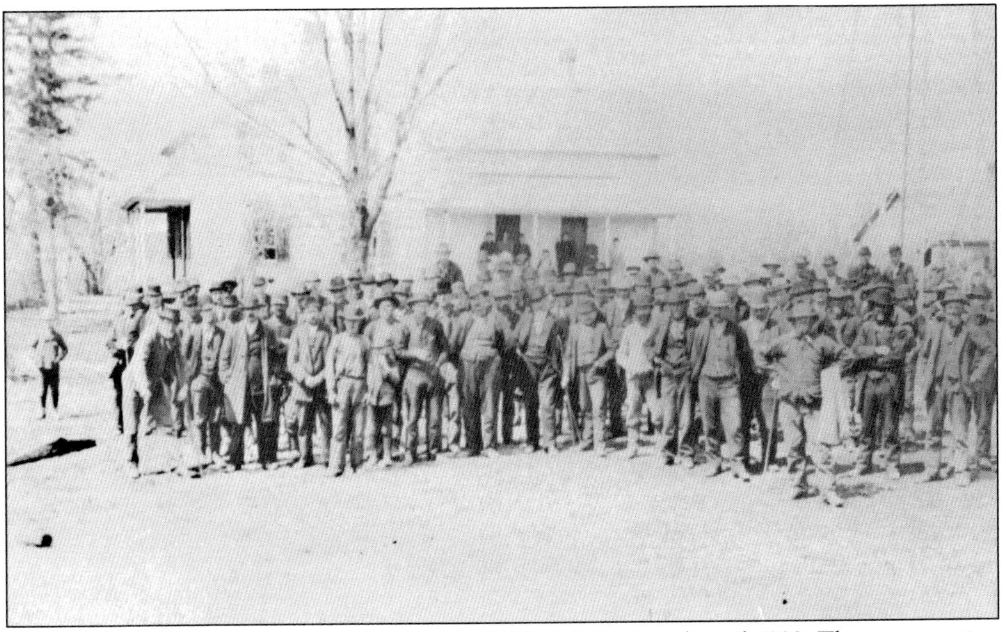

The Cal-Sag Channel construction began in 1911 and continued until 1922. The construction created jobs and brought people to Worth, which led to its incorporation in 1914. Pictured here is a rare group photograph of canal workers at the beginning of the project in the Worth section of the canal. Workers were welcomed to many local businesses, as they helped make way for small improvements and increased business in town.

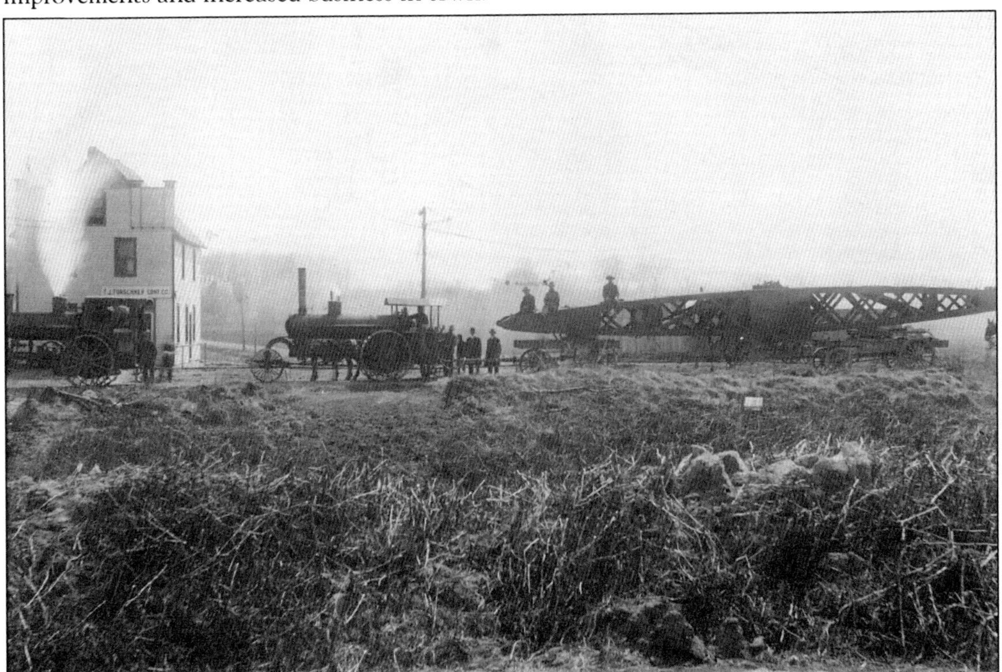

Machines came parading proudly through town down 111th Street, making their way toward the canal construction site. Workers and townspeople alike were amazed at the new technology of the steam-powered engines that were transforming their lives.

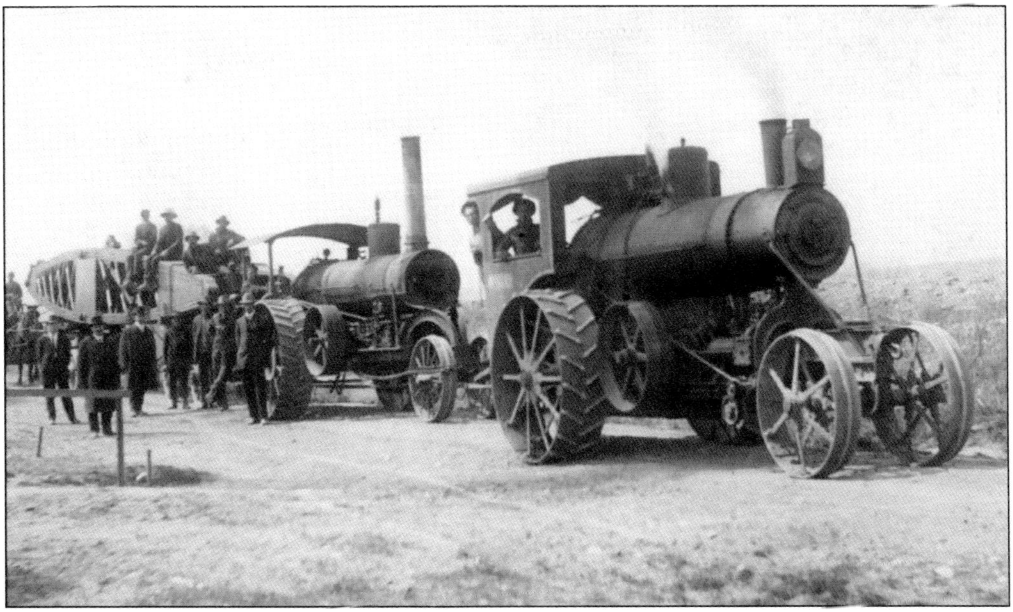

The Cal-Sag Channel is 16 miles long and originally 60 feet wide. It flows from the Calumet River on the southeast side of Chicago and runs into the Chicago Sanitary and Ship Canal. The Wabash cannonballs used in the construction are seen making their way down Harlem Avenue to the location in the Worth section.

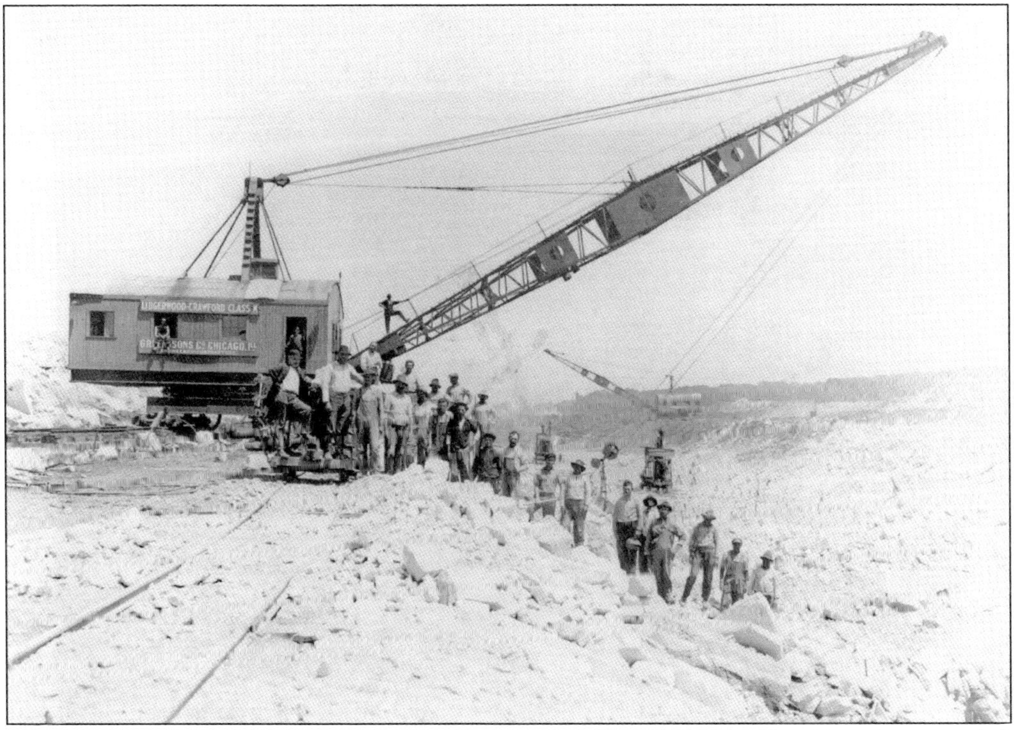

Canal workers endured long hours and removed, often by hand, many boulders that were left over from blast sites. Boulders were many sizes and ranged in weight. This photograph illustrates the varying sizes of boulders in comparison to the men.

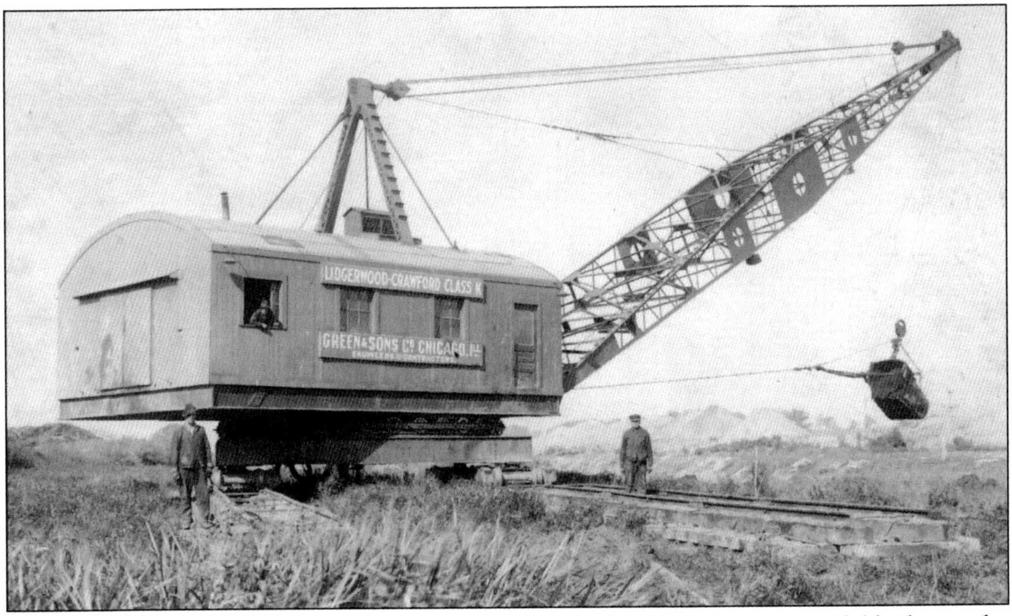

In 1914, Worth's population sharply increased as hundreds of jobs became available due to the construction of the Cal-Sag Channel. At left is Jake Smith, an uncle of Frank Homerdin, and at right is Louie Smith, Frank's grandfather. Homerdin was a Worth Park District commissioner for 32 years.

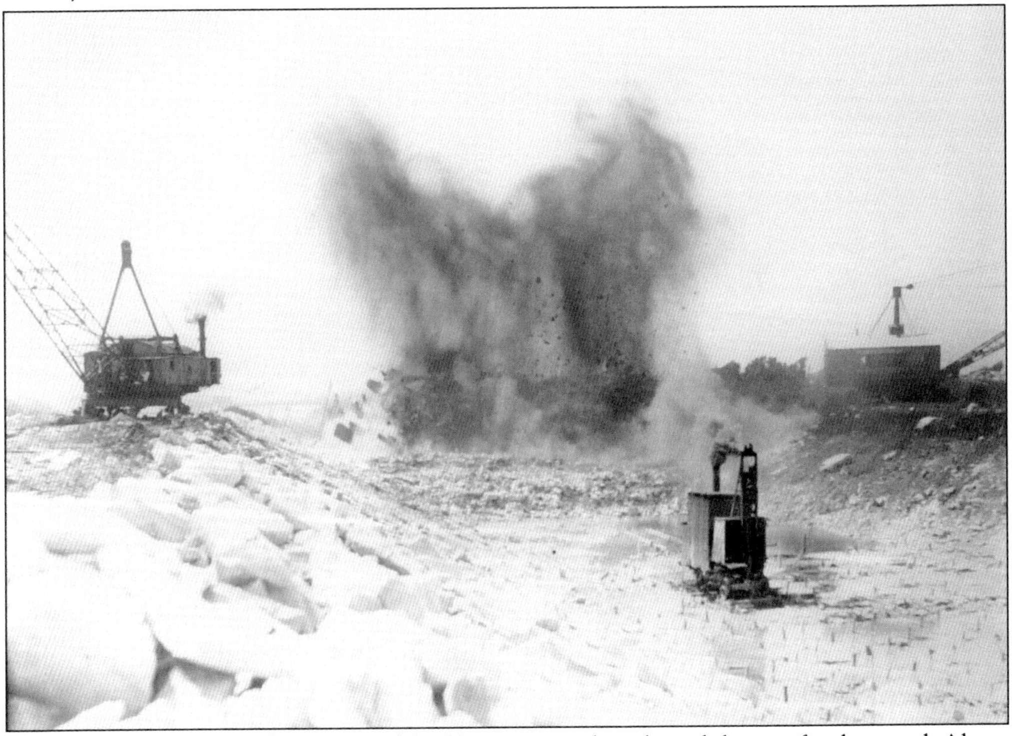

This photograph depicts the impact of the blasting sites that cleared the way for the canal. About 1,800 pounds of dynamite were used, and 103 holes were dug for the dynamite to be placed into. This photograph was shot in the Worth section on August 18, 1915.

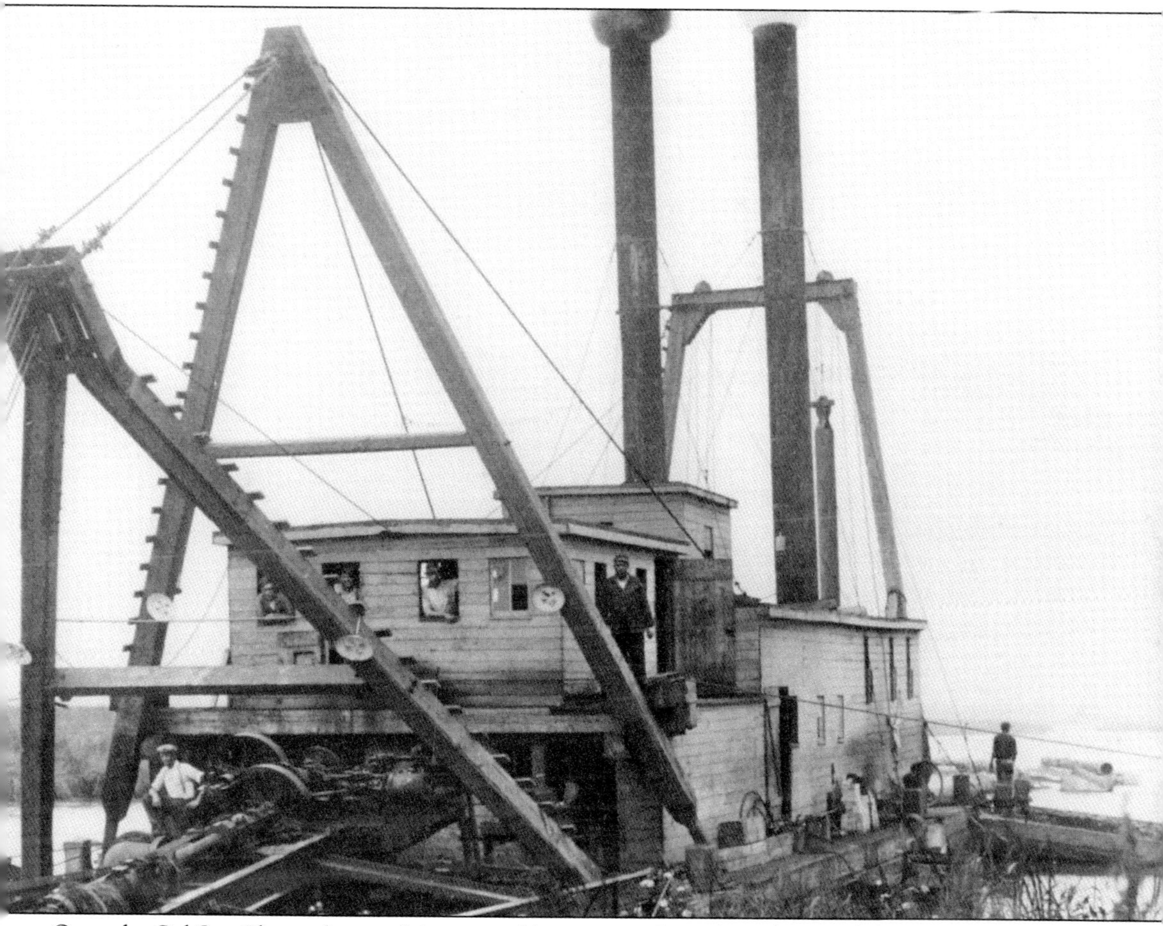

Once the Cal-Sag Channel opened, barges and boats went through to clean and clear the bottom of large boulders. This is a photograph of an early dredge boat making its way down the channel.

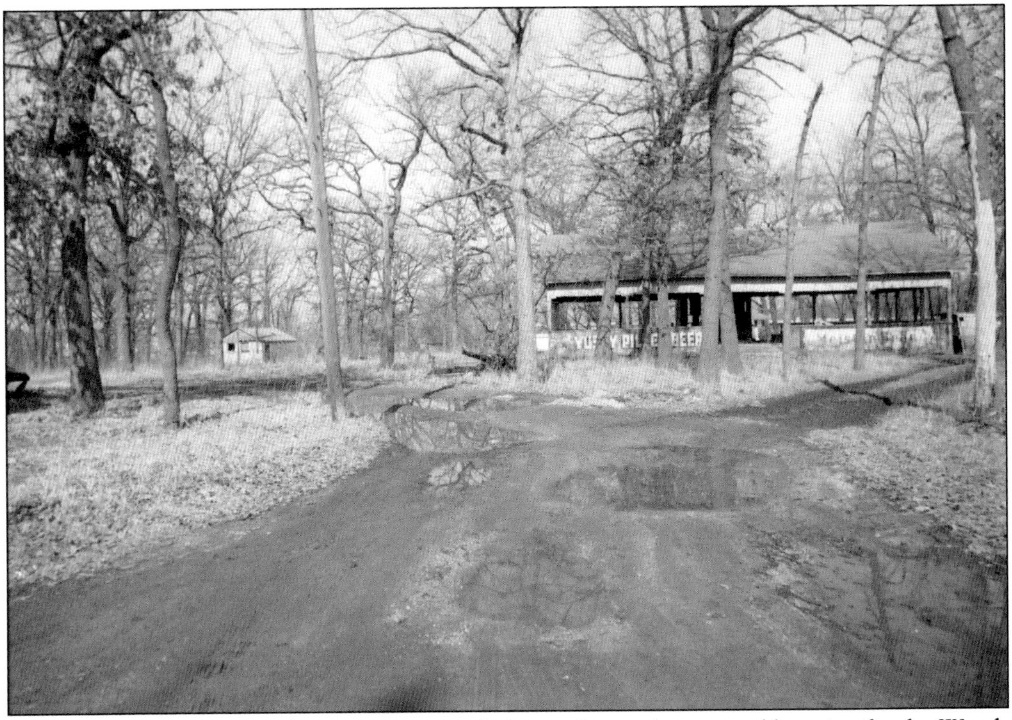

Diesing's Grove was located at 7500 West 111th Street. It was the original location for the Worth Days picnic. The Diesings built a pavilion and held big dances every Sunday in the summer for 42 years. After Mr. Diesing passed away, Florence, his wife, only opened the grove for Worth Days picnics until it moved to the Wilson Wagner Field. Florence married W. Grange Mahaffay and built a home at this location.

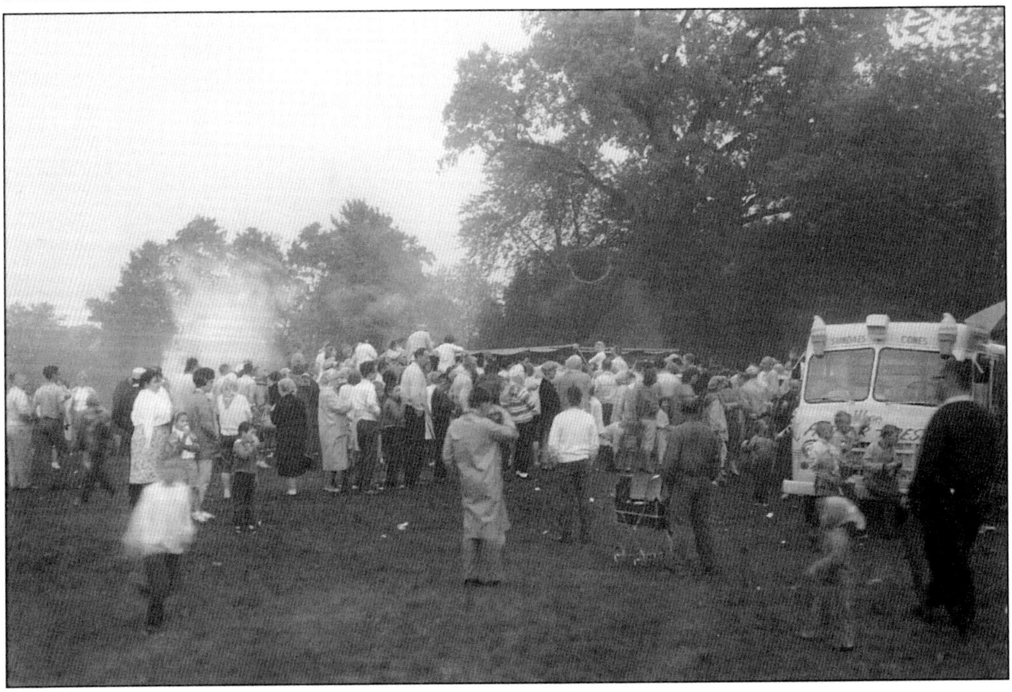

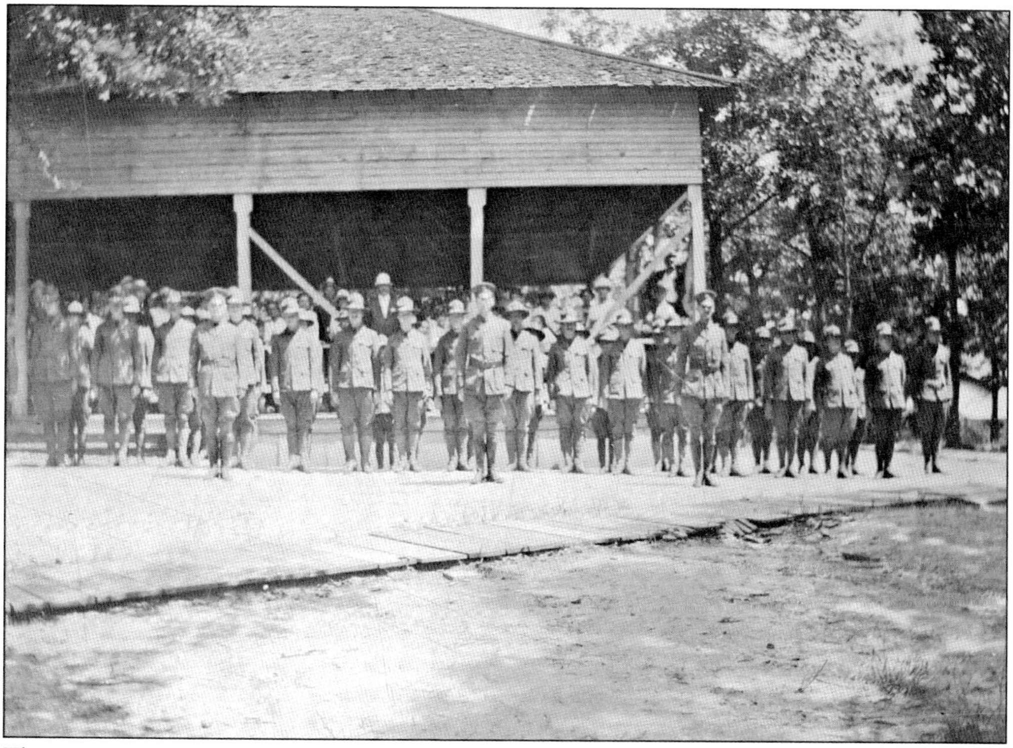

The grove was used during World War I as a training and picnic ground for the home front. These photographs were donated by the Lucas family, and members from the family recalled relatives discussing their training was close to home.

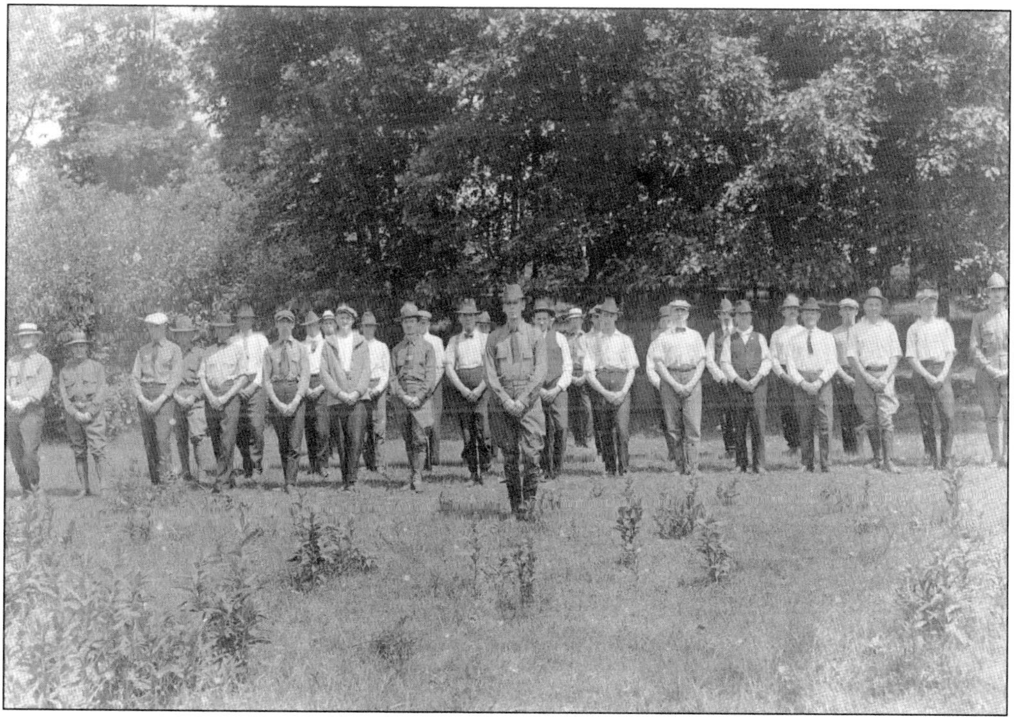

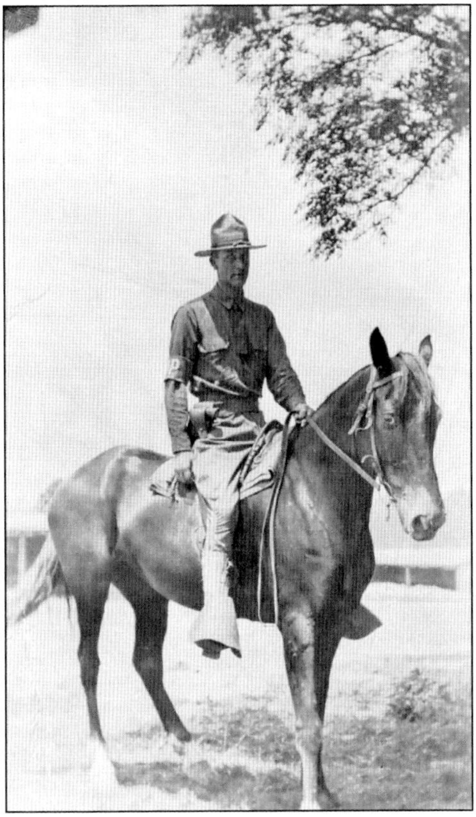

The foundation of the American Legion came about during World War I. A post was not established in Worth until 1946, and the Marrs-Meyer name was derived from two local servicemen. Raymond Marrs, seen on horseback, was a signal corpsman who died on April 11, 1919, during World War I in France. His wife was Mary Martin, a resident since 1907. Mary Martin worked for the railroad and is seen holding the mailbag. She was employed by the Wabash Railroad and was the local depot agent, responsible for catching the bag as the train went by. She and her husband lived in the first train depot in Worth, which was where her husband's homecoming was.

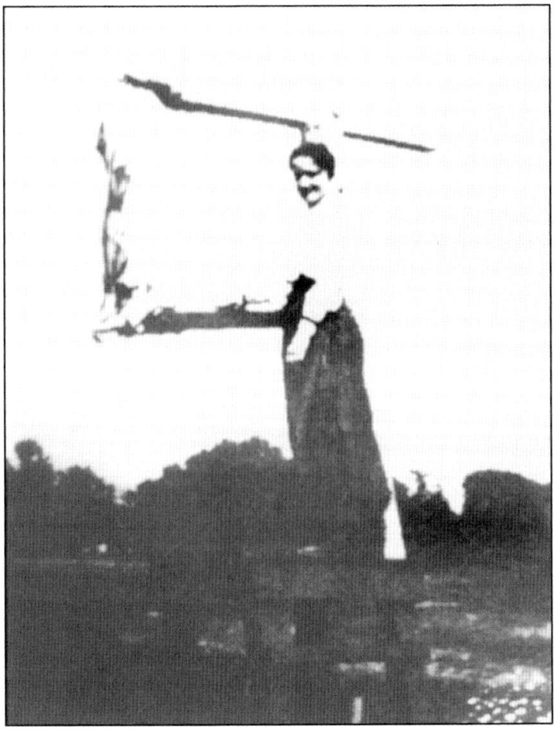

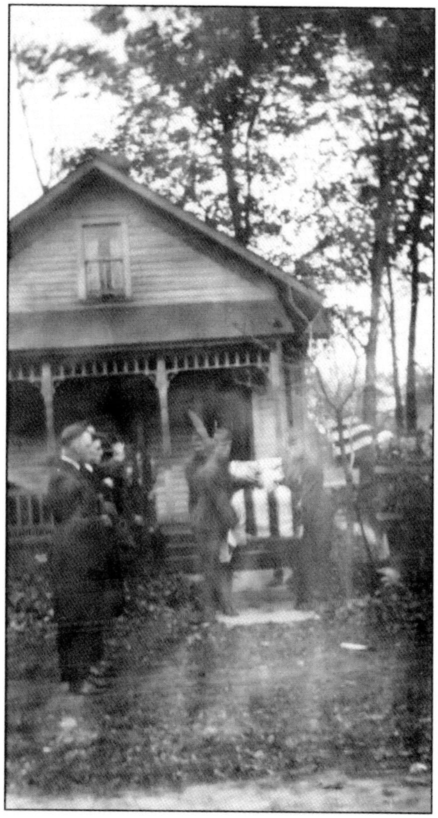

Walter Meyer is the second half of the namesake of the American Legion post. Walter Meyer was an infantryman who was fatally wounded in Italy and died on September 26. His wife, Vivian Meyer, and daughter Loretta were involved in the establishment of the American Legion Women's Auxiliary. Loretta never met her father.

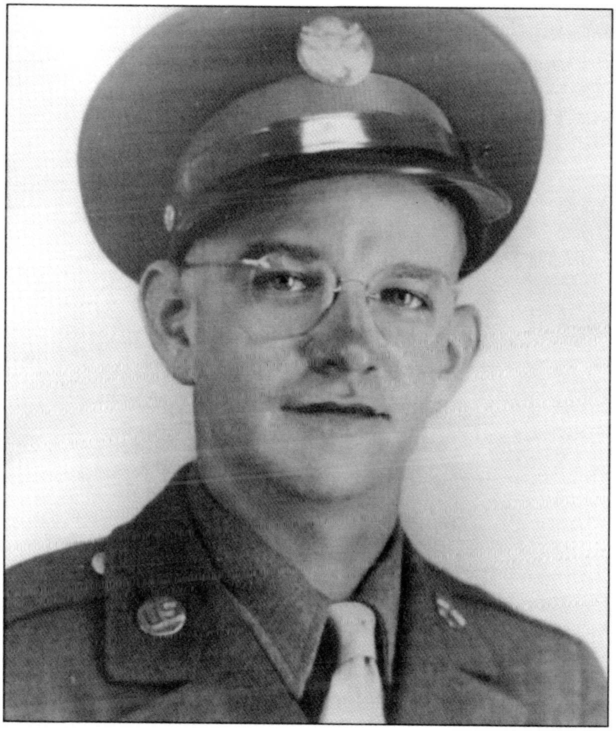

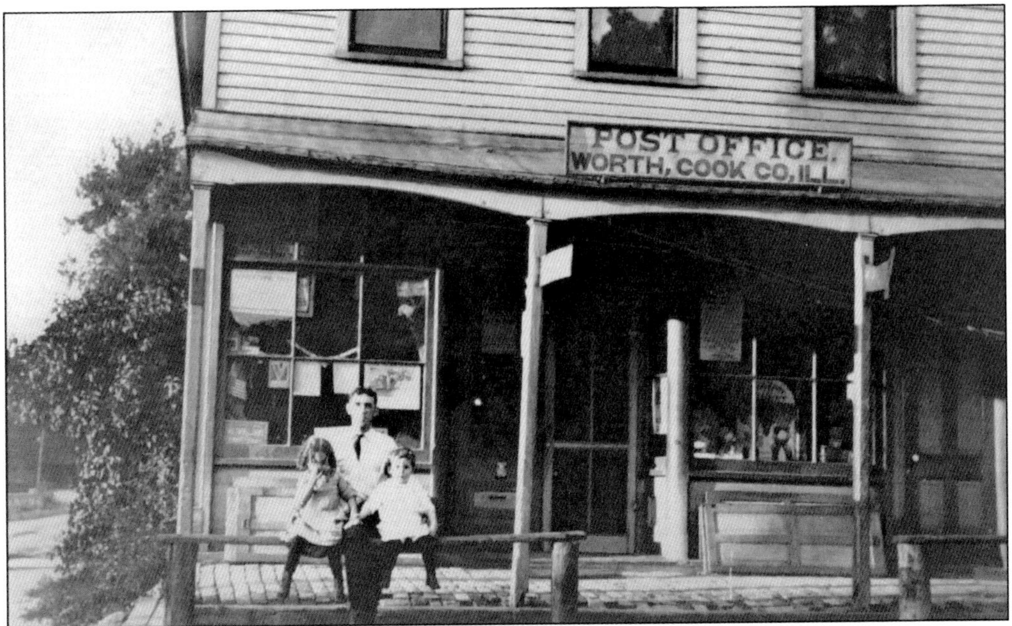

Carl Bishop, the eldest son of the late Edward Bishop, assumed the responsibility of managing the family store into the 1930s. This photograph was taken in the late 1920s. The small-town charm is still noticeably the same as it was during the establishment of the store. Carl is seen holding his daughter Leah Rose and son Bud.

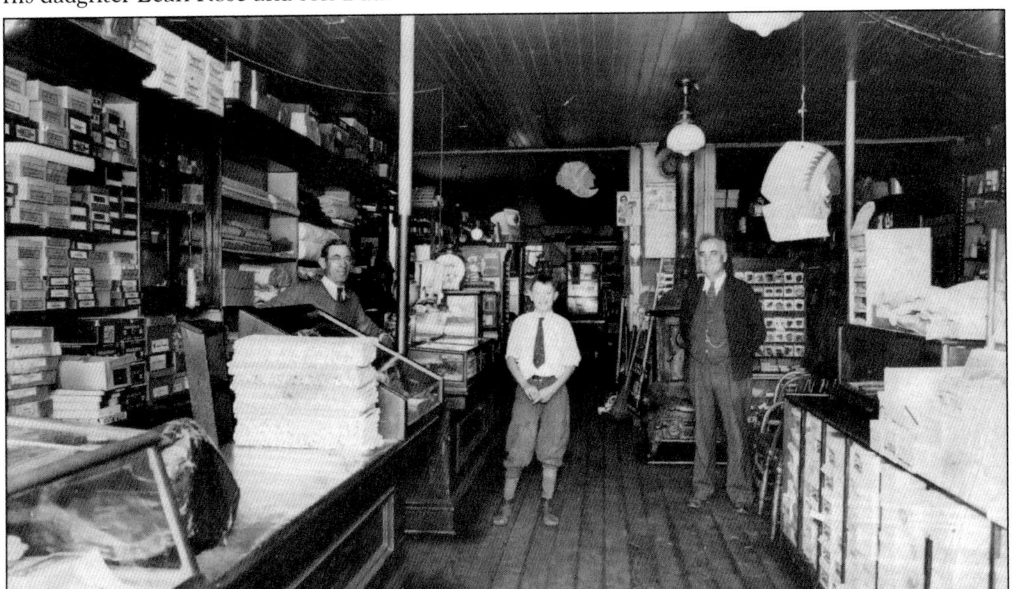

This interior shot of Bishop's store shows the condition in 1930. Larry Wyma is in the center of the photograph, and store operators George Monroe Peterson (left) and Carl Bishop, in front of the potbellied stove, get ready for a busy day. The store became the hub of activity for people throughout the area. Bishop's store sold items like candy, groceries, lunch meats, and candles and offered the only outdoor scale in the vicinity. George Peterson was the first village clerk and instrumental in the incorporation of the village. The two men partnered in the store until 1940. (Courtesy of Karen Caldwell.)

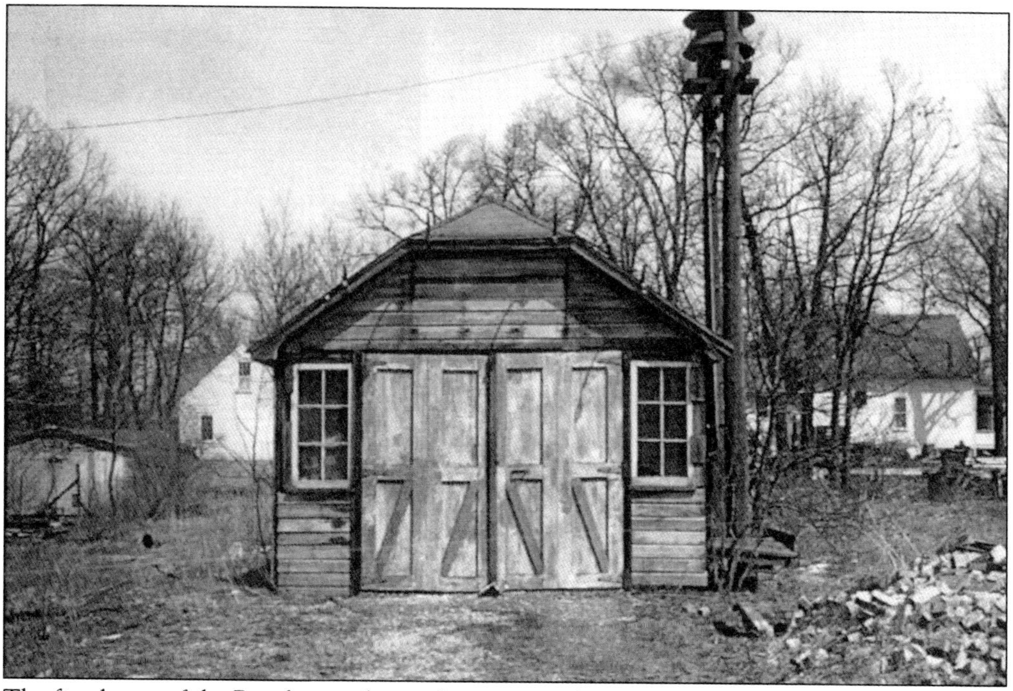

The first home of the Reo fire truck was this converted carriage house. It was moved from 111th Street just west of the Worth School where it was a candy store. When the Dodge-Chrysler plant was forbidden to use a siren for its workers during World War II, the five horsepower siren was secured for the fire department and mounted above the garage. When the fire department obtained a new building, the siren was moved along with the equipment..

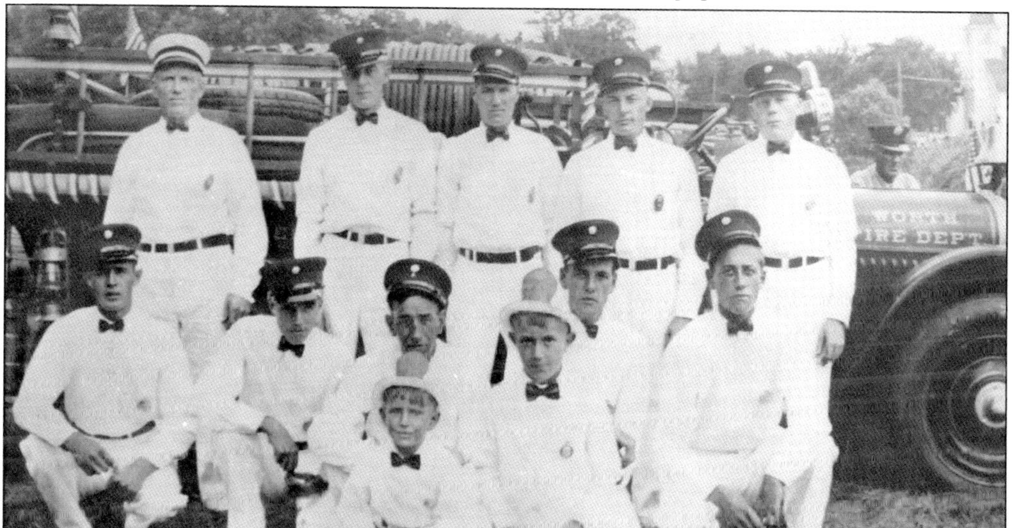

Worth's first volunteer fire department was established in 1925. The men are posing in front of the first fire truck, the Reo, at a 1933 picnic. From left to right are (first row) Robert Ferrin and Bill "Stogie" Conway, son of the captain of the department; (second row) Harold Russert, Earl Teason, Mike Poorman, Elmer Lysen, and Edward Conway Jr.; (third row) Chief Conway, also president of the Village of Worth; Arthur Plahm; Edwin Rolfe; George Plahm; and Ed Plahm.

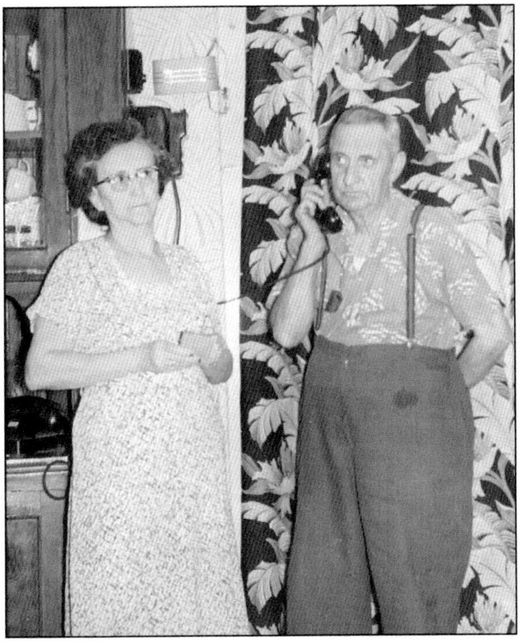

Art and Louise Meyers were an integral part of the fire department. Shown at their home and tavern on 109th Street and Depot Avenue, the couple would answer the outside telephone and set off the siren atop the village hall by pushing the remote control button, seen located over Louise's head. When the firemen arrived at the fire station, they would crank the handle to ring the bell on the phone that Art is holding. This was the first intercom system and dispatch set up in the village. The Meyerses were not compensated for their service.

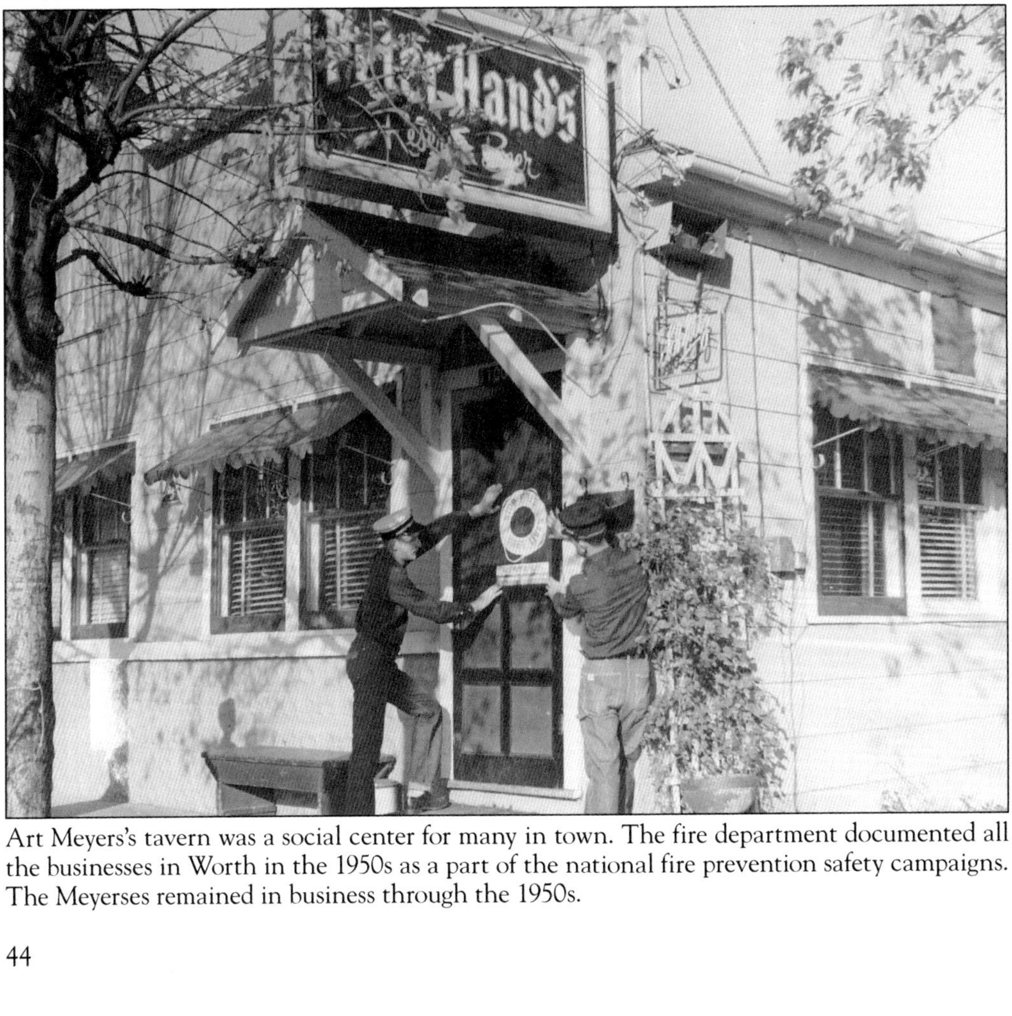

Art Meyers's tavern was a social center for many in town. The fire department documented all the businesses in Worth in the 1950s as a part of the national fire prevention safety campaigns. The Meyerses remained in business through the 1950s.

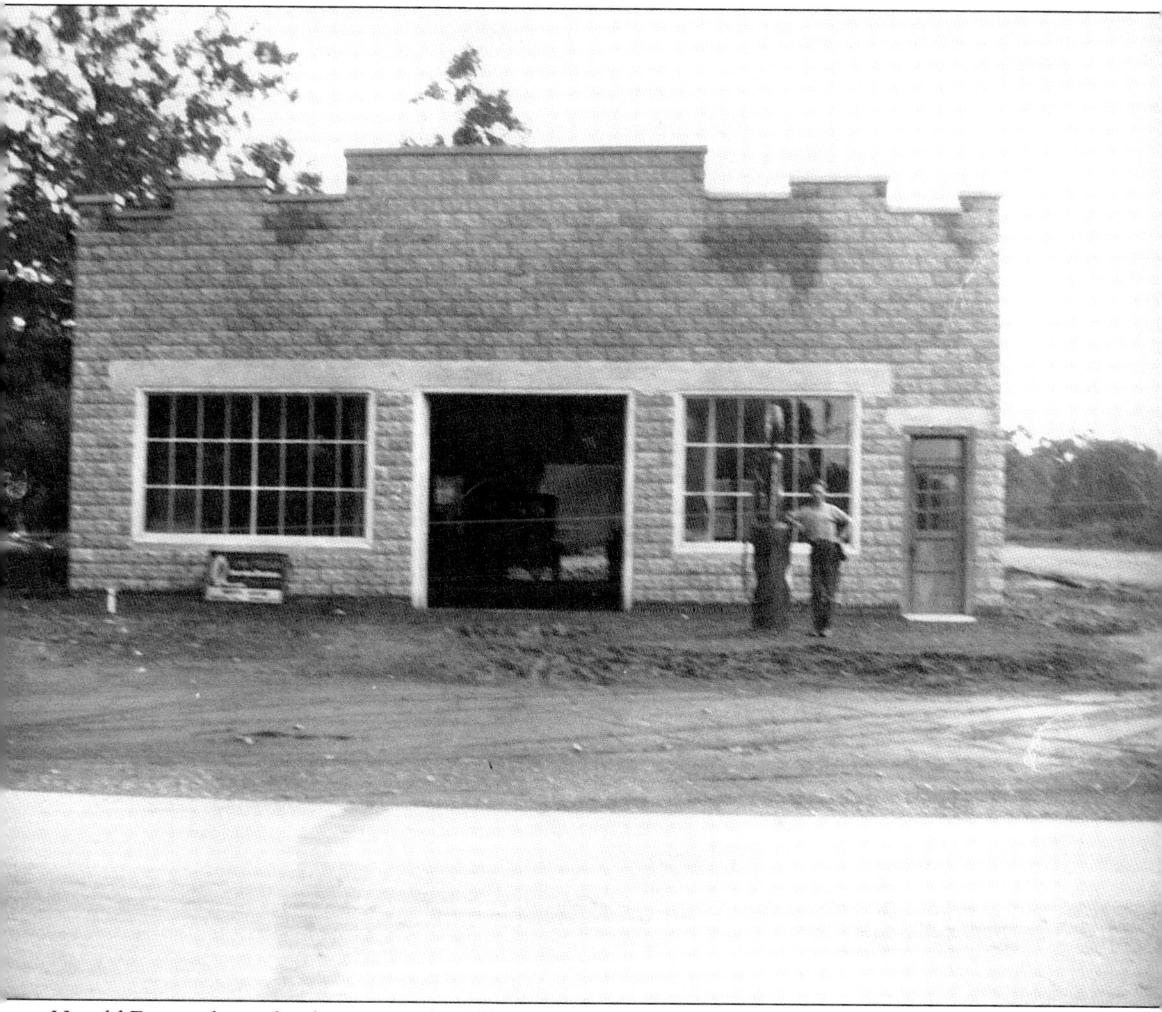

Harold Ferrin chose this location to build his garage because he knew that Worth was becoming a crossroad from country to city. His building stands were the Palmer Ice Cream Parlor stood, yet another sign of progress in the small town. As cars made their way to the country, Ferrin provided the only garage service in the area. Ferrin's Garage later became Vicki's, a popular place to shop in the 1950s and 1960s, and is currently a mortgage company. (Courtesy of Chuck Templin.)

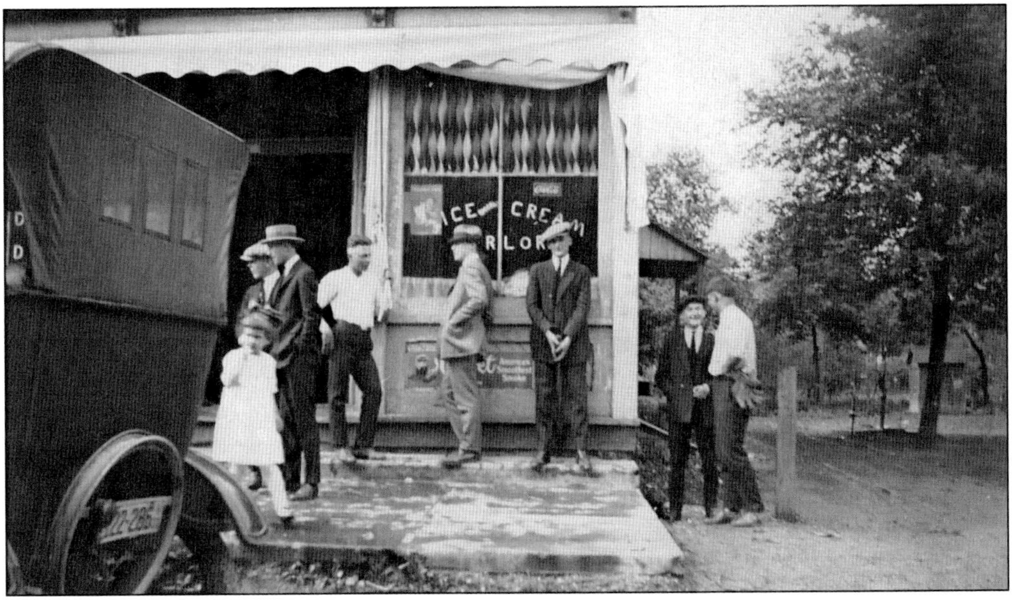

Located on 111th Street, Russert's Ice Cream Shoppe became a favorite for people to come and visit. It was conveniently located across the street from Ferrin's Garage and gas station, which was the perfect place to fuel up for a ride in the country. In 1915, one of the first roads to be paved was 111th Street. Franklin Russert was village president from 1943 to 1949.

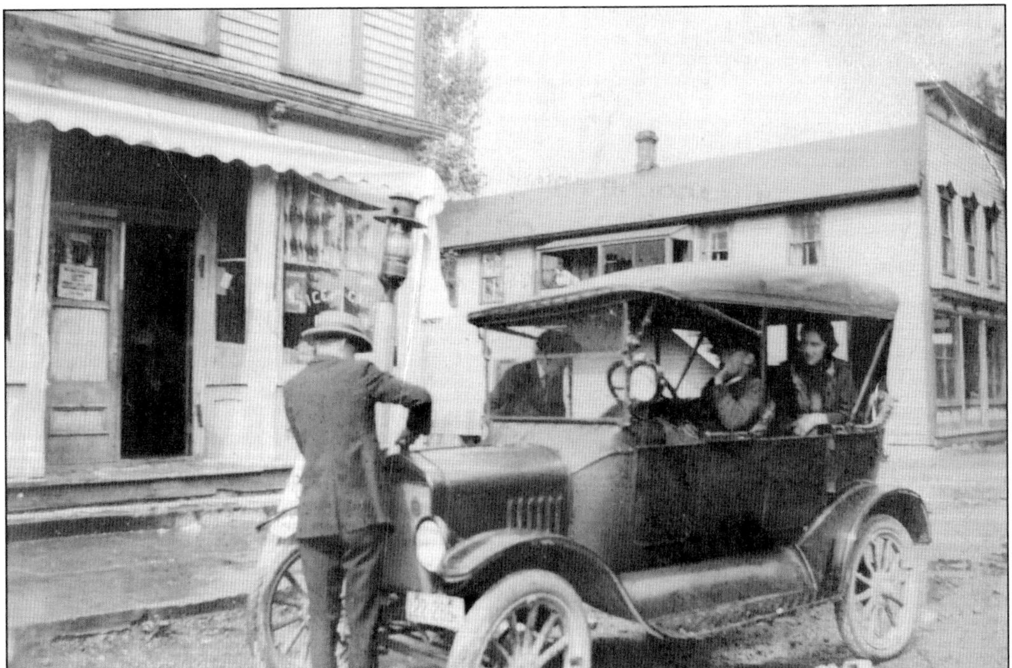

After enjoying some ice cream in the country, a patron is seen checking his engine before making his way back to the city. In the background, one can see the building that was known as Harrington's Tavern, later a grocery store owned by a distant Crandall relative. The buildings were located at 111th Street.

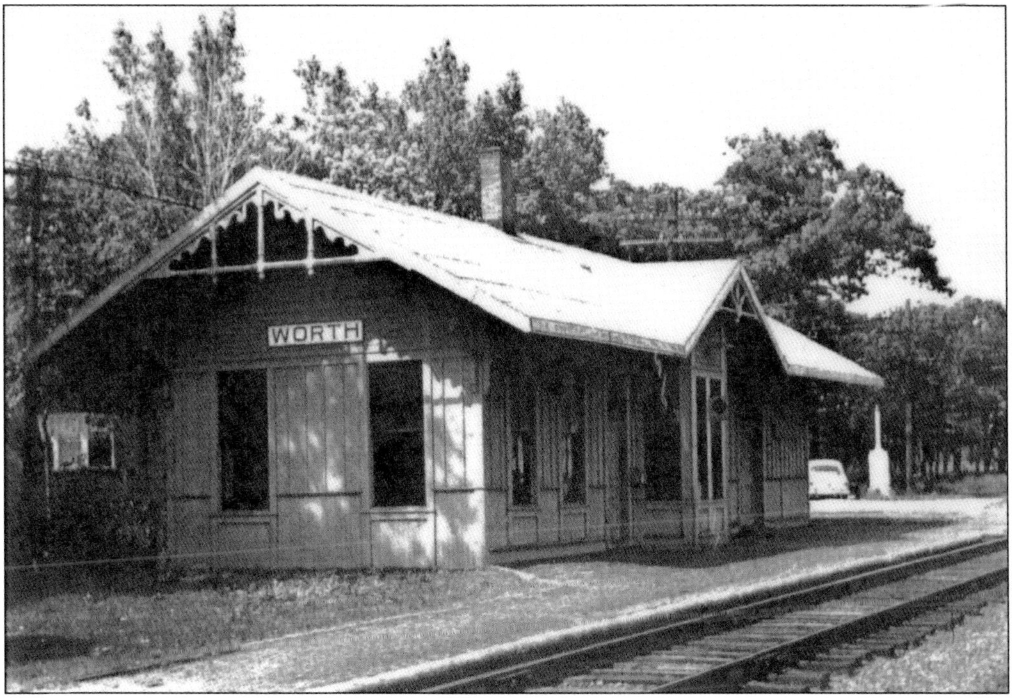

The Worth Train Depot modernized in 1908 once the establishment of a business district was made. The new train station accommodated anywhere from 5 to 15 passengers at a time. By building this station, it allowed for commuters to move easily back and forth from the city to the country. This station also brought visitors into the area and established Worth as a destination for travel and commerce.

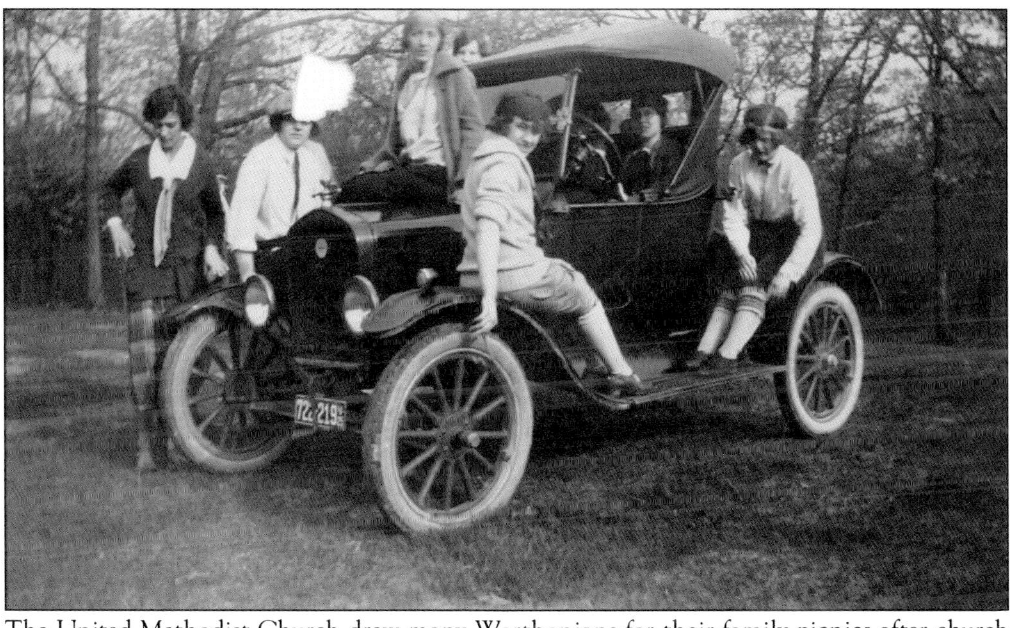

The United Methodist Church drew many Worthonians for their family picnics after church services. Here, the youth group members from the church admire another member's new wheels in the grove behind the church. This photograph was taken in 1931.

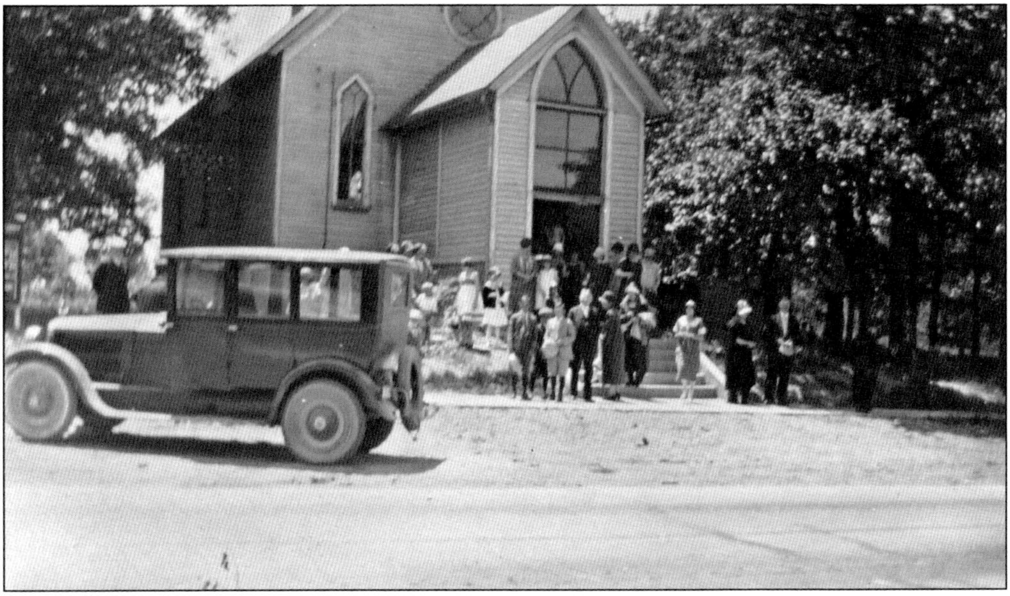

Outside the church after celebrating the 50th anniversary, patrons of the church stop to display their Sunday best. Under the direction of Reverend and Mrs. Guy, many church picnics and neighborhood celebrations were held throughout the summer. In 1946, a new church was constructed at 112th Street and Depot Avenue after fire devastated the original building. The brick building still stands today.

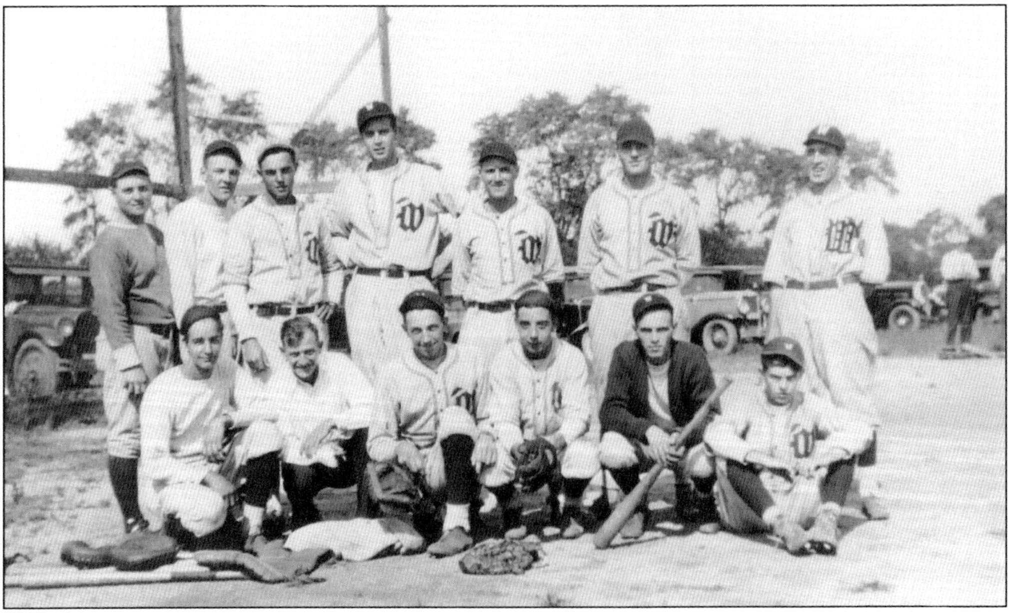

Worth had some powerful ball players in town during the early 1930s. Pictured are, from left to right, (first row) Herb Foyle, Smitty Smith, Norman Hanchett, Charles Beck, Franklin Russert, and Herb Stewart; (second row) Fred Behrends, Edward Lysen, Edwin Teason, Ken Lucas, Edwin Rolfe, Ray Miller, and manager George Monroe Peterson. Herb Stewart assisted Don Hanski in creating the first Boys Club, a baseball little league in Worth.

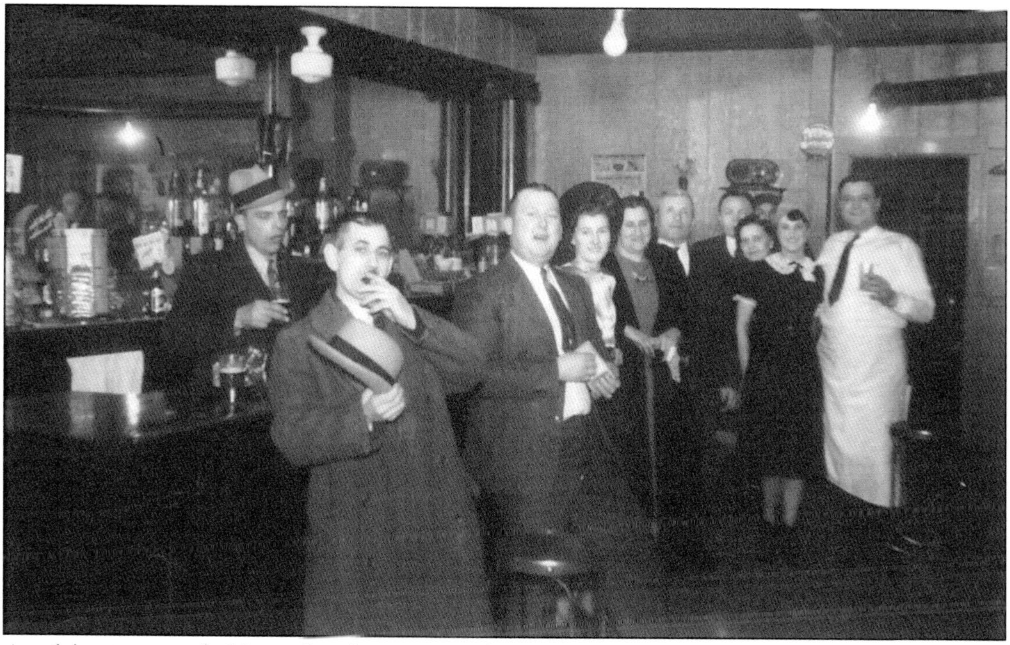

A celebration was held in a local tavern not long after the election in 1927 that gave Edward Conway, fifth from the front, the title of village president until 1941. Conway was the second president in town and was also the fire chief and resident blacksmith. Gert Conway is pictured fourth from the front. She was the first president and founder of the PTA in Worth in 1934.

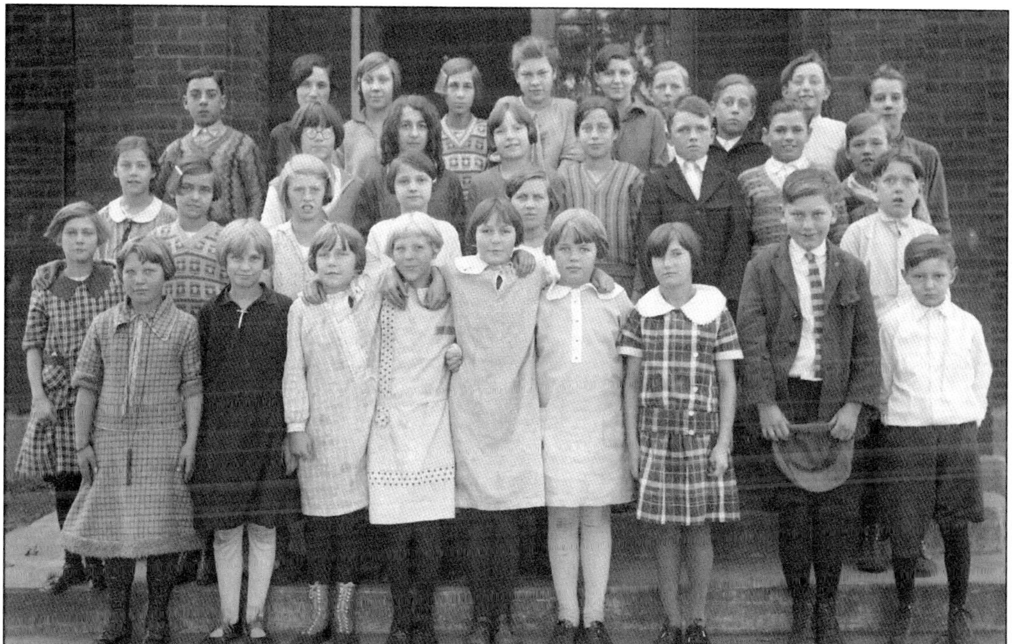

In 1924, student enrollment was up to 50. It was during the mid-1920s that the students from Chicago Ridge left the Worth School because a new district was formed. Prior to this year, students would come from Palos Township and nearby Chicago Ridge. As the population began to increase, the need for more options occurred.

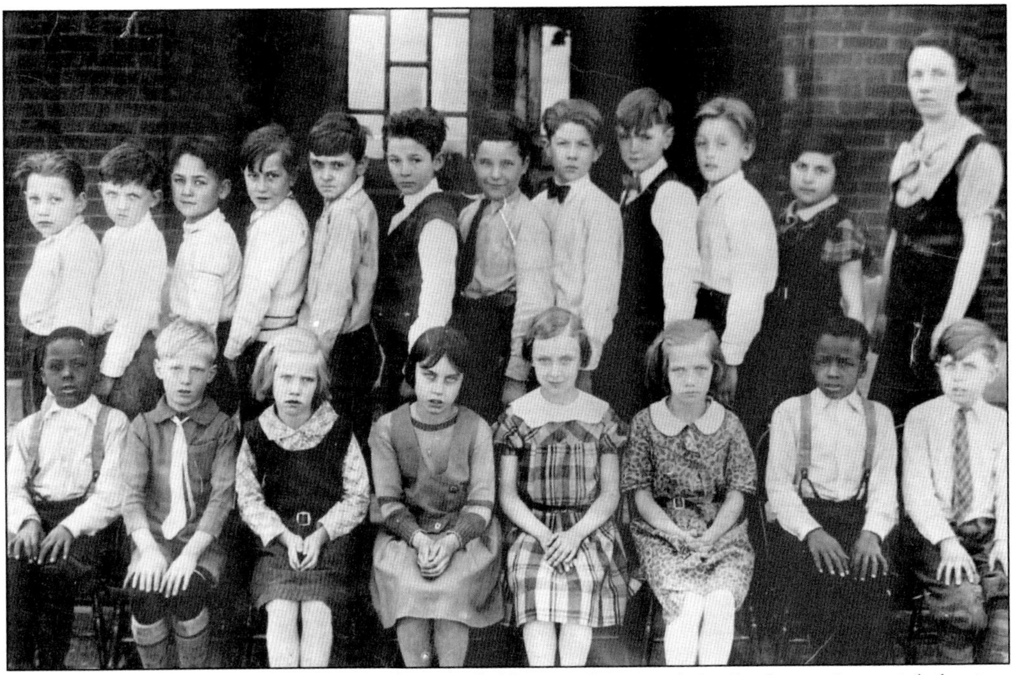

The class enrollment of 1934 increased to 84 children and strained the facilities. A special election was held in August 1935 for the purpose of authorizing an addition to the school. As a result, one classroom, an auditorium, two washrooms, and the basement were built, with 35 percent of the cost coming from the Federal Emergency Administration of the Public Works Grant. Pictured in this 1931 class are, from left to right, (first row) Willie Dancie, Casey Lode, Adrianne Lode, Irene Peterson, Helen Hoffman, unidentified, Eddie Dancie, and Jim McEathron; (second row) Art Kagabine, George Langlon, Fred Goodwin, Bill Conway, Alan Scheipper, Norvil Godvin, Dave Zuidema, Alvin Prebbe, Rich Foyle, Ray Johnson, unidentified, and Alice Reilly.

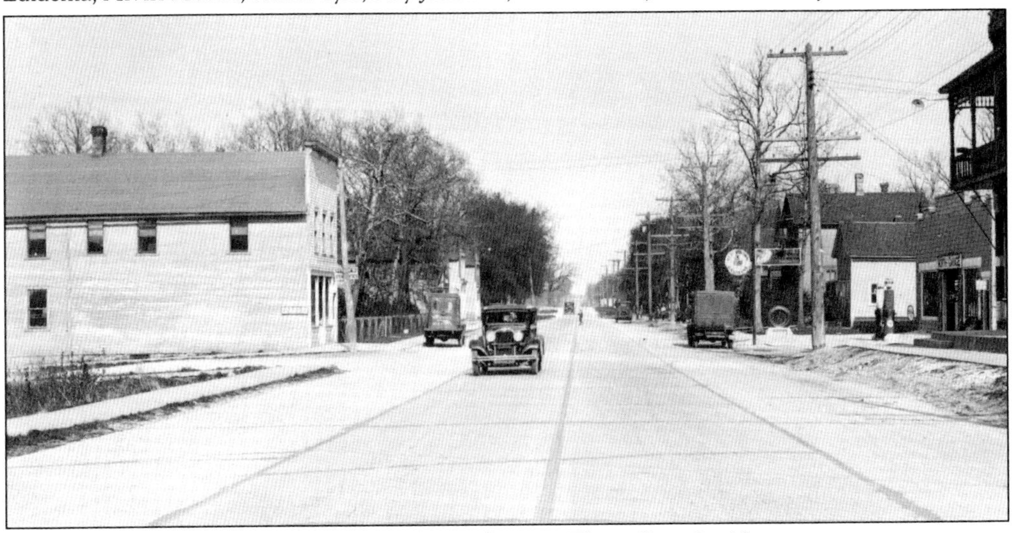

In 1934, the operating budget in Worth was $8,798. The village had begun to concentrate on the infrastructure of the village as more people began to move to the area. Flooding was not uncommon, and many cars were often stuck in the mucky roads in the country village. This photograph is looking down 111th Street, one of the first roads to be paved.

Looking south from 110th Street and Harlem Avenue, this car travels smoothly down Harlem Avenue after it was paved. The paving that occurred led way for many changes to come to town. After World War I, people started going places in automobiles. Before long, the auto builders outstripped the road builders, and traffic jams became more common.

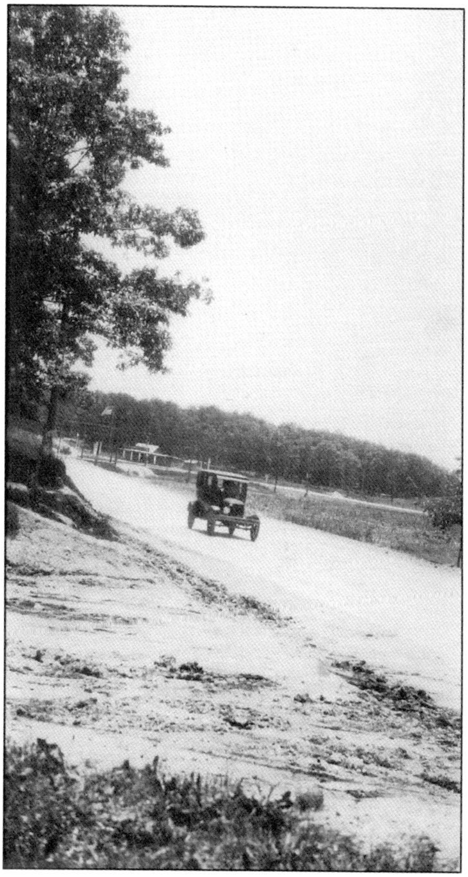

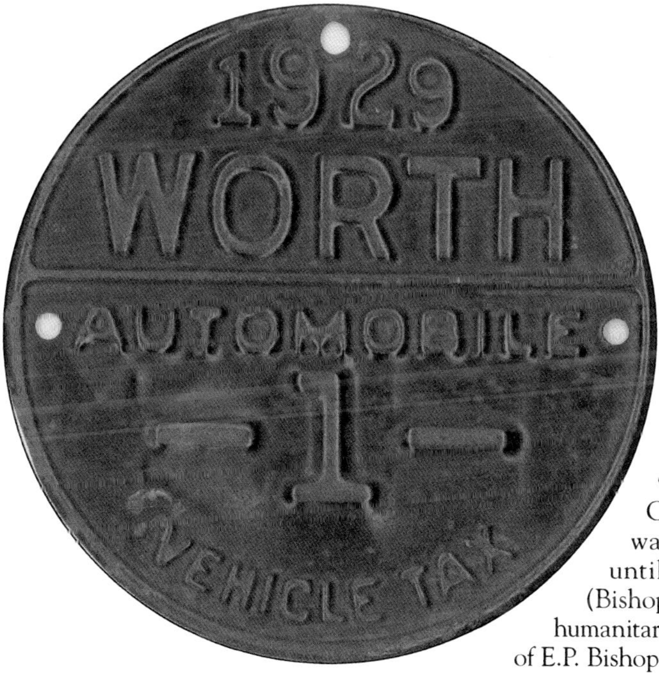

The village began distributing and selling licenses for automobiles. This vehicle tag was donated by Chuck Templin. Chuck's father, Vernon Templin, was village president from 1956 until 1961. His mother, Leah Rose (Bishop) Templin, a schoolteacher and humanitarian in the village, was the daughter of E.P. Bishop.

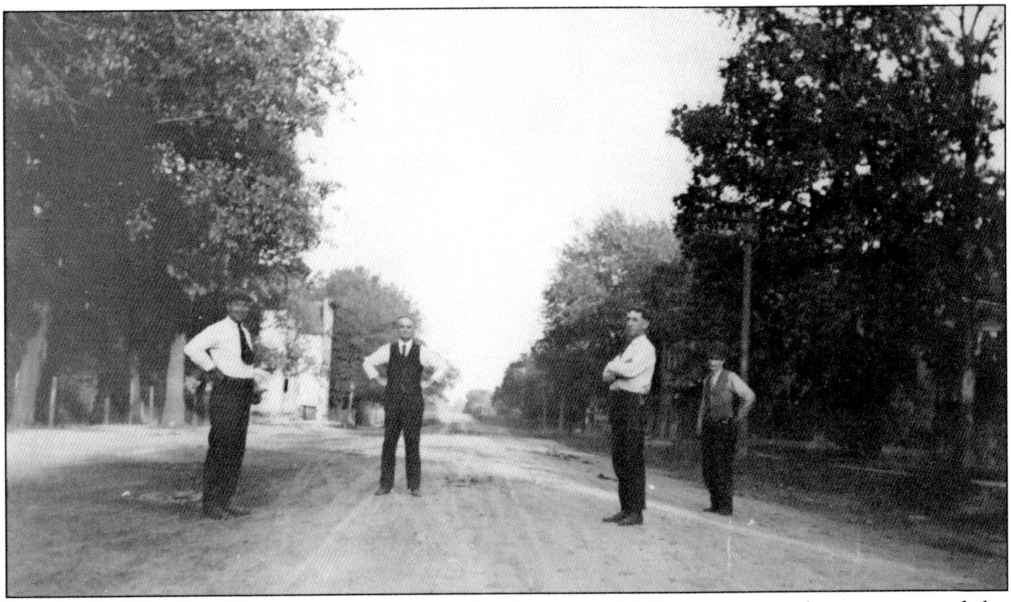

As the local businessmen congregate on 111th Street in 1932, one can only reminisce of the pioneers that did the same before them. Many in the village of Worth were reluctant to see change come in the form of increased transportation and population and paved roads.

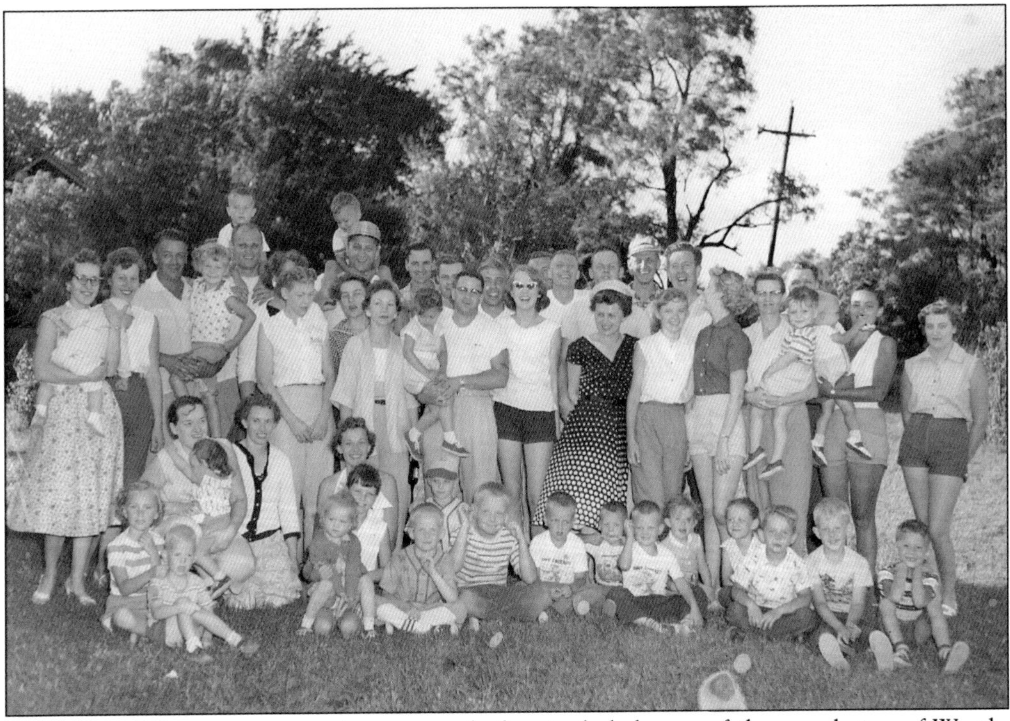

Family reunions were common in town and often included most of the population of Worth. While the population grew, new neighbors were spotted at these events in addition to distant cousins, aunts, and uncles. This photograph depicts the Lode, Plahm, Kerkstra, and Kittle families in the mid-1950s. Many of these family members were directly involved in building the village of Worth in the 1950s.

Three

Sleepy Hollow to Boom

Cities are wonderful places to live. There is growth, and governing bodies make decisions that often change the landscape to urban places. The village of Worth had its biggest growth spurt in the early 1950s. Post–World War II suburbia began to grow as the US government offered incentives to settle the southwest suburbs. In 1952, a sign that read, "Worth 700," greeted travelers through town. By 1955, the sign read, "Worth 7,300." For the greater part of the 20th century, Worth was a "Sleepy Hollow" town, where nothing ever altered or happened. The 1950s gave Worth a face-lift, and rapid transformations could be seen with the replacement of old, wooden buildings with modern strip malls. With increased needs for the establishment of professional departments, the fire and police departments saw improvements. While the majority of the members were volunteers, the village began to properly fund the departments with the influx of residents.

As families flocked to the suburbs to seek the open air of the country, it was not uncommon for schools to experience overcrowding. Much expansion occurred during this time at the elementary and parochial schools in the area.

While the early pioneers cited tales of being stuck in the "muck of the sloughs of the preserves" that nearly forced some to take up residence right at the location where they were stuck, it was not the case for the residents of the 1950s. Many came because of the small-town charm that Worth had to offer. This chapter explores the development of municipal services and key factors that influenced change at the municipal levels of government.

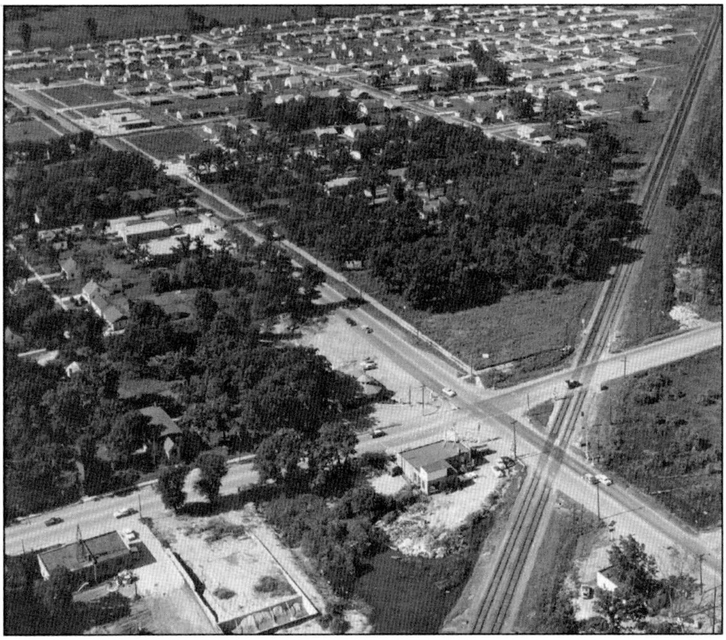

In 1956, Worth was growing by the hundreds. This aerial view shows the increase of post–World War II frame homes that were constructed. According to a special census, there were 934 homes built between 1951 and 1953. This photograph shows the intersection of Harlem Avenue and 111th Street prior to the addition of the underpass on the northwest corner. The village hall can be seen on the left-hand side of the photograph.

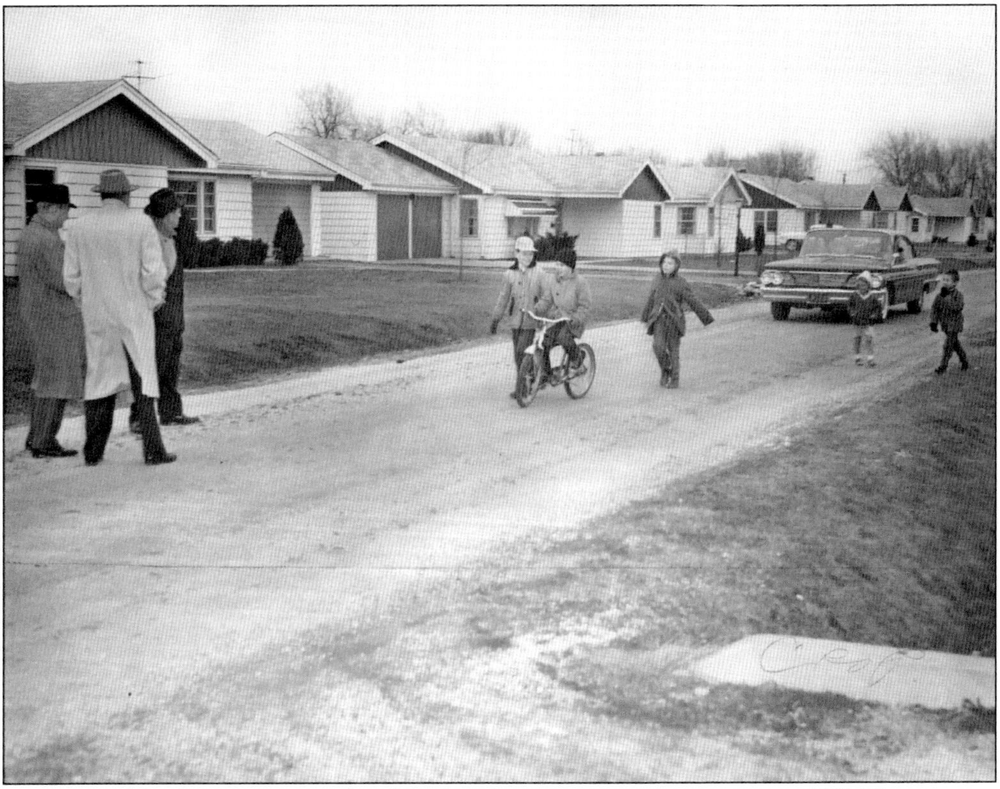

Box homes, like these constructed on Natchez Avenue, were very common in 1955. The majority of homes were built on a slab due to the terrain and many underground springs in the village. The average cost of a home in Worth in 1955 was $10,000.

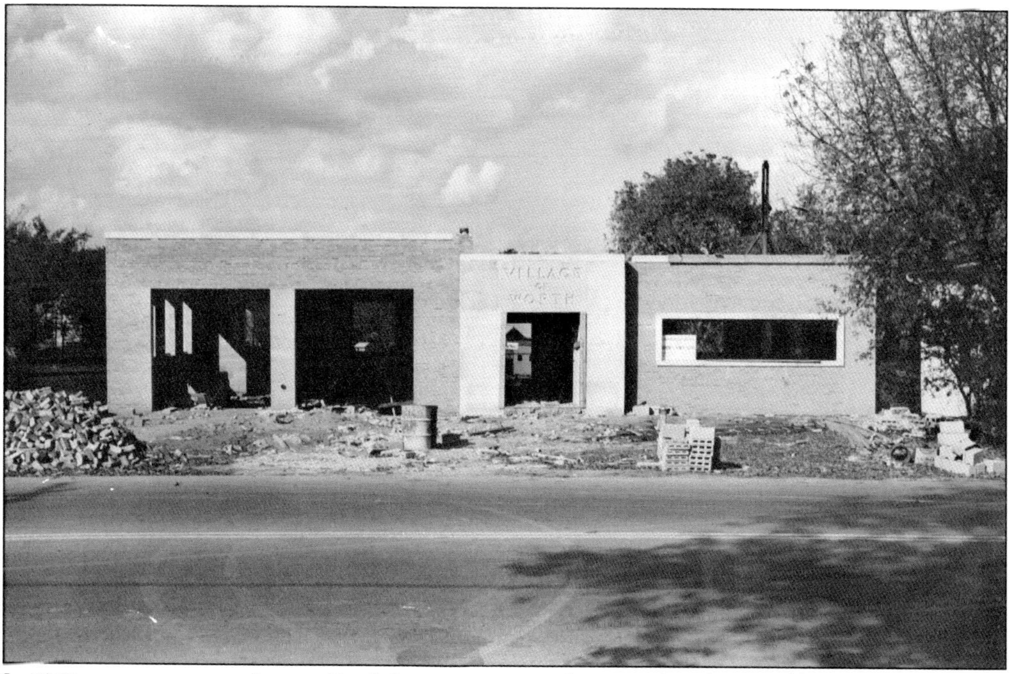

In 1941, government workers realized that a permanent location for a larger village hall was needed. Prior to the construction of the village hall, meetings were held at various locations, including the old Featherstone building on 111th Street. When that caught fire in the late 1940s, it was determined that a modern building was needed to address the needs of the residents.

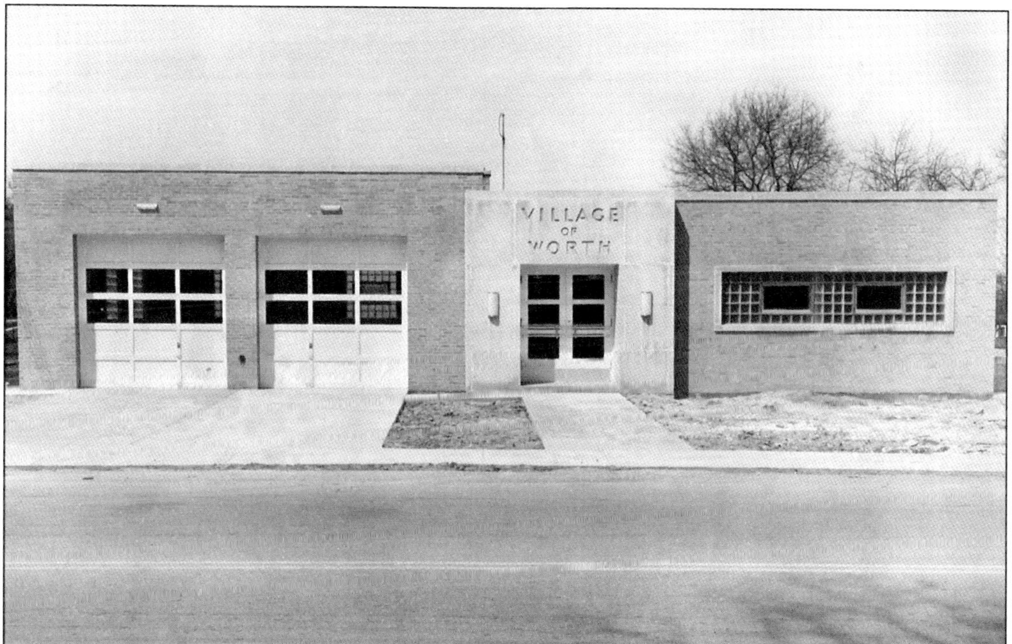

Construction was completed in 1950, and the building shared space with the police and fire departments. The village board and president Francis E. McDonough passed a special bond for $30,000 to construct the building.

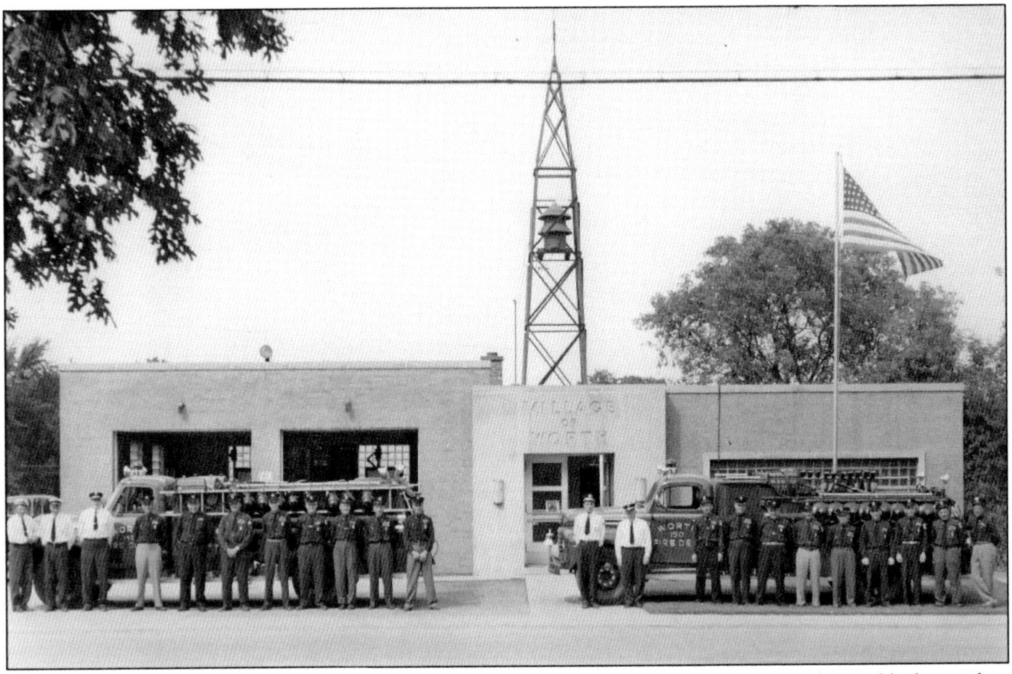

The 1954 fire department consisted of two 500-gallon-per-minute pumping trucks and belonged to the Community Firemen's Association, an organization that included 65 towns and memberships. The department had over 44 volunteers, and the chief was Bert Lode. In these photographs, the firemen line up to show the importance of fire safety. Local fire departments would compete in safety tournaments throughout the state. Hundreds of photographs were taken by fire safety training officer Ed Emond to demonstrate to the public and to the department the importance of fire safety in town. The siren located on this building was the original that had been used on the old wooden barn.

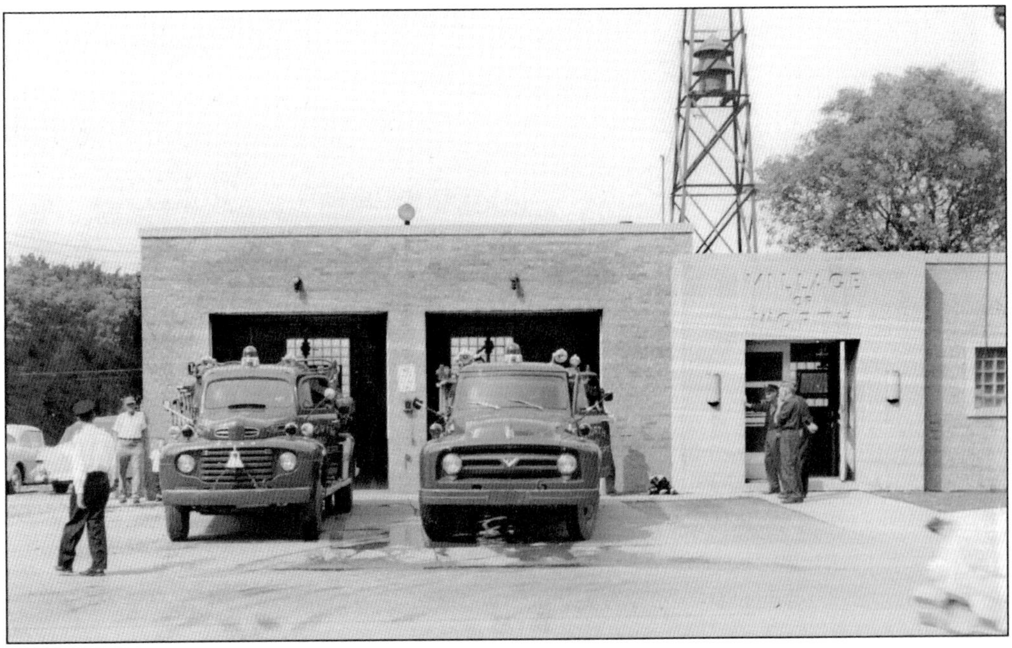

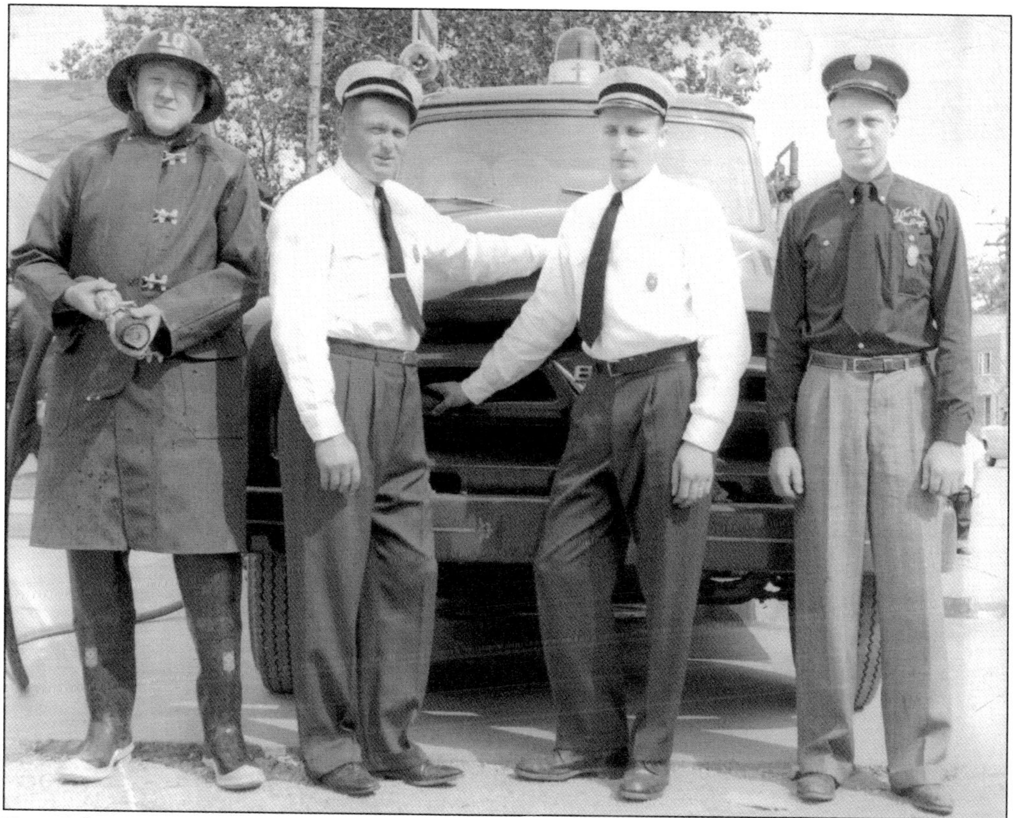

From left to right, Len Teason, Chief Burt Lode, assistant chief John Zuidema, and Casey Lode stand in front of the newest member of the truck team. Burt Lode was fire chief from 1952 to 1963.

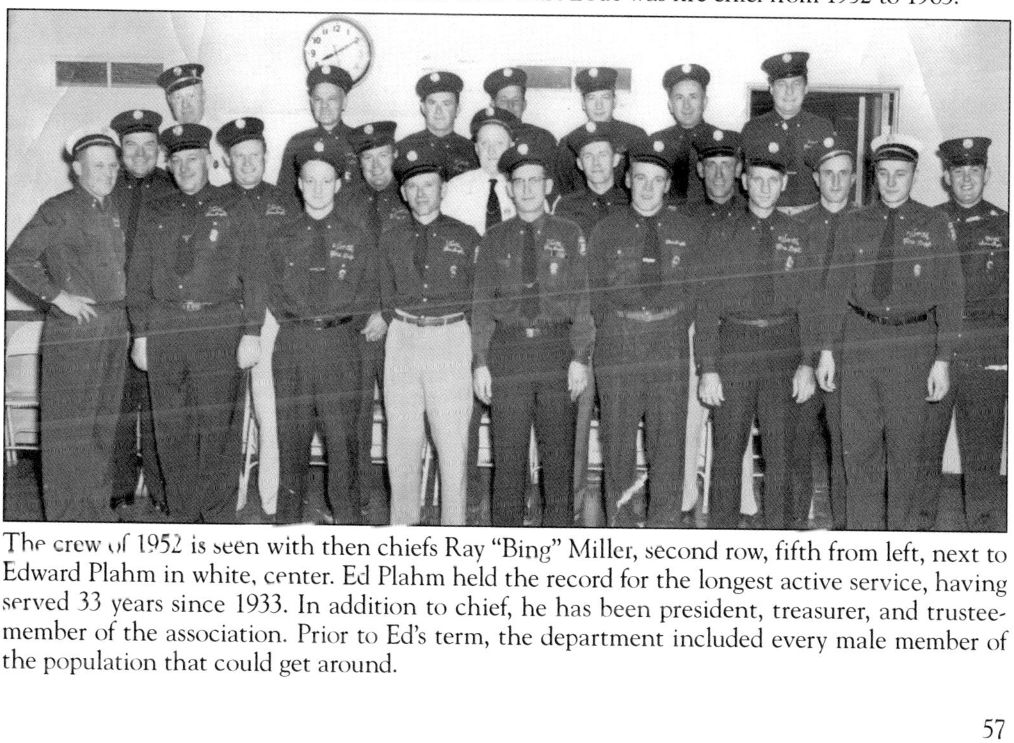

The crew of 1952 is seen with then chiefs Ray "Bing" Miller, second row, fifth from left, next to Edward Plahm in white, center. Ed Plahm held the record for the longest active service, having served 33 years since 1933. In addition to chief, he has been president, treasurer, and trustee-member of the association. Prior to Ed's term, the department included every male member of the population that could get around.

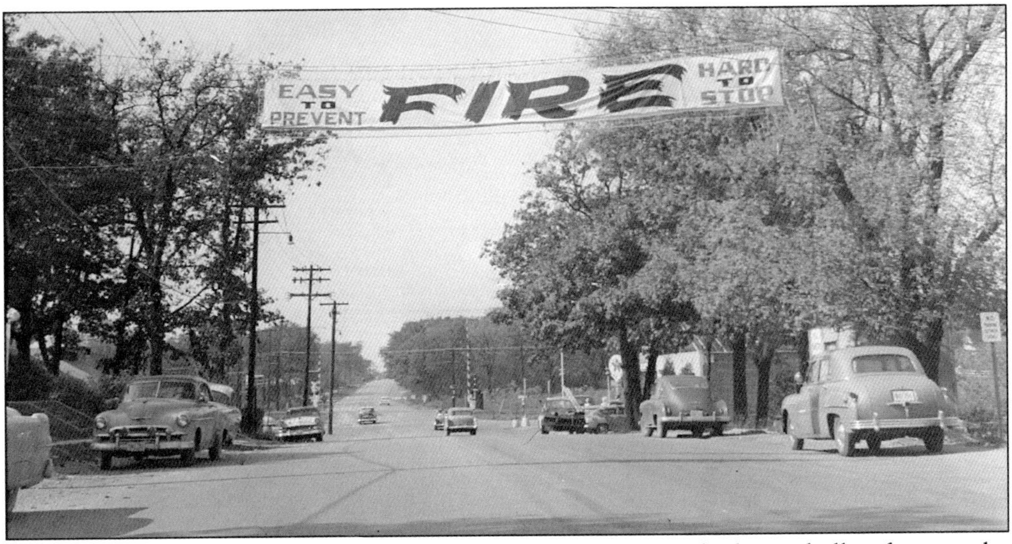

A full banner is stretched across the street from the firehouse to the legion hall, informing the community and all who pass through that the second week of October each year is "Fire Prevention Week." This was in honor of the Great Chicago Fire. Fire Prevention Week was a very active and exciting time for all that lived in town. Firemen staged drills around town that would engage residents on the importance of fire and home safety.

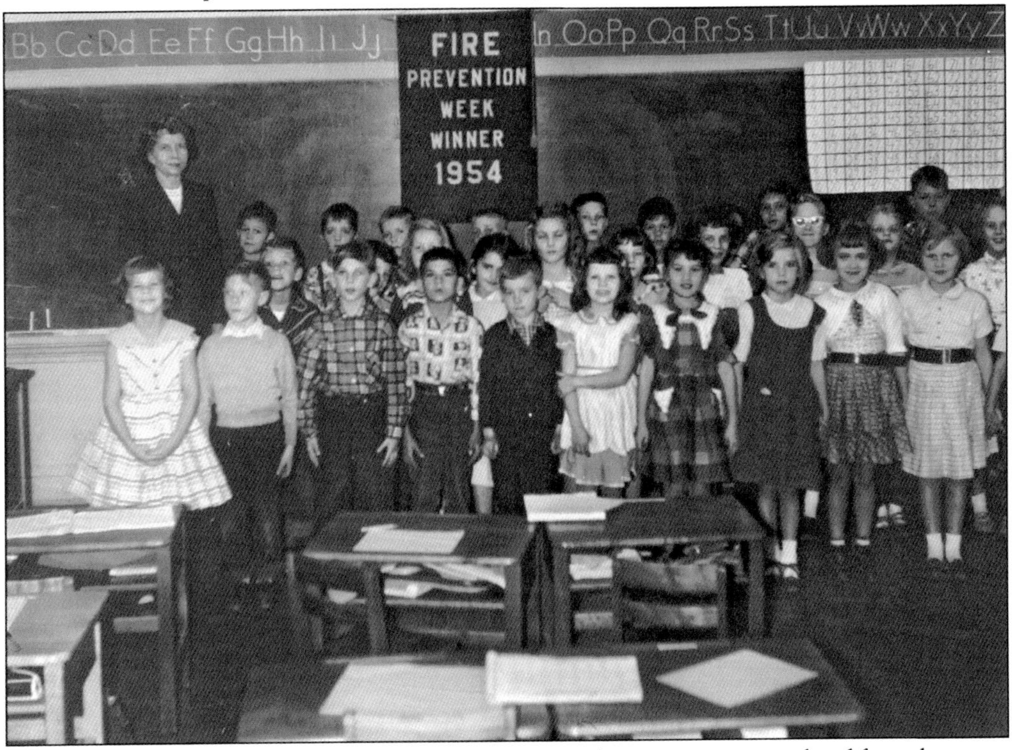

In 1954, this class received a special banner for turning in the most essays completed for a classroom that discussed the importance of fire safety. Poster contests, essays, and school demonstrations were just some ways that firemen would engage the community. For several years, Fire Prevention Week activity chairman Ed Emond and Chief Bert Lode held events throughout town.

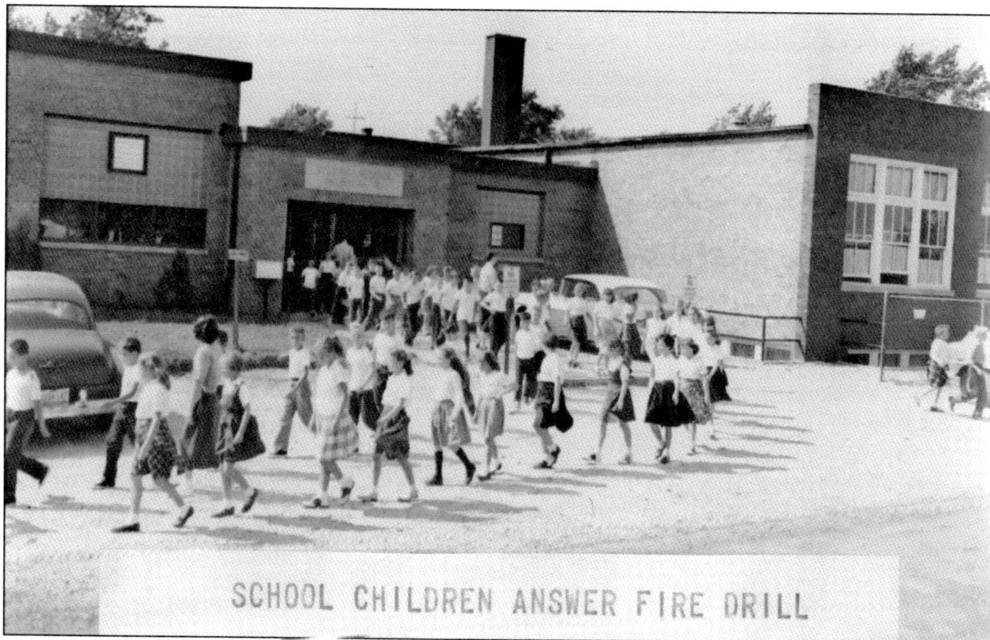

School evacuations were common during Fire Prevention Week. These students from Worth Elementary School evacuate safely out of the north exit after the new edition was put on in the late 1950s.

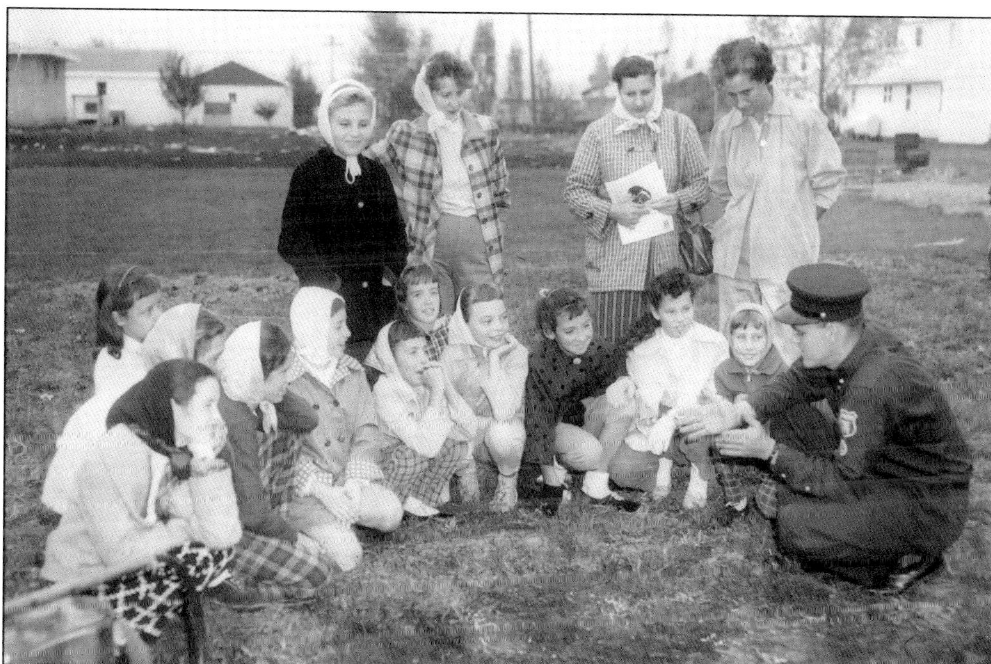

In an effort to make fire prevention a hands-on experience, firemen would go into the community and offer training sessions on items that could be purchased and put in homes. This photograph shows instructor and volunteer Kenny Dunn demonstrating fire techniques to the Intermediate Girl Scout Troop 253 in 1960. The girls listen intently and answer questions on how to prepare and be safe.

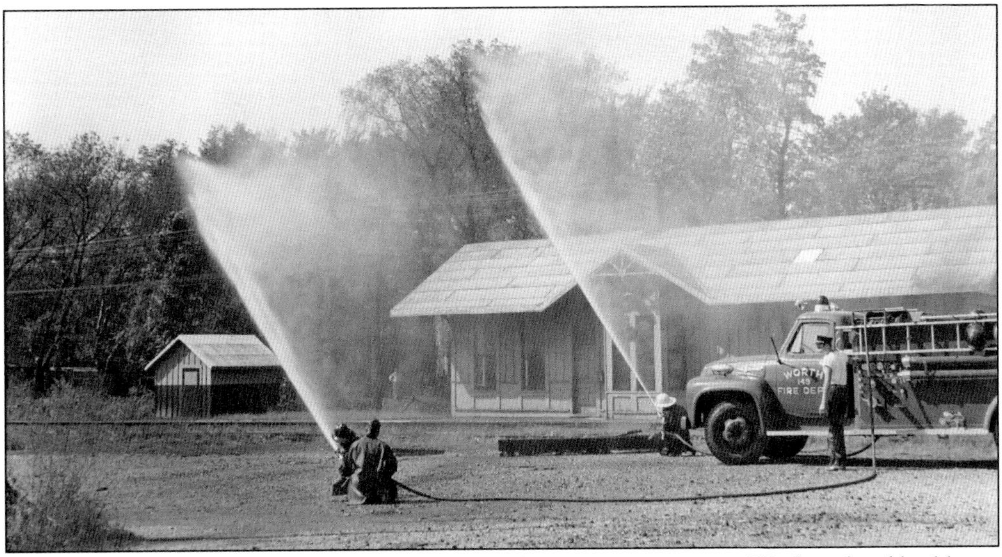

Demonstrations by the fire department were done during Fire Prevention Week on local buildings. Here is a photograph taken near the Worth train station. Oftentimes, the fire department would display their preparedness on local buildings prior to a demolition or after a fire. In this instance above, members of the department were cleaning hoses and keeping shop. The train depot was located behind the fire department.

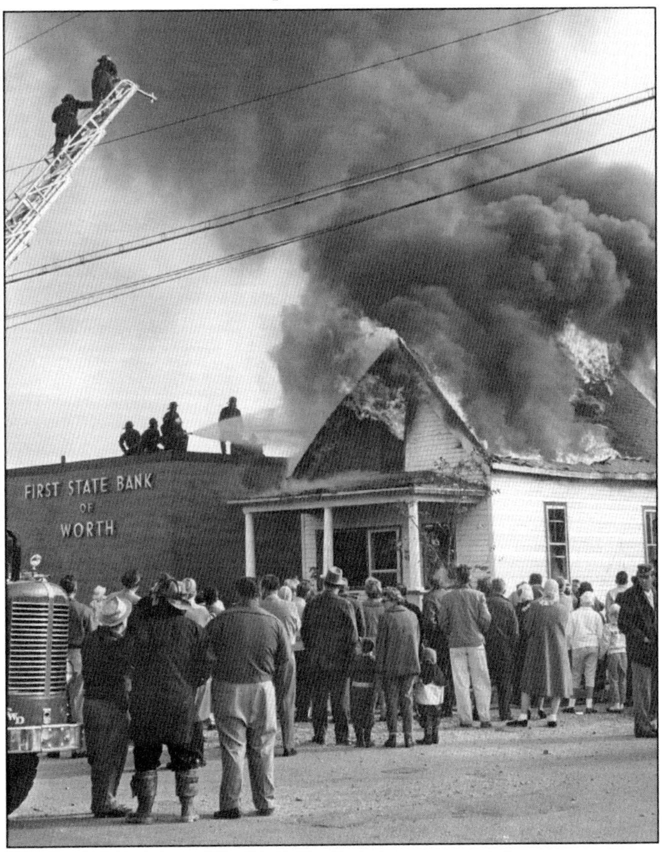

It was not uncommon that many homes of the original pioneers were demolished. These homes were often used as working farm homes or livable homes. The village does not have a historic home ordinance, due to the specifications and cost it would take to designate these areas on the homeowner. This home, originally built by the Crandall family, was located next to the First State Bank of Worth. The home was demolished to make way for a parking lot and building expansion for the bank.

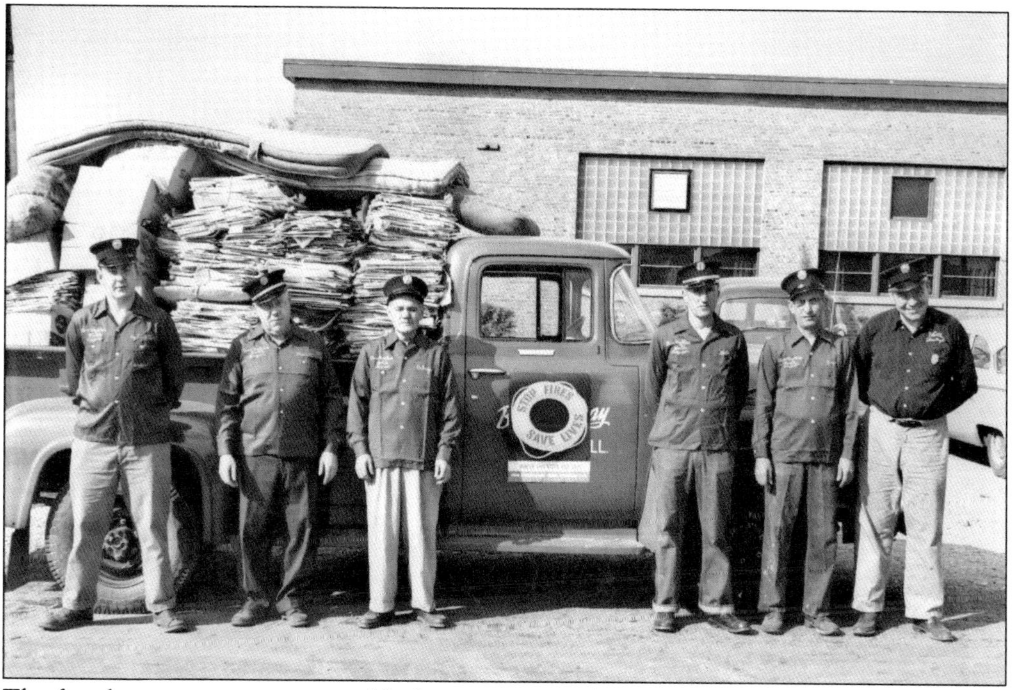

The fire department was responsible for various recycling programs. Often, the department would turn in papers to local plants for funding. The department was made up of volunteers and relied on its booster club for funding. The paper drives were an opportunity to inform residents on containing their garbage and to reuse and recycle items often. In 1958, the fire department responded to 108 calls to homes. There were 41 volunteers, and they were not supported by the village tax levy.

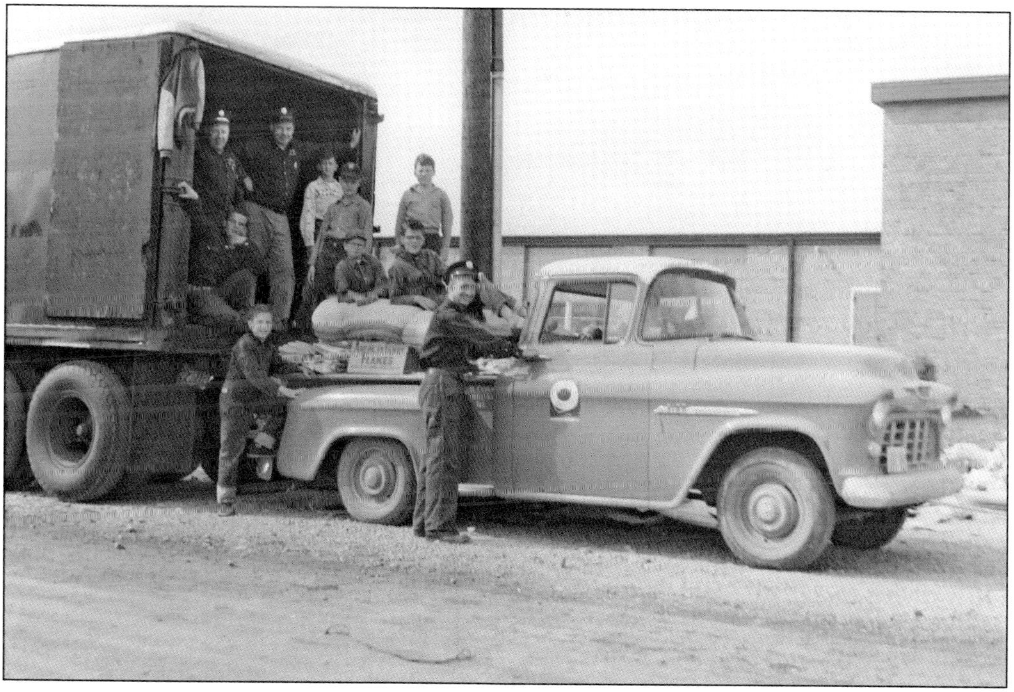

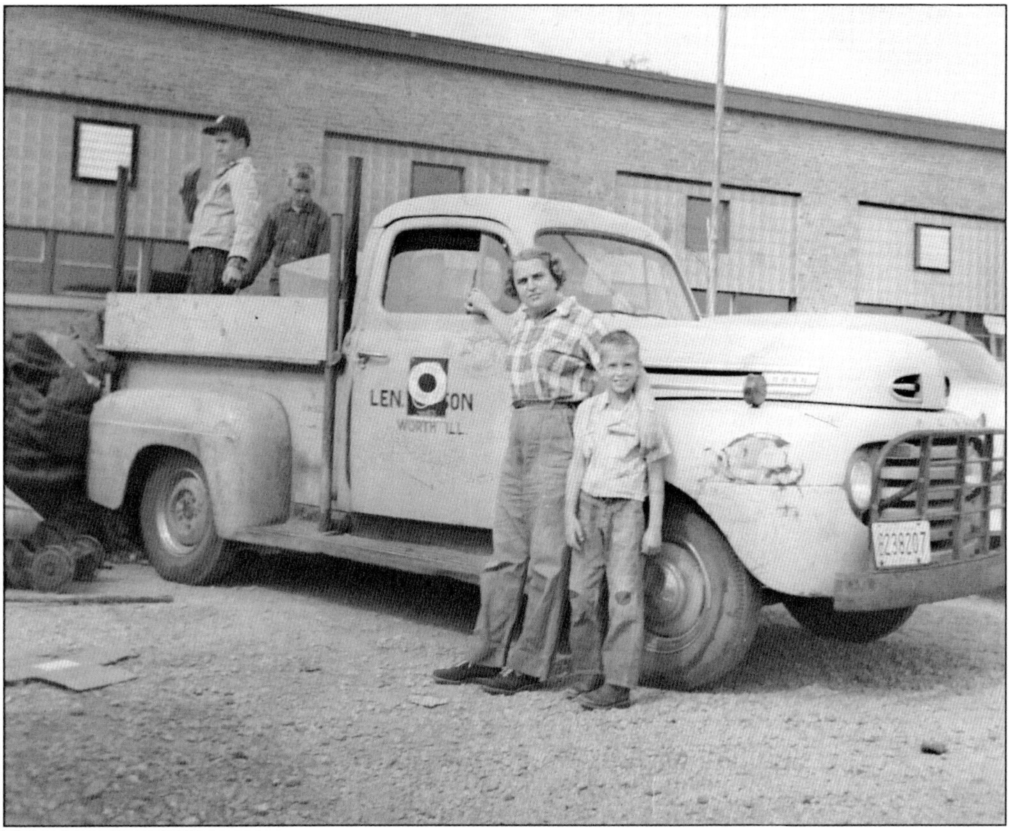

Ester Foyle Lode and her three sons often assisted in the paper drives that were held by the fire department. Ester Lode was one of the founders of the *Worth Record*, along with Agnes and John Daniels. The *Record* was a local newspaper that was published in Worth.

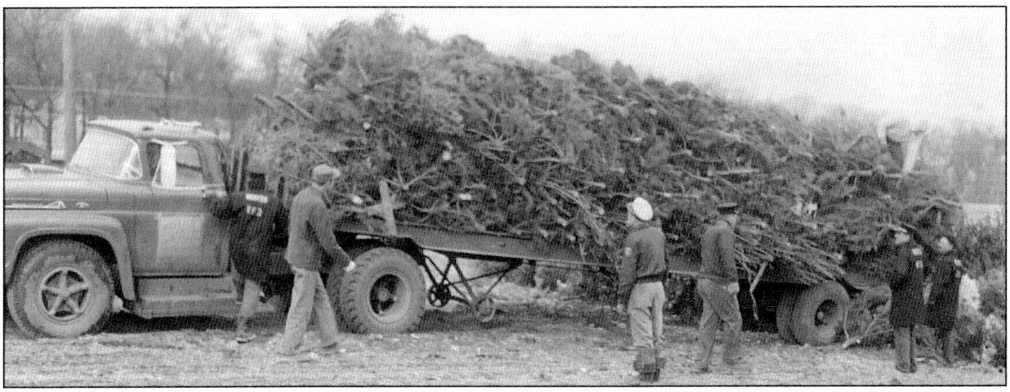

The Sunday after the New Year, the fire department would drive around town collecting all the trees used during the Christmas holiday. They would use the trees for a large, controlled bonfire that would be held behind the village hall. This was done to demonstrate the dangers of having dried out trees and also to control garbage left in the village.

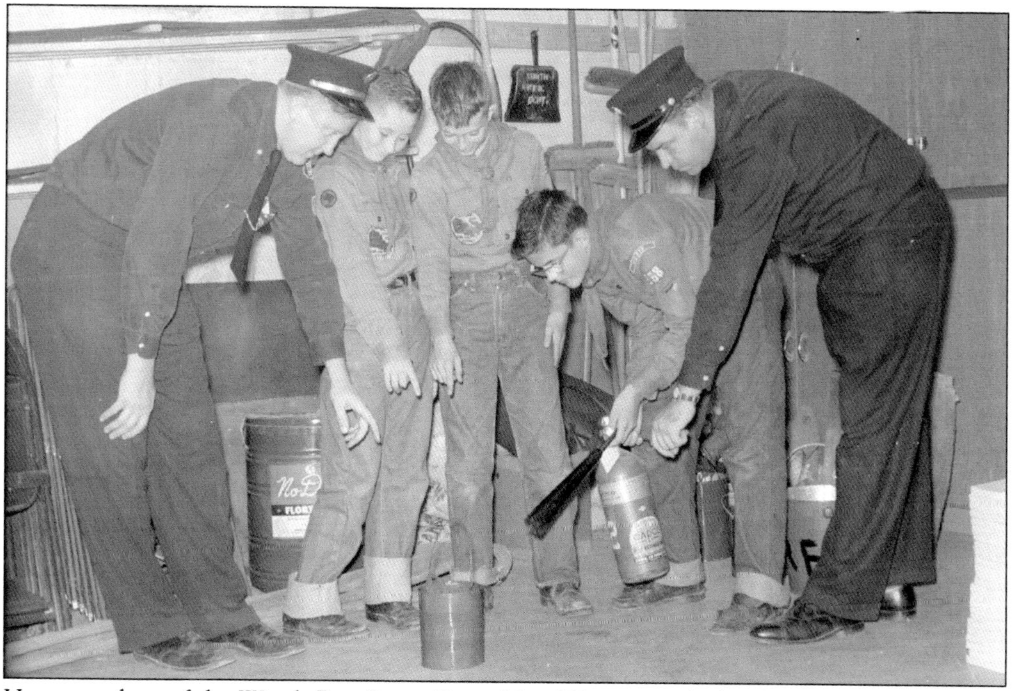

Here, members of the Worth Boy Scout Troop No. 668 meet with the fire department to learn about fire safety. Both the Boy and Girl Scouts were instrumental in assisting with outreach programs for youth. Many of the parents of the Scouts were also volunteer firemen.

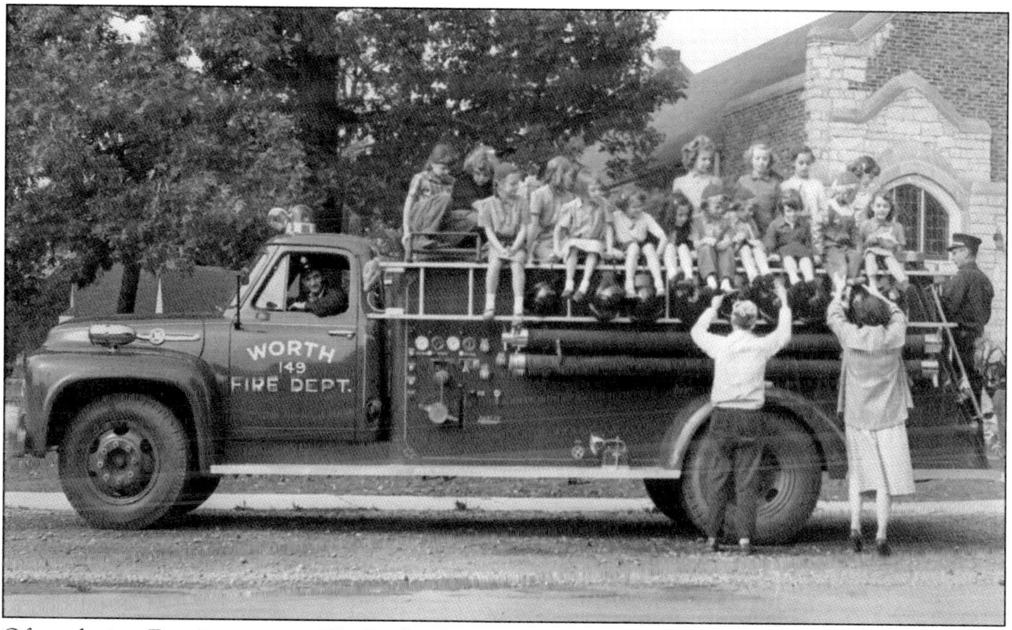

Often during Fire Prevention Week, the fire truck would be seen driving around with children and community groups to promote awareness. This 1953 troop came out of their meeting at the United Methodist Church, seen in the background, to take a photograph with the firemen. The troop leader is making sure all the girls fit on the truck. The Methodist church moved to this location in 1949 after a fire destroyed the original building.

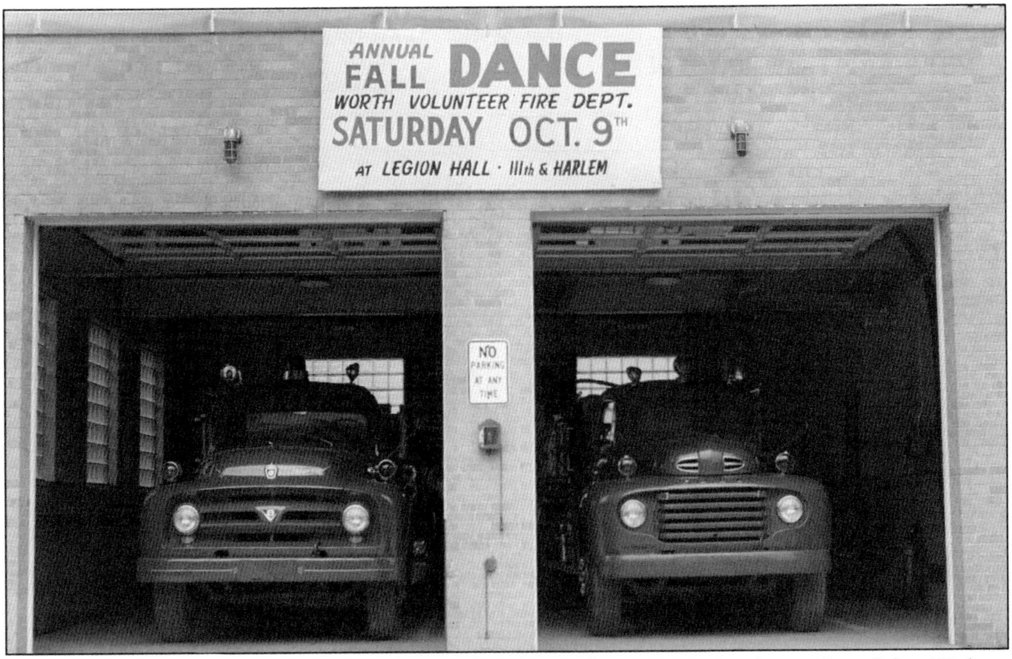

Fire Prevention Week would wind down with a dance for teens and a dance for adults. Tickets were sold by the fire department for the whole month of October, and dances were staffed by volunteers from local civic organizations (such as the Lions Club, PTA members, and the Methodist Church). Money raised would go toward much-needed fire equipment.

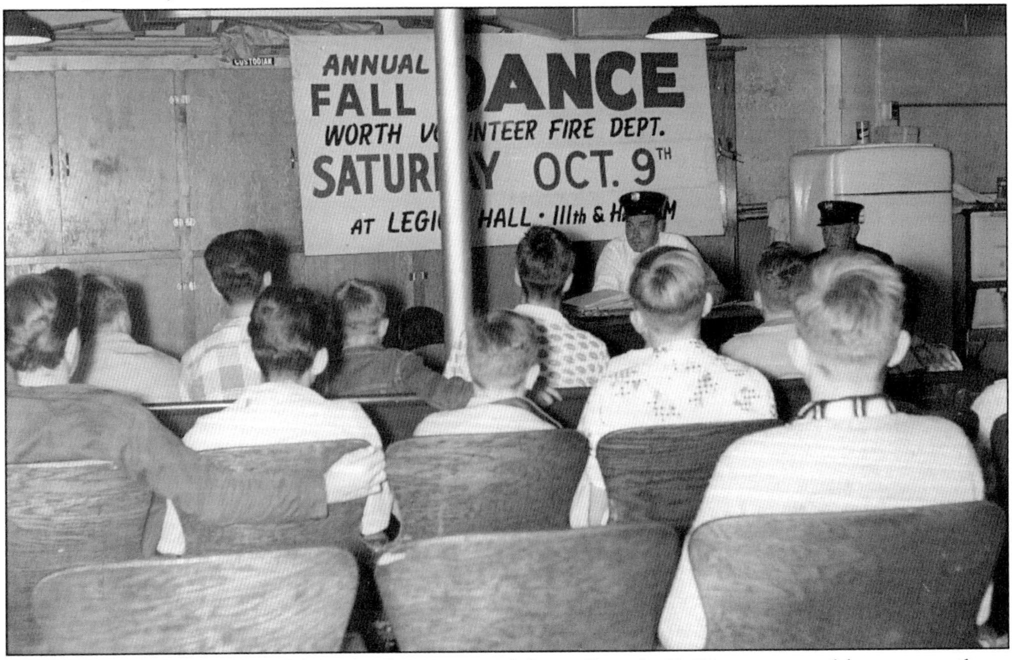

Meetings for teens were held in the basement of the village hall. Teens were able to contribute to the planning of activities, such as the dance during Fire Prevention Week. Entertainment and local talent were important in this community-wide event. The Keen Teen Program was created out of these events.

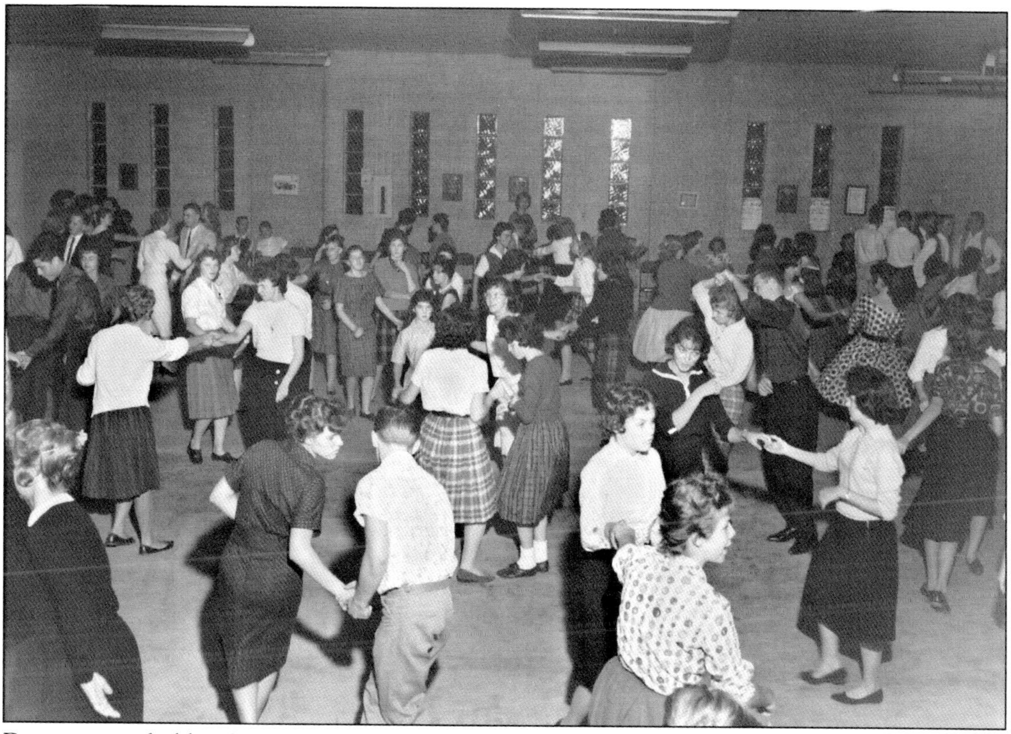

Dances were held at Diesing's Grove, Bachelor's Grove, Hildebrand's Hall, above the Worth Hardware, and Ferrin's Garage. These photographs depict the dancing-room-only events that were held in the basement of the American Legion.

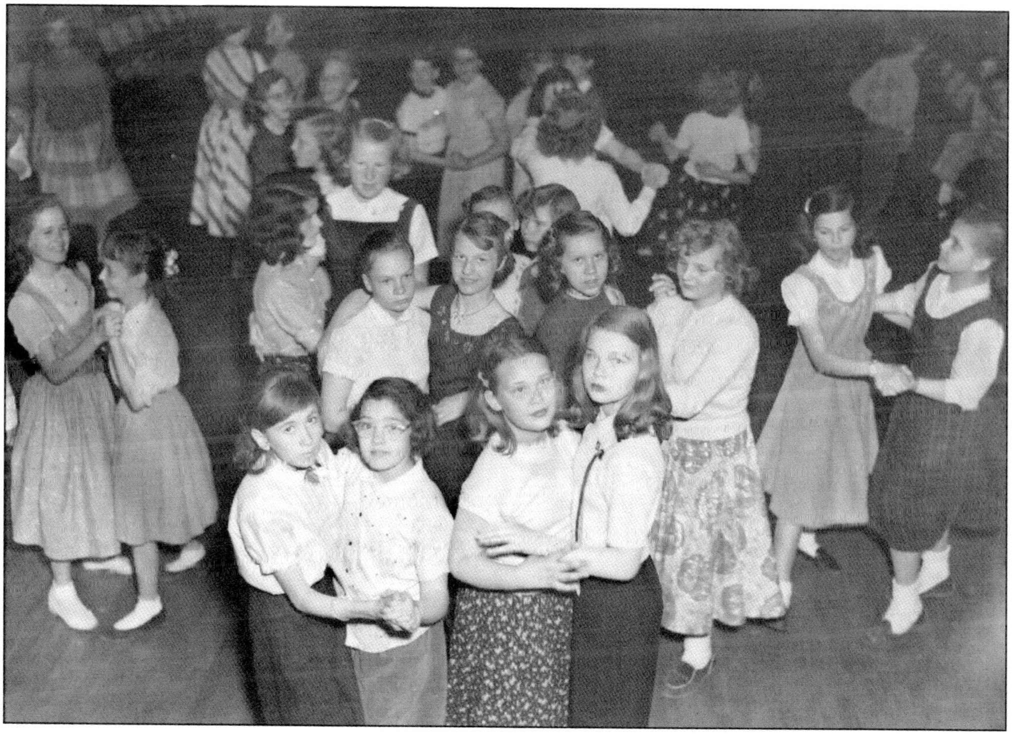

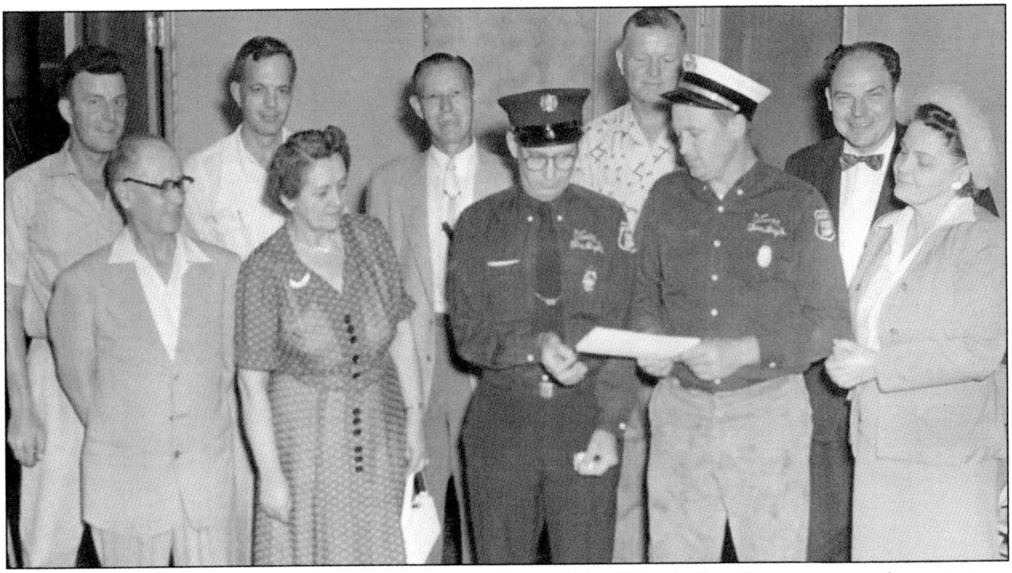

In 1956, during the term of Carl Korbitz, president of the Worth Fire Department Association, the mortgage on the first truck, No. 250, was burned. Pictured are, from left to right, (first row) trustee Charles Peske, clerk Mary Plahm, Carl Kprbits, Bert Lode, and trustee Ina Sundquist; (second row) trustees Edward Bishop, Ernest Hedlun, Charles Hart, and Henry Boersma and village president Vernon Templin. While the fire department operated independently of the village board, it did partner with them, and a trustee was assigned to attend meetings and report back to the village board.

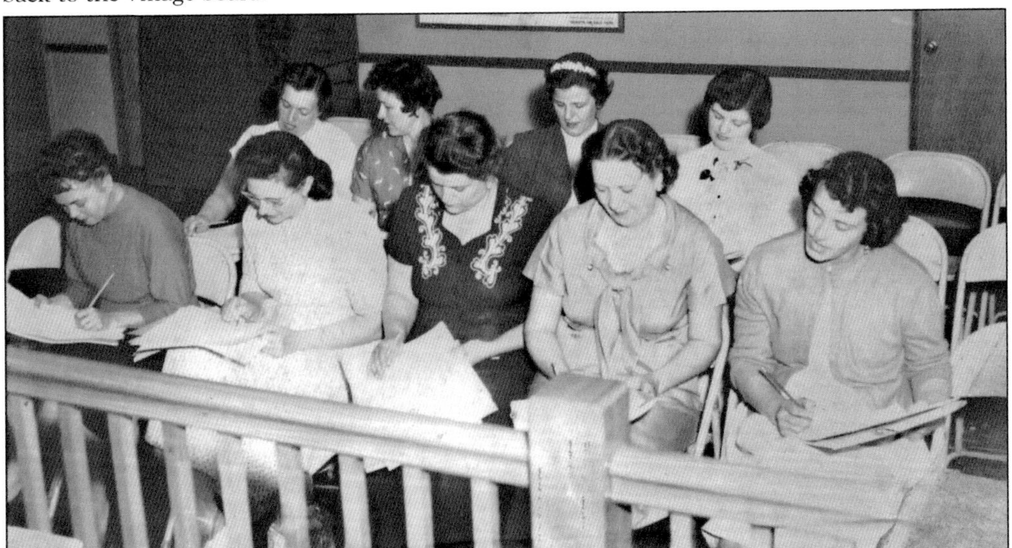

A special census was requested in 1953 in order to obtain more motor fuel tax to assist in the growing infrastructure problems in town. In 1957, Northwestern University graduate students did a special assessment to determine the land use and the needs of the village of Worth. Seen here are members of the special census committee obtaining information and directions on completing their task. Pictured are, from left to right, (first row) Eleanor Webber, Lucille Thiele, Ethel Coats, Beulah Broniecki, and Edith Dick; (second row) Marie Ralston, Stella Lysen, Clara Moore, and Maralyn Zeman.

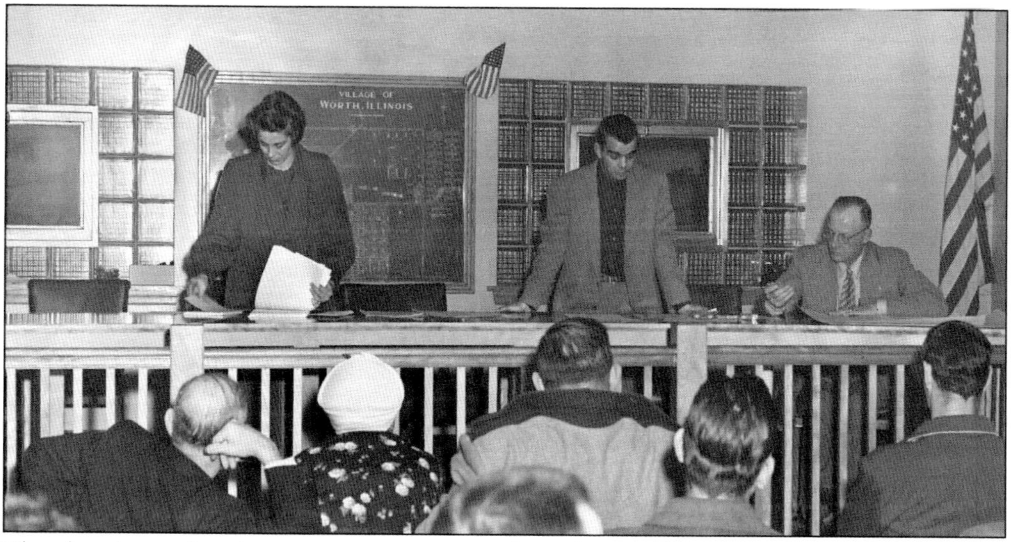

The planning and zoning commission was quite busy during the 1950s and 1960s. Many zoning changes and ordinances were introduced to the village at this time. Aggie Daniels, standing, was the owner and publisher of the *Worth Record*. She was also the chairperson of the planning and zoning board. She worked alongside many administrations to ensure that the integrity of the village remained intact. Aggie was often seen as the moral watchdog of village officials. Also in the photograph are Howard Ballard (center) and clerk George Plahm (right). This photograph was taken during a meeting in 1954 to discuss the toll road expansion.

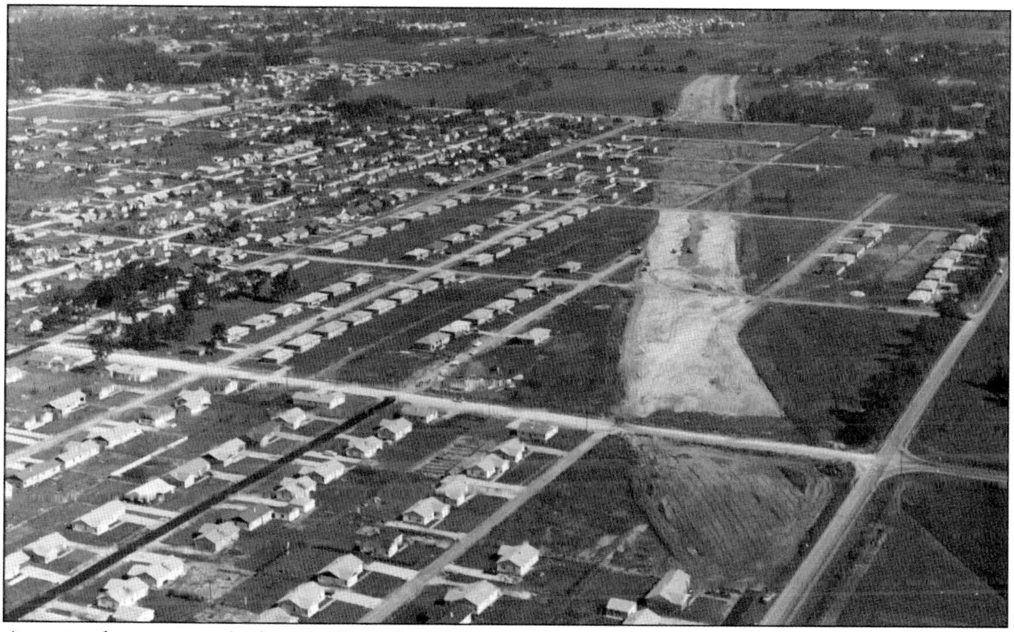

A major decision put before the board was discussed when the village became physically divided with the construction of Interstate 294, which cut off the eastern end of the village. After many debates and discussions, a committee was formed in the 1950s to oppose the expansion. It was determined by the committee to fight for the toll road to pass on building an entrance and exit on 111th Street, fearing the further separation of the townspeople and local businesses along the business district. Construction began in 1957.

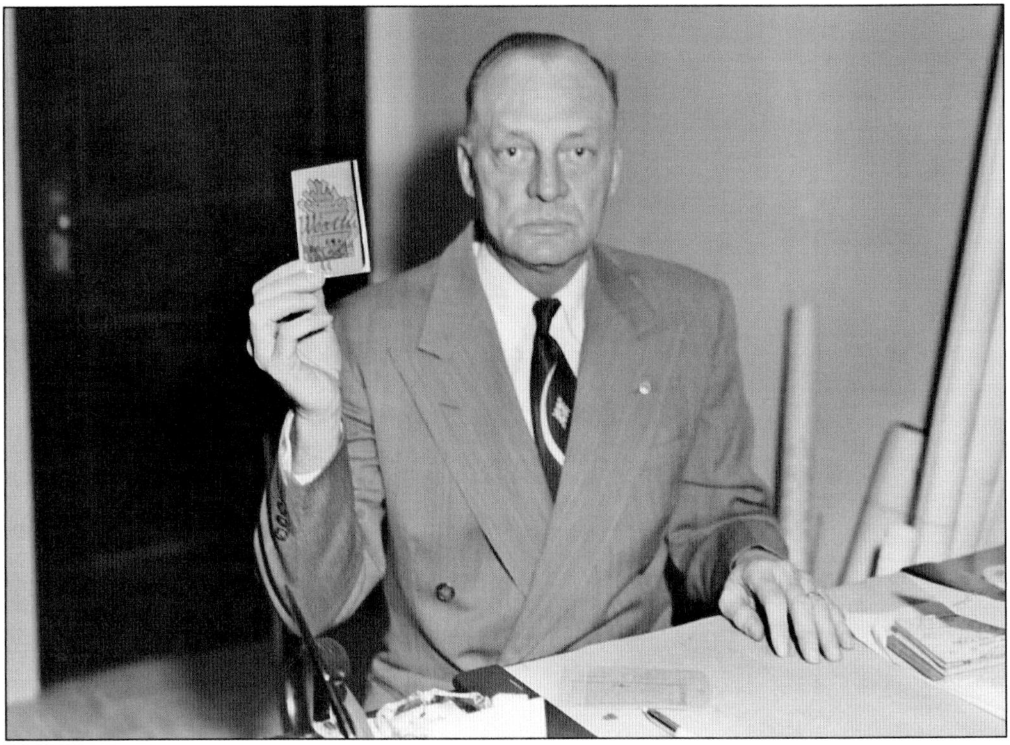

In 1928, George Plahm was elected clerk in the village. He served the village for 27 years as clerk as well as in fraternal organizations in the community. Clerk Plahm was a charter member of the Lions Club, chief of the volunteer fire department from 1949 to 1952, and served on the rationing board during the war. Also, all knew him as "father confessor." George's first job in the village was as a water boy during the construction of the Cal-Sag Channel. While he was involved in so many things, he was a modest and humble man. He is seen in this photograph showing the latest village car sticker in 1954.

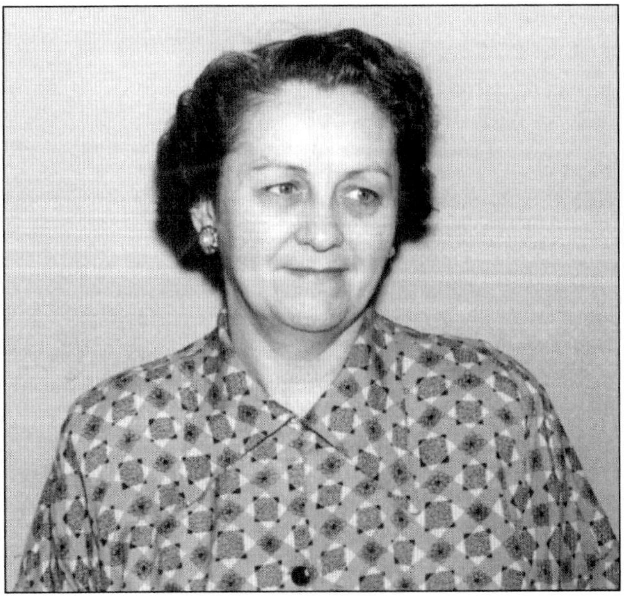

Mary "Pansy" Plahm, pictured here in 1961, replaced her husband as village clerk after his untimely death in 1955. Like her husband, Pansy was involved in many benevolent organizations in town. She resigned after eight years as clerk in 1963 due to an illness. The Plahm family home stands at 113th Street and Worth Avenue. It was built by the Booster Club of Worth, a benevolent society that assisted with many village projects in the 1950s.

Water systems in Worth were quite a hot discussion during this time of growth. Many residents operated on a well system until 1965, when Chicago water made its way to Worth. From left to right, Paul Zeman, Speed Kittle, L.J. McCauley, Jack Harper, and Wilber McCauley celebrate the achievement as they survey the first water that was drilled underneath the village hall in 1962.

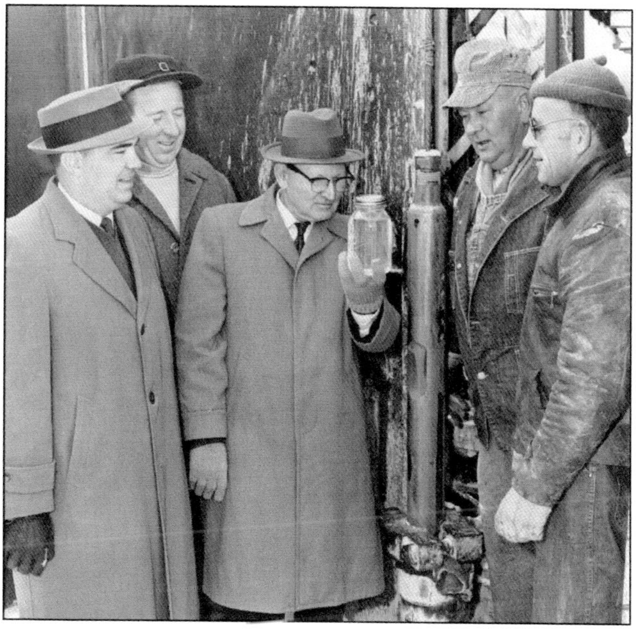

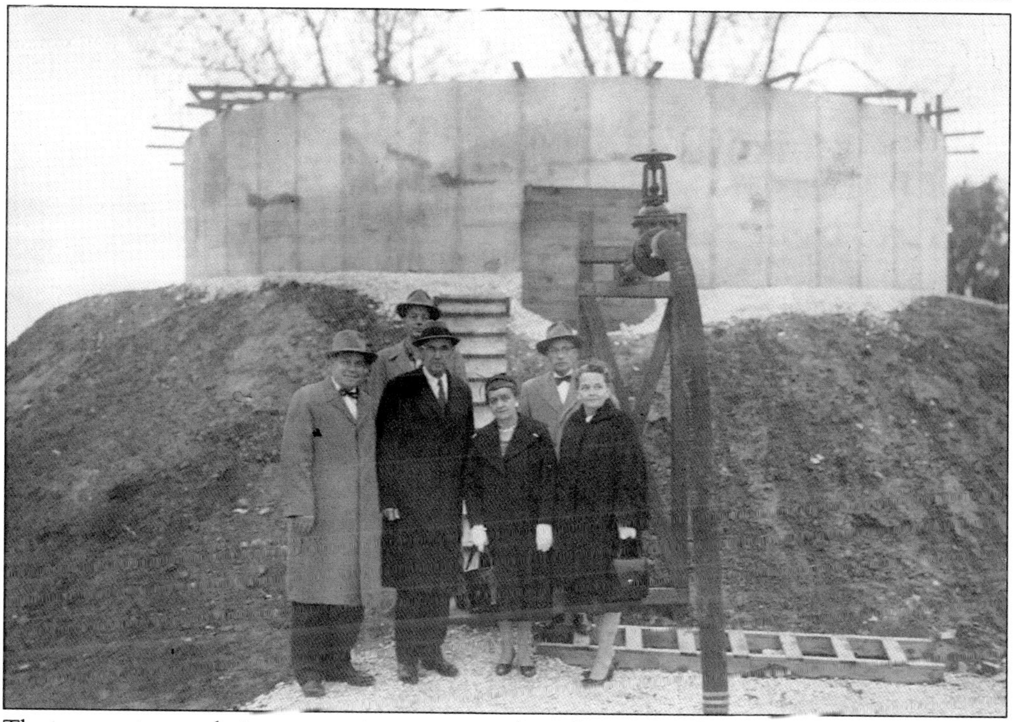

The increase in population was putting a strain on the infrastructure. Many new improvements came to the village in the form of sewer and water systems. During the Vernon Templin administration, the village board approved a sewer system to replace septic tanks. This photograph, taken in 1959, shows, from left to right, (first row) Vernon Templin, Walter Baltis, Mary Plahm, and Ina Sundquist; (second row) Ernie Hedlum and Marshal Beaver standing in front of the newly constructed water reservoir in the southeastern end of town. Residents in this section of town had a private pumping system, known as the Percy Cump system.

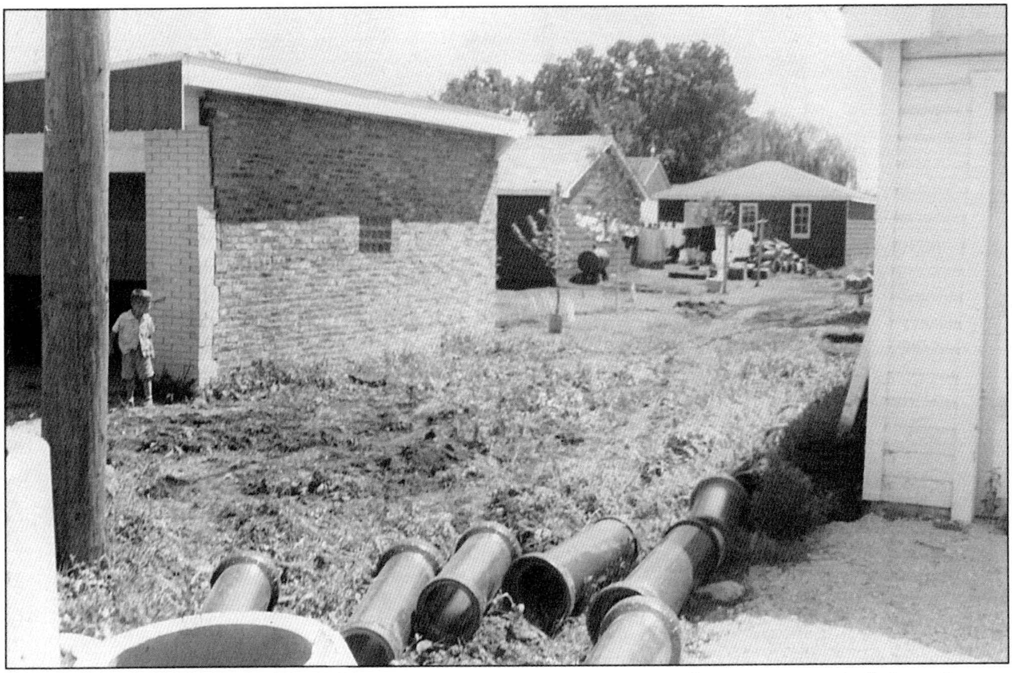

Sewer tiles were laid in Worth home easements in preparation for getting rid of the odorous septic systems in 1959.

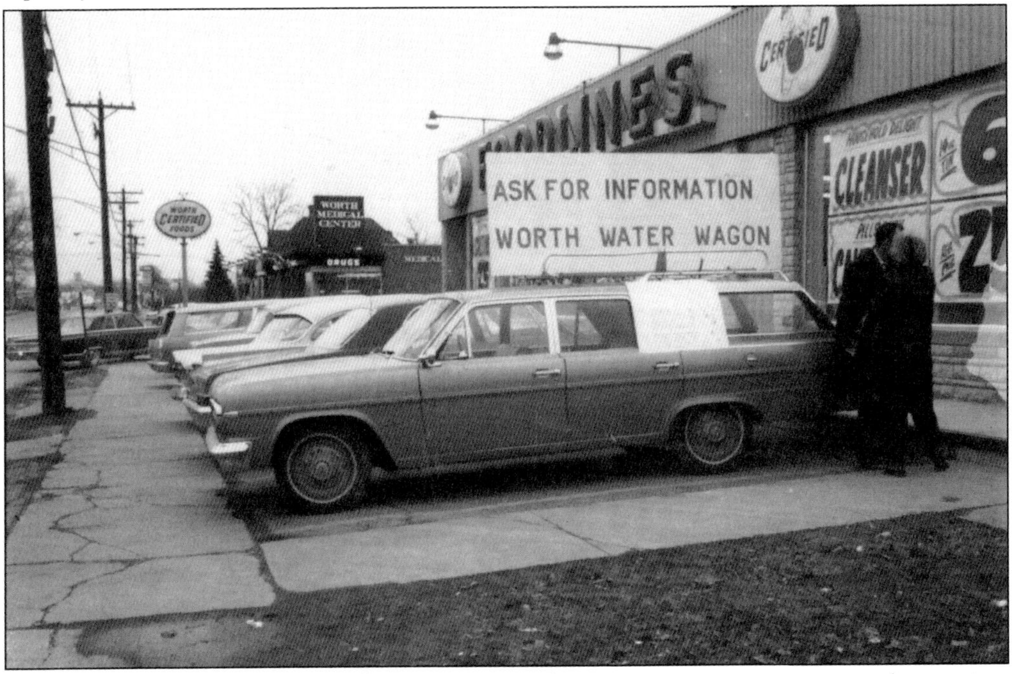

While the village was making way for improvements for sewers, water systems were under scrutiny. Hundreds of homes built in the southeastern section of town were on a water system built by Percy Cump. The original drilling in town was done in 1925. By 1964, a group called the Committee of 39 formed to advocate for a municipal water system. Water cars would be seen around town to educate residents on the improvements.

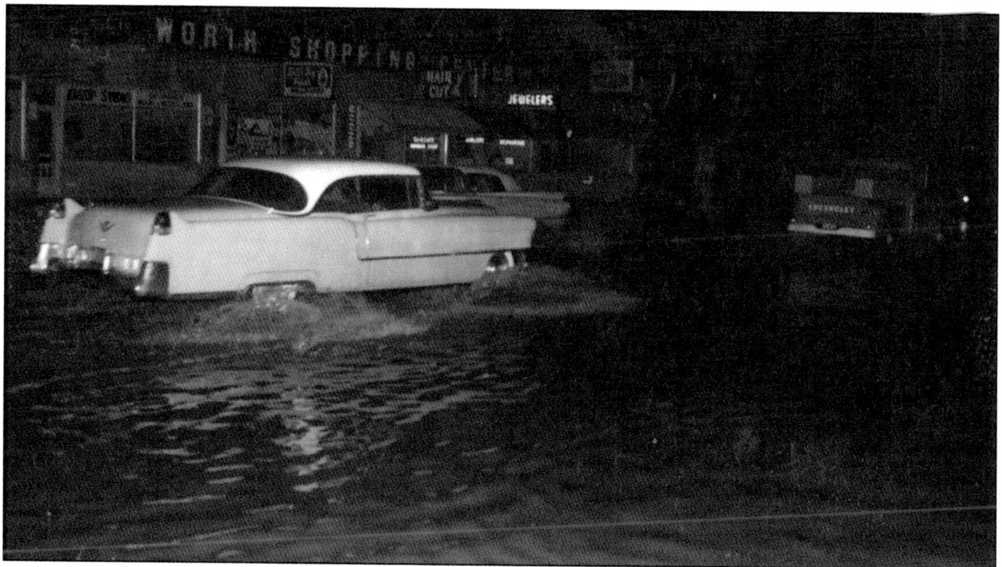

By the 1970s, the village again had to deal with sewage and drainage issues. Just as the pioneers had to endure flooding along 111th Street, so did modern-day residents. The pooling trends of the water issues in town were realized, and it was not until the late 1970s that the village replaced sewer lines that traditionally held large amounts of water. This 1967 photograph shows the difficulties of living on a moraine.

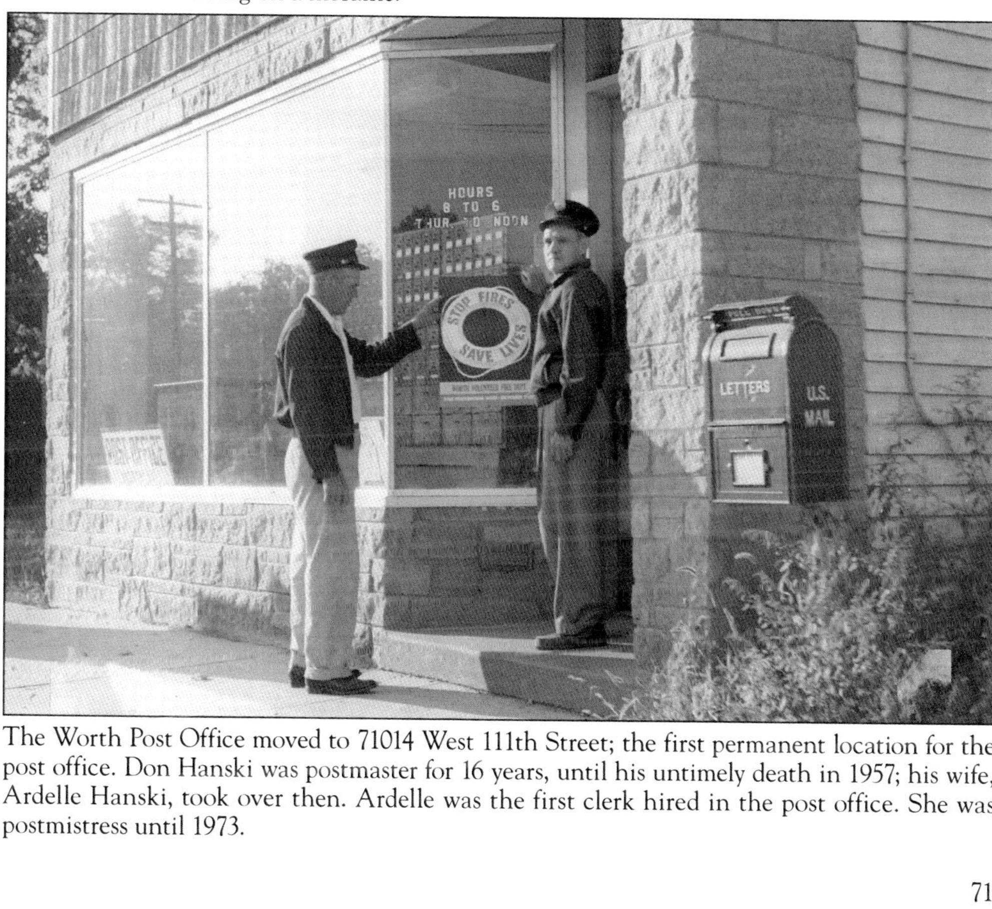

The Worth Post Office moved to 71014 West 111th Street; the first permanent location for the post office. Don Hanski was postmaster for 16 years, until his untimely death in 1957; his wife, Ardelle Hanski, took over then. Ardelle was the first clerk hired in the post office. She was postmistress until 1973.

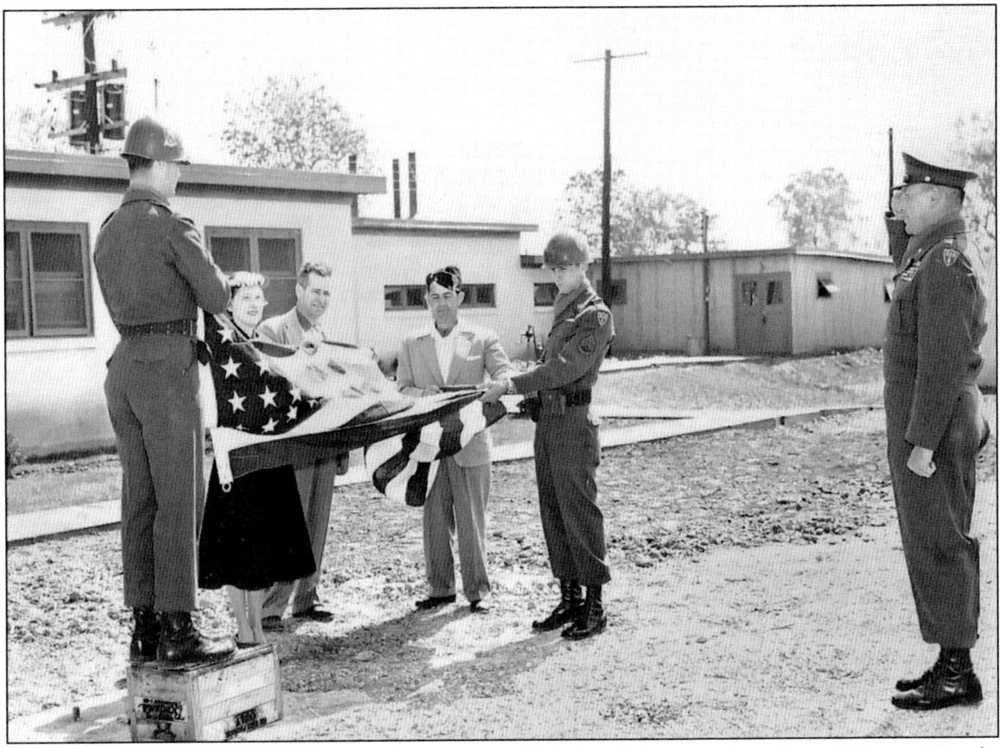

Nike Air Base C-51 was located at 116th Street and Ridgeland Avenue along the Cal-Sag in Worth. It was operational from 1955 until 1972. The base housed surface-to-air missiles and was among 22 bases spread throughout the Chicago area. In this photograph, civilians Marge and Frances McDonough (second and third from left) and George Frain (fourth from left) are seen dedicating a flagpole along with officials. Francis McDonough was village president from 1950 to 1956.

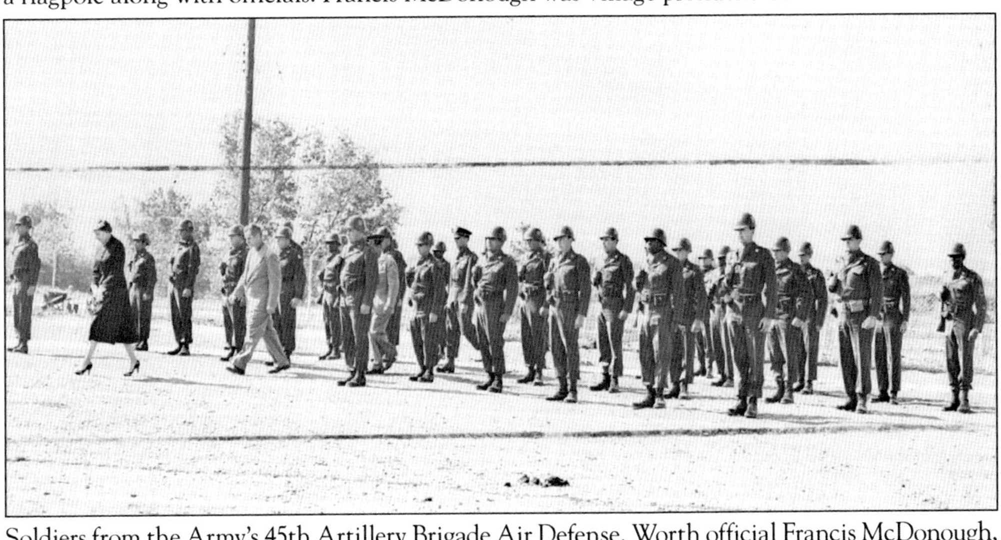

Soldiers from the Army's 45th Artillery Brigade Air Defense, Worth official Francis McDonough, and others return from a review of the flag dedication on May 15, 1955. The base contained Nike Ajax missiles, named for the Greek goddess of victory. The American Legion and local VFW would often visit and provide entertainment in the form of bingo games and local talent for the soldiers deployed to the Worth base.

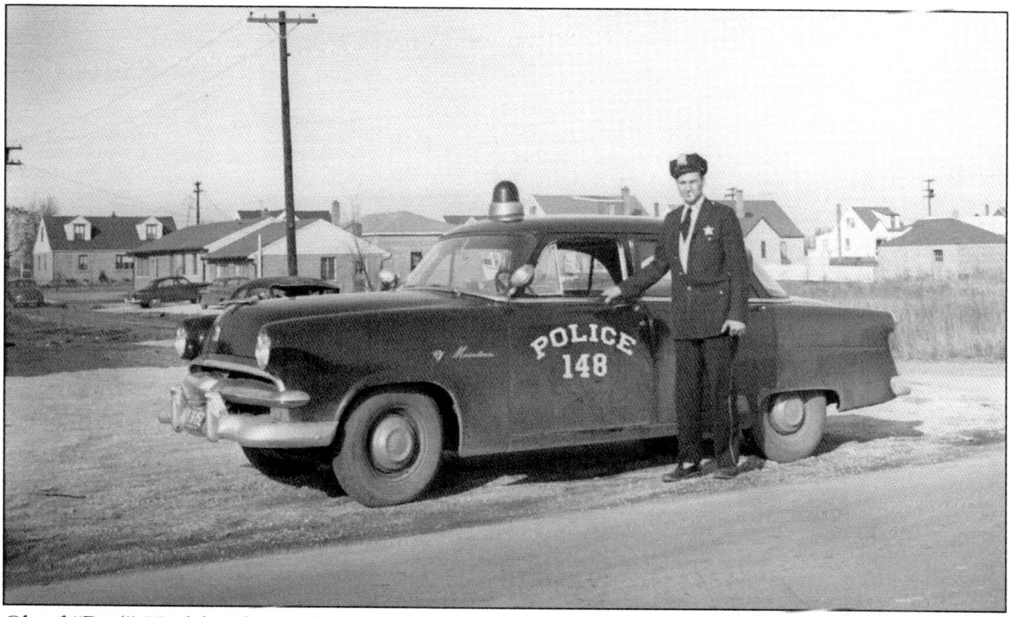

Chief "Red" Highland proudly displays the first police car that the village purchased. The photograph was taken in 1953, looking on the north side of 111th Street at Crandall and New England Avenues. The chief lived in town, and his home is shown directly behind the car.

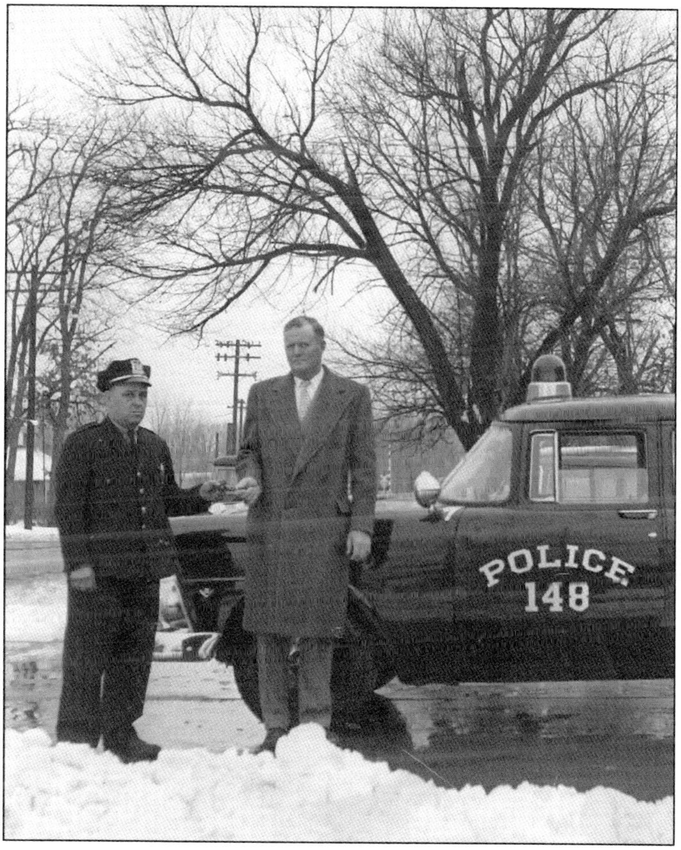

Chief Frank Gerenger and an unidentified officer reveal the keys to the second police vehicle owned by the village. On September 23, 1957, the village board voted to pay just under $500 for a 1957 Ford squad car. In 1957, there was only one full-time officer. The chief was part-time and others—10 patrolmen, a lieutenant, and a sergeant—were on a semi-volunteer basis and a part-time schedule too.

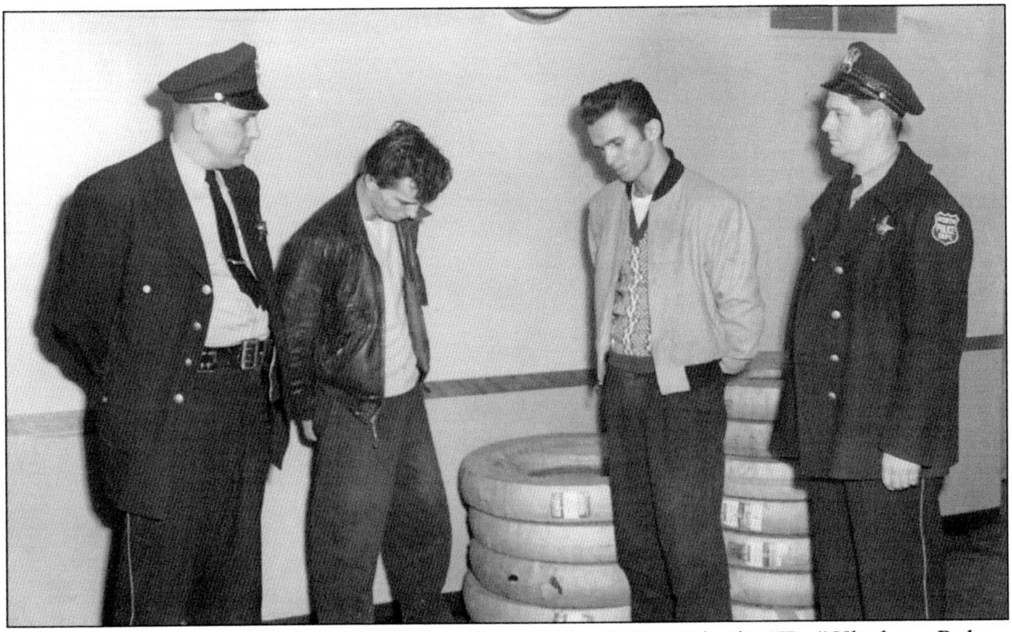

Shown on Friday, February 22, 1956, are, from left to right, Officer Charles "Tex" Kluchins, Robert Leninger, Nick Gironda, and Officer James Horvath. The officers were on duty and apprehended the two youths about midnight on the previous Sunday following their theft of tires from Ed Lode's Texaco Station.

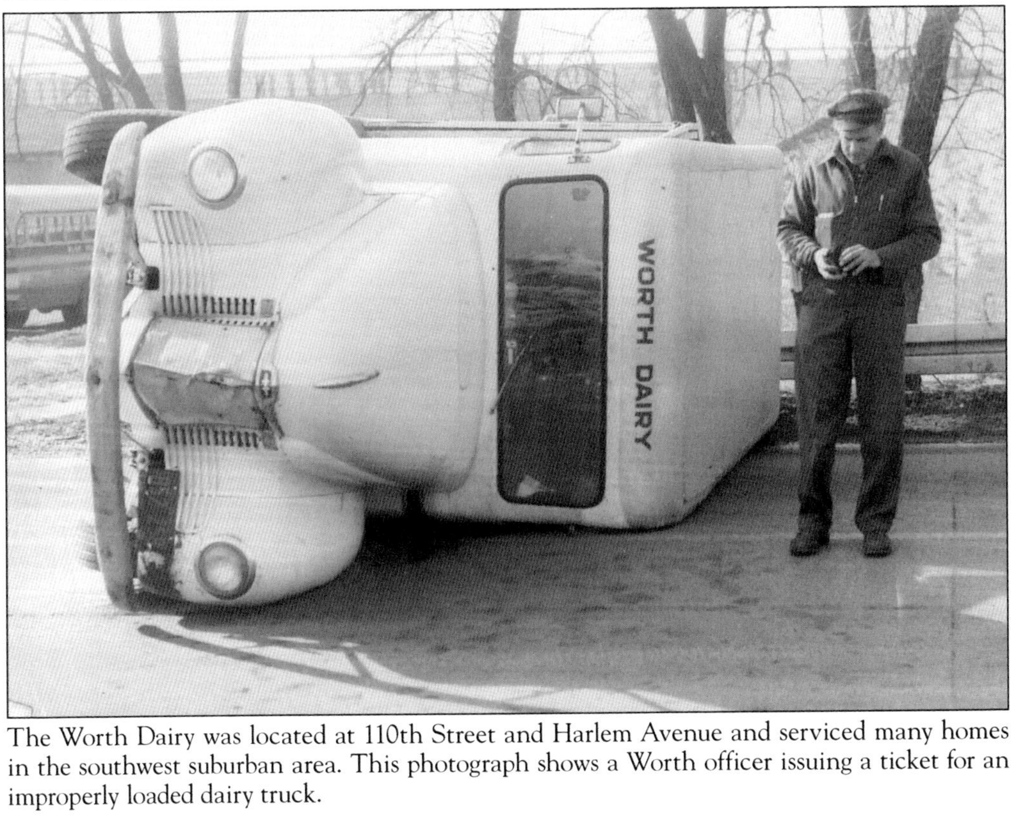

The Worth Dairy was located at 110th Street and Harlem Avenue and serviced many homes in the southwest suburban area. This photograph shows a Worth officer issuing a ticket for an improperly loaded dairy truck.

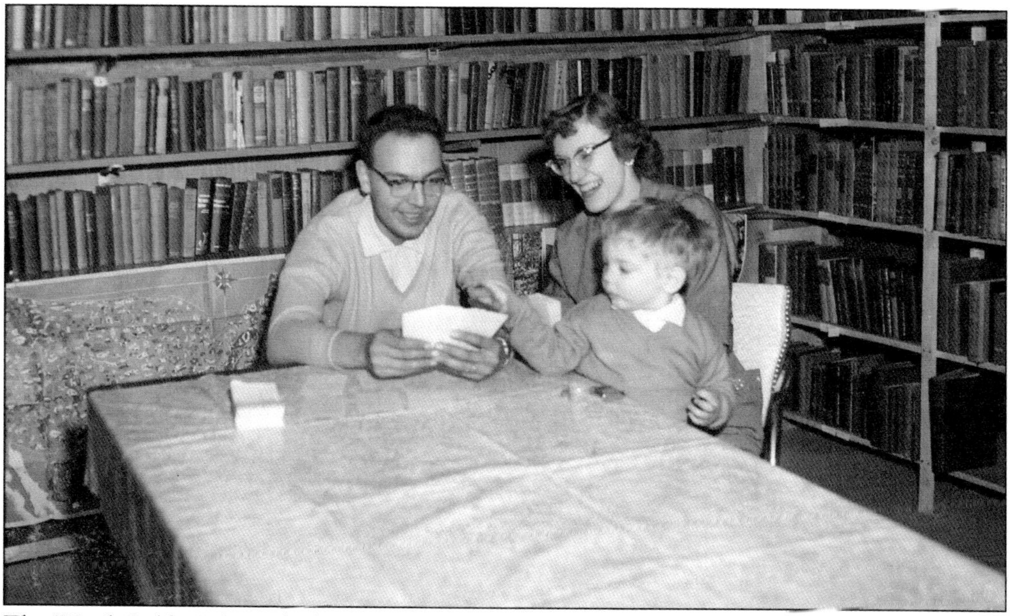

The Worth Public Library had its beginnings in the basement of Delores and Donald Goodline's home at 7008 West 114th Street on December 16, 1956. Delores, a graduate of the Chicago Teacher's College, catalogued the books according to standard library methods. Donald published a newsletter, titled the *Worth Bookshelf*, to inform residents of recent donations, hours, book reviews, and news about community organizations. The Goodline library was the first free library in the state to exist without state or federal funding.

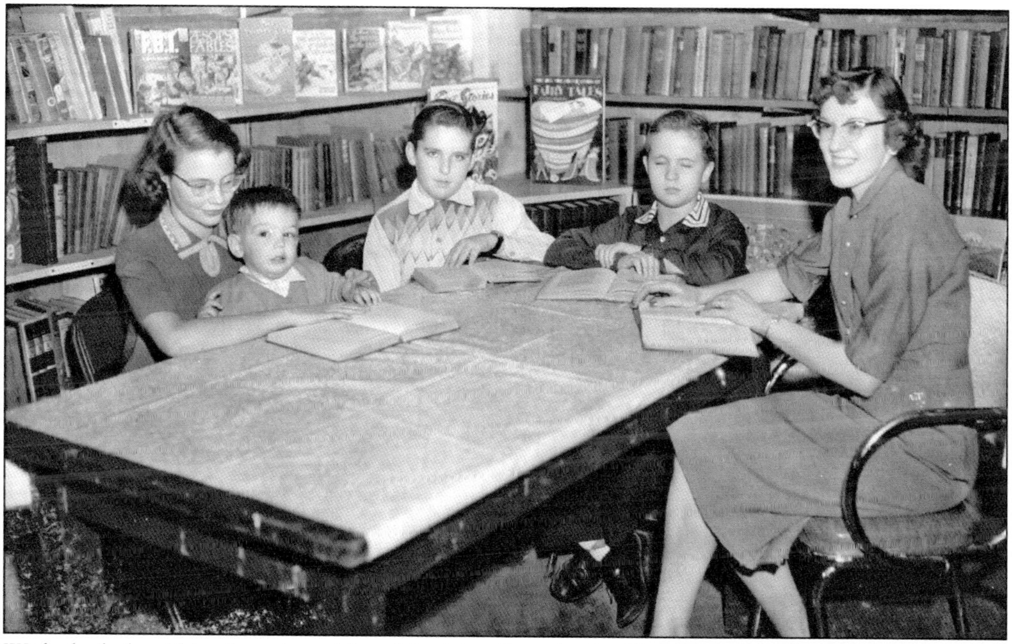

With the help of friends and neighbors like John Daniels, the Worth Lions Club, and the Cub Scout Pack No. 3668, donations for the library reached into the hundreds. Borrowing from the library was free unless books or items were returned late or lost. By March 1957, over 600 people registered for a library card. The Goodline library had outgrown its quarters and needed to expand.

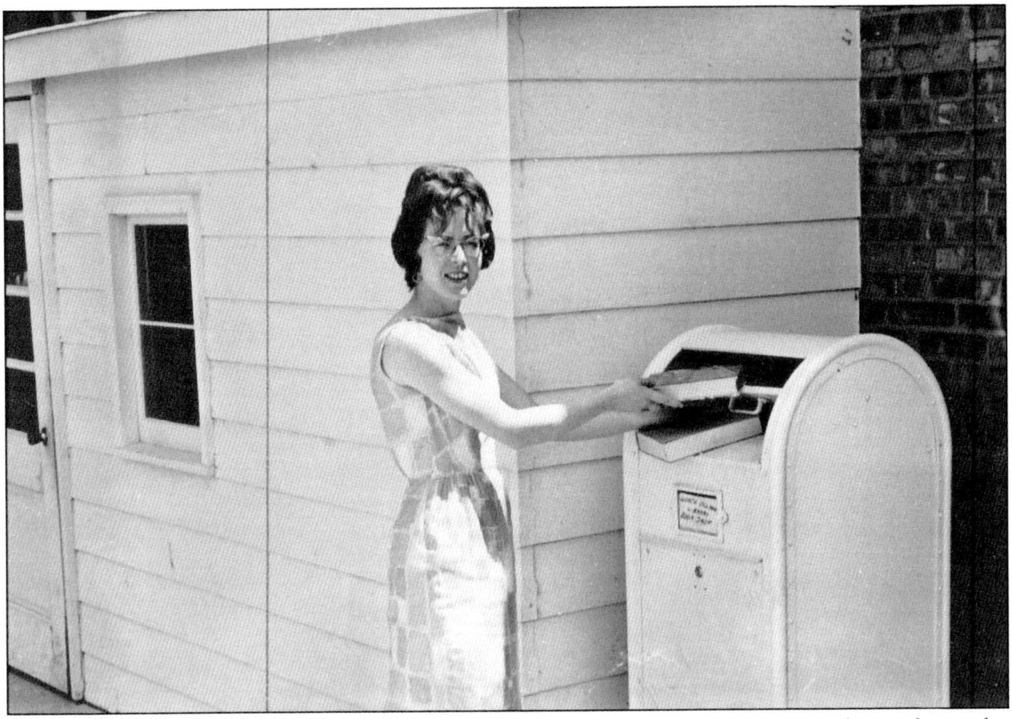

The library was open from 2:00 to 5:00 p.m. and 6:00 to 9:00 p.m. Patrons were admitted into the library upon pressing a buzzer. A book drop was added to assist in avoiding late fees.

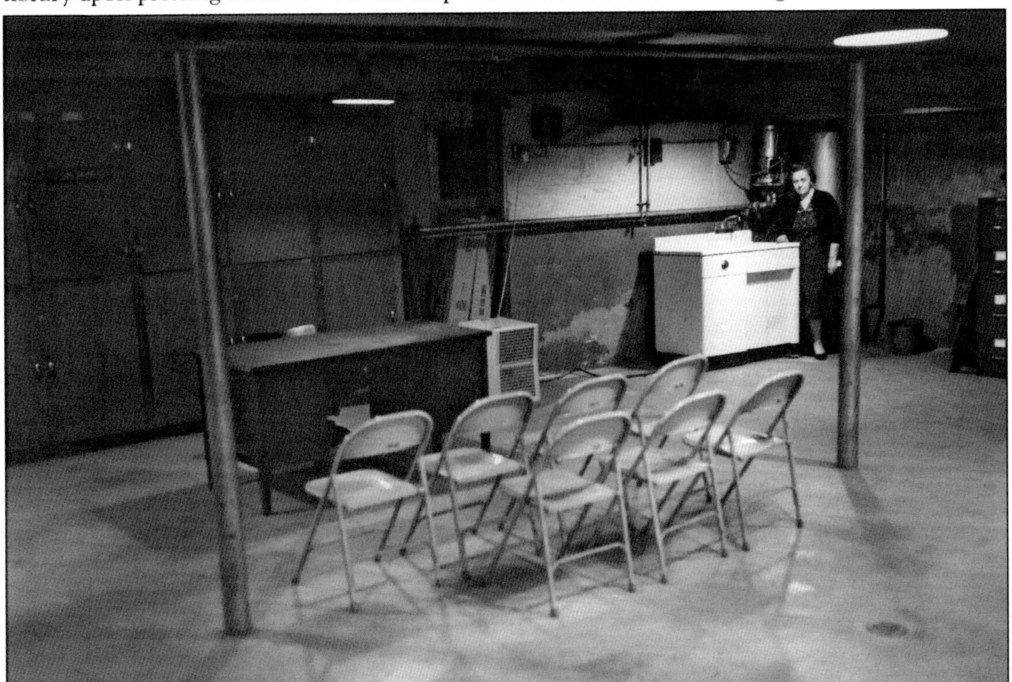

In May 1957, the administration of Templin determined the need to introduce a referendum to establish a library board as a separate taxing body. In the same year, the library became a member of the American Library Association.

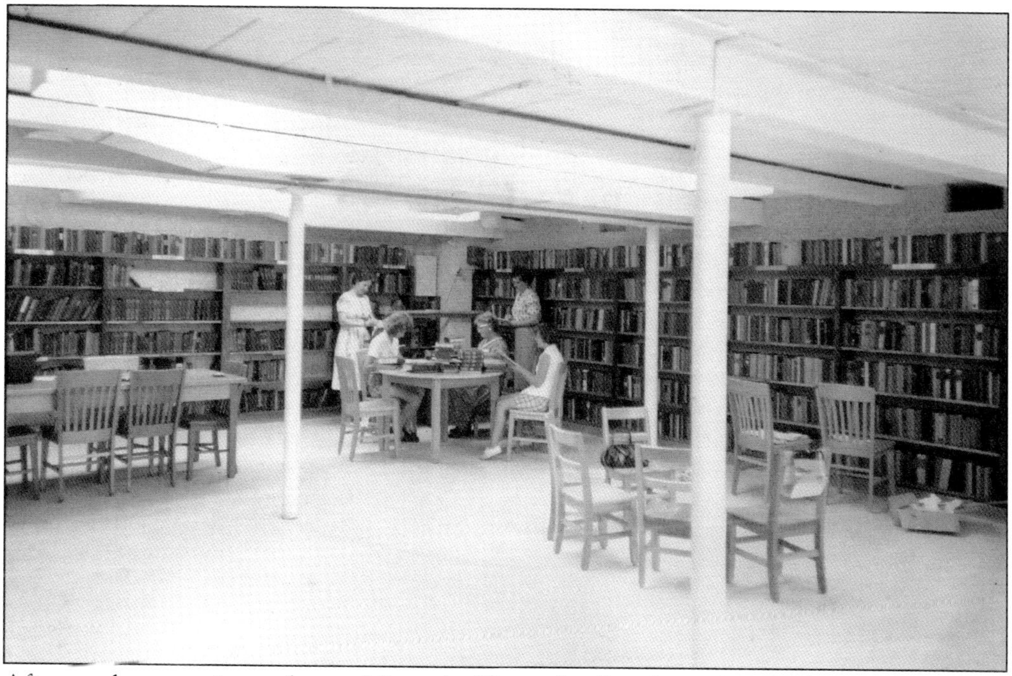

After much renovation and remodeling, the library finally relocated to the basement of village hall in 1961. This new location only allowed the library 1,500 square feet and a total of 6,000 volumes of books.

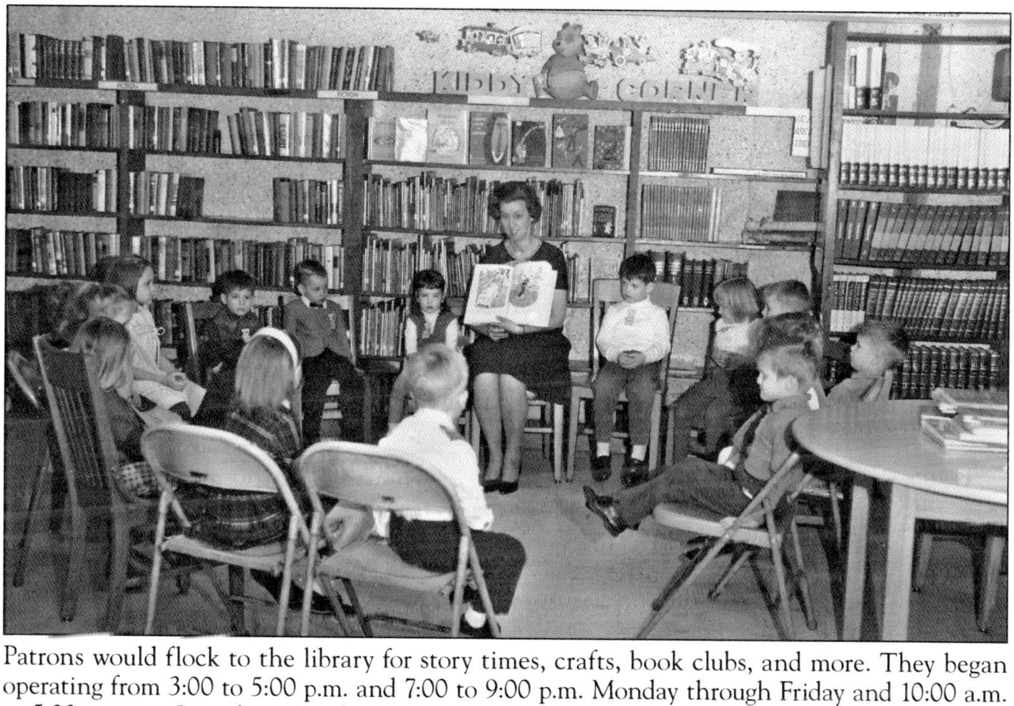

Patrons would flock to the library for story times, crafts, book clubs, and more. They began operating from 3:00 to 5:00 p.m. and 7:00 to 9:00 p.m. Monday through Friday and 10:00 a.m. to 5:00 p.m. on Saturdays. Residents ages six and older were eligible for cards. A limit of three books could be checked out, and books were kept for two weeks. The fine was 2¢ per day for any late books. Nonresidents were charged $1 per card.

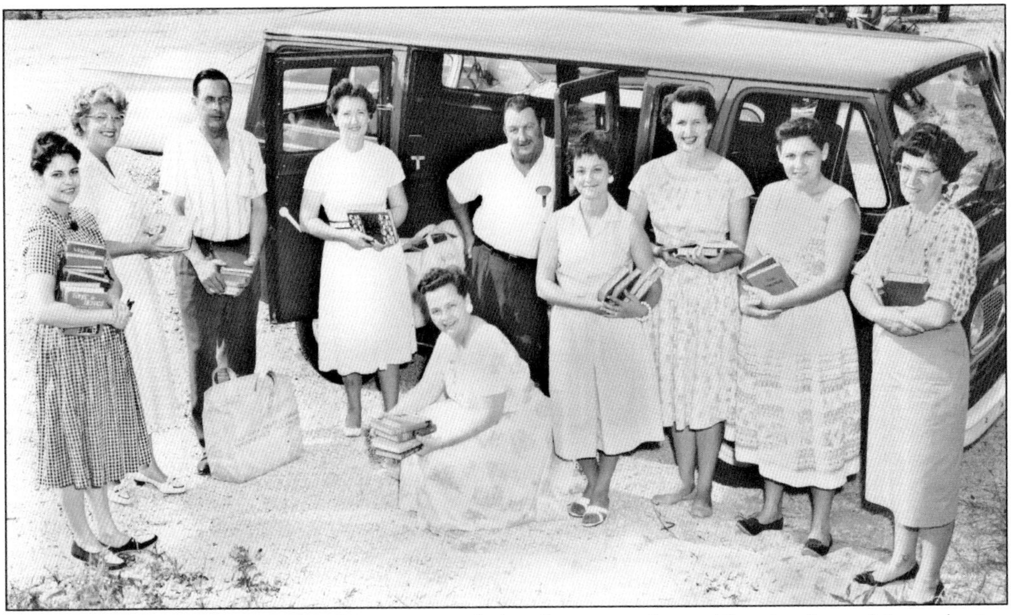

On April 1, 1961, trustee Ina Sundquist reported that the regional state librarian James Montedonico had met with the commission and confirmed the loan of 1,500–2,000 books, depending on the number of books the commission was able to procure. During the same year, the Friends of the Library was formed to assist in managing donations and collections.

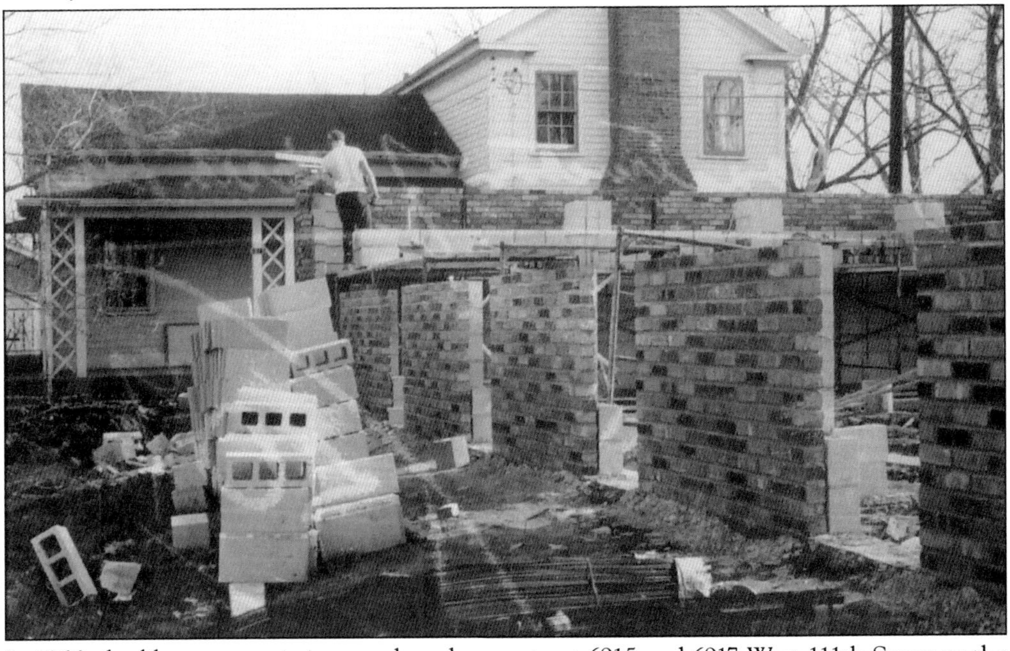

In 1966, the library commission purchased property at 6915 and 6917 West 111th Street as the village library had again outgrown its quarters. The site of the new library was where settlers John and Jane Crandall had built their first home in Worth in 1858. The home remained until 1977, as the original structure of the library was built on the front half of the property. After two failed referendums in 1968, a referendum was passed in 1979, and construction began on the new library.

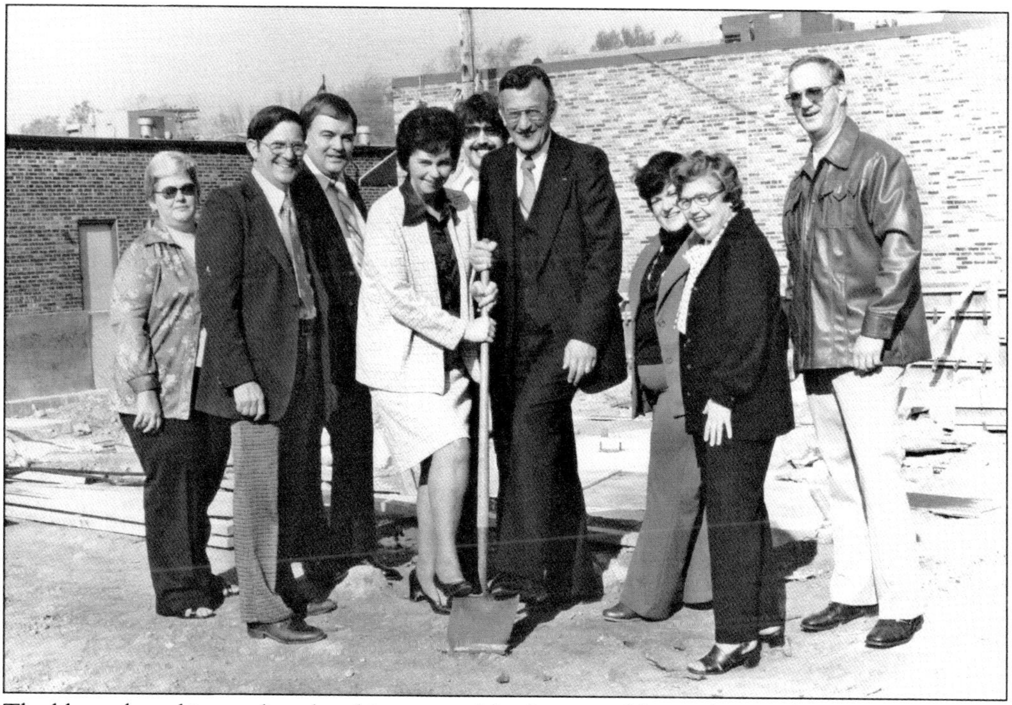

The library board is seen here breaking ground for the new addition that would include an upstairs reading and meeting room, elevator, and foyer. Included in no particular order are Connie Evans, trustee Gil Dobslaw, trustee Dorke, Shirley Christine, Don Christine, Jean Fickes, Bob Fickes, and two unidentified library board members. The foundation was finally laid in the spring of 1978, after being defeated in the spring referendum of 1977. It passed in the fall referendum of 1977 and cost about $625,000 to build. It was during this time that the last home on the property was demolished. The home belonged to settlers John and Jane Crandall.

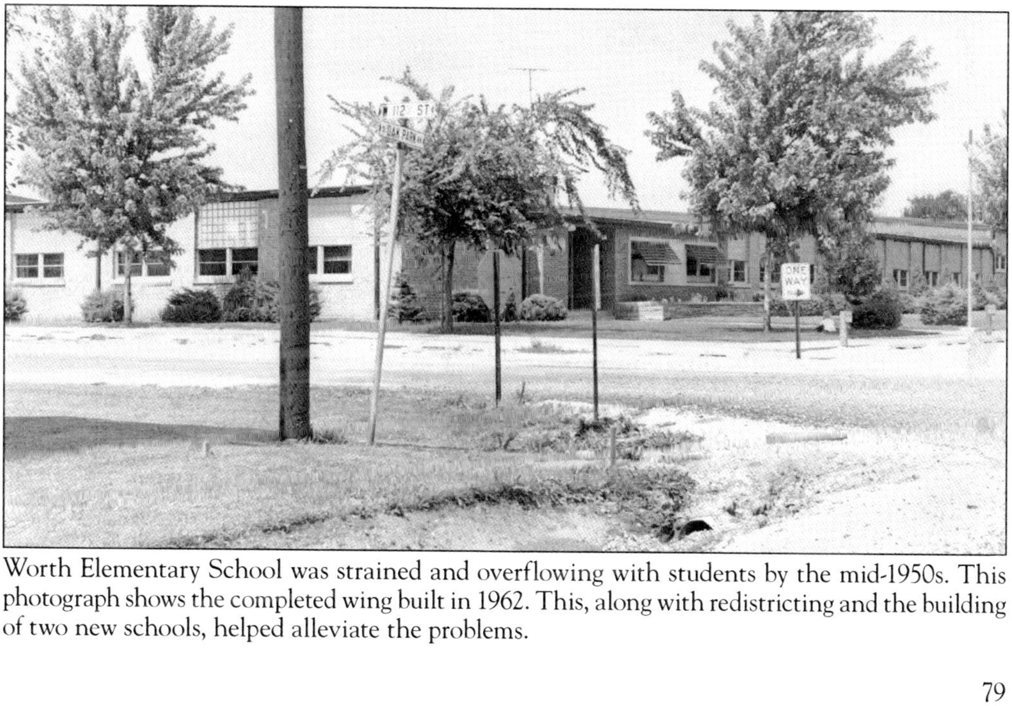

Worth Elementary School was strained and overflowing with students by the mid-1950s. This photograph shows the completed wing built in 1962. This, along with redistricting and the building of two new schools, helped alleviate the problems.

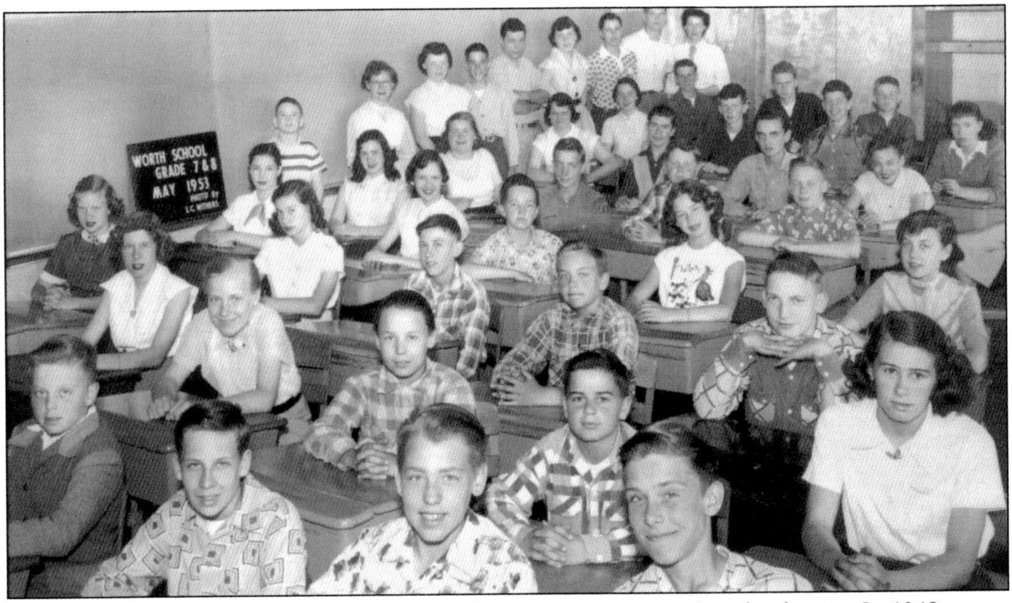

From 1949 to 1959, a dramatic increase in students was experienced in the district. In 1949, it was noted that only 35 students were registered for two classrooms. By 1958, each classroom had 65 students in it—an unexpected number! Most students were seated two to a chair. The basement was converted into a classroom in 1949, and again, an addition was put on but was quickly outgrown by 1952. Students were taking split-shift classes. This 1953 class seems to be smiling, not only because they enjoy school, but also because of their schedules.

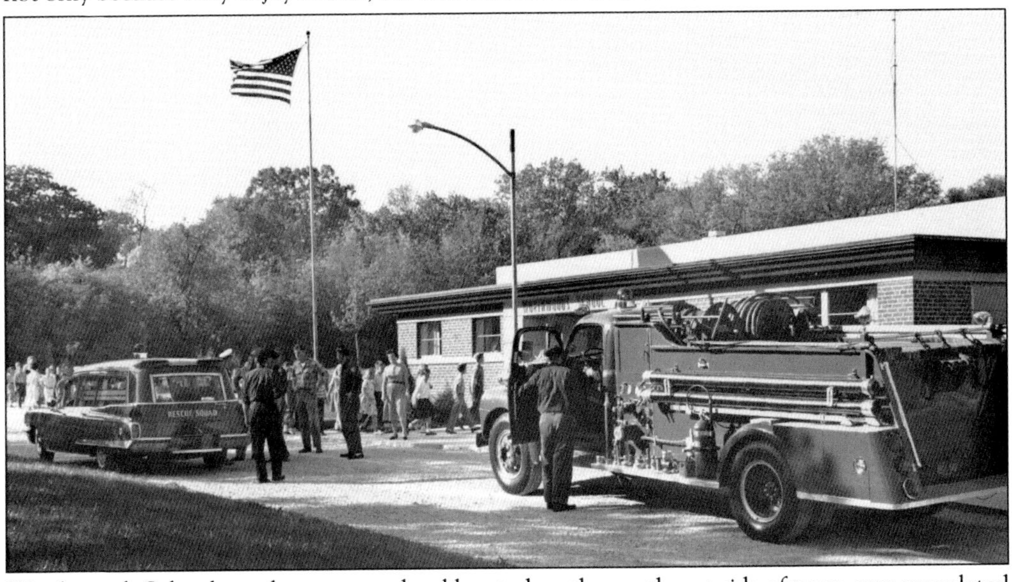

Worthwoods School, an elementary school located on the northwest side of town, was completed in 1960. Voter approval for construction of new buildings did not always keep pace with the needs of the district. Half-day sessions continued until the 1962–1963 school year. By the late 1960s, the district began to grow with the help of an interest-free loan from the State of Illinois. Worth Ridge School was built by 1963, as was Worth Terrace. Seen here is the first fire drill of the year at the new Worthwoods building. There were 190 students at the school, seven classrooms, and seven teachers. On this day in 1960, it took the students 48 seconds to exit the building.

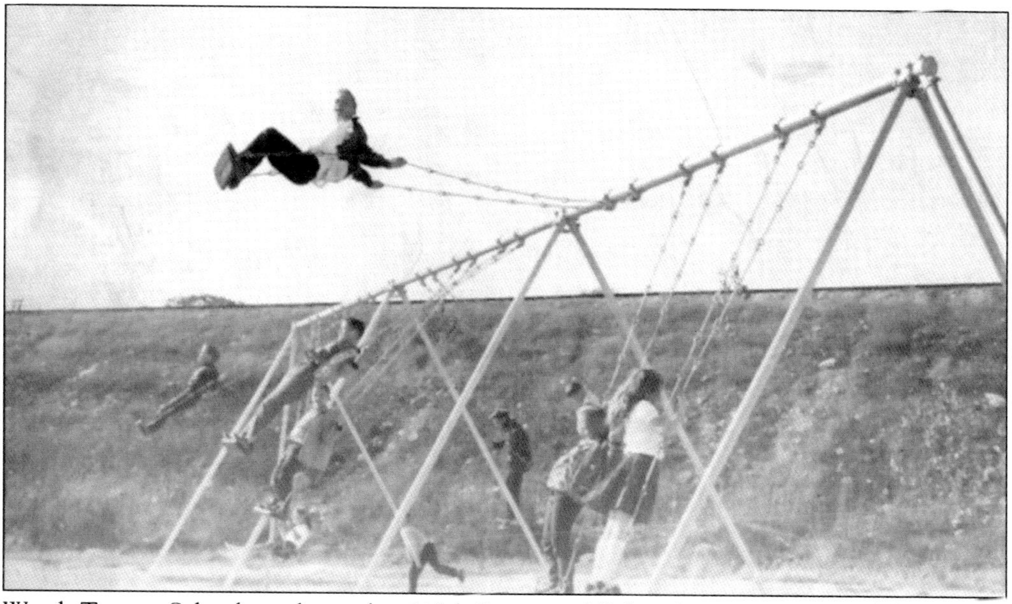

Worth Terrace School was located at 115th Street and Beloit Avenue, near the Cal-Sag. This school closed in 1980 due to the loss of enrollment. The building was purchased by the Worth Park District in 1985 and was renamed the Charles Christensen Terrace Center after a longtime resident and public servant.

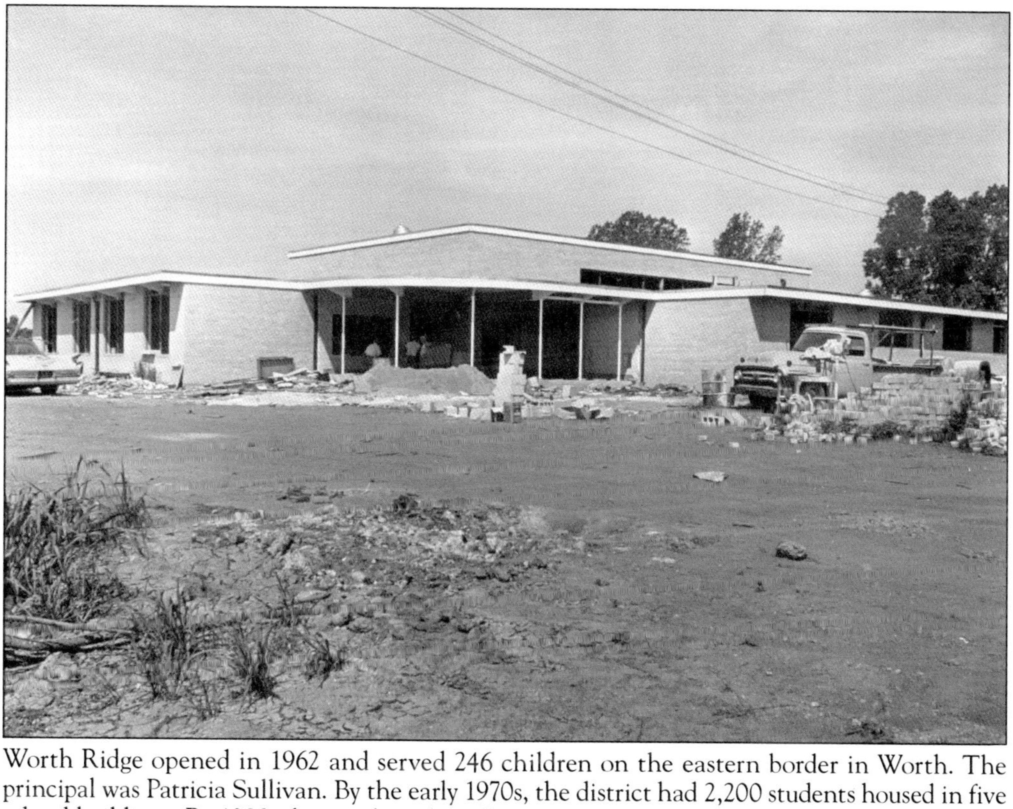

Worth Ridge opened in 1962 and served 246 children on the eastern border in Worth. The principal was Patricia Sullivan. By the early 1970s, the district had 2,200 students housed in five school buildings. By 1980, the numbers dwindled to 1,100. Worth Ridge was closed in 1982.

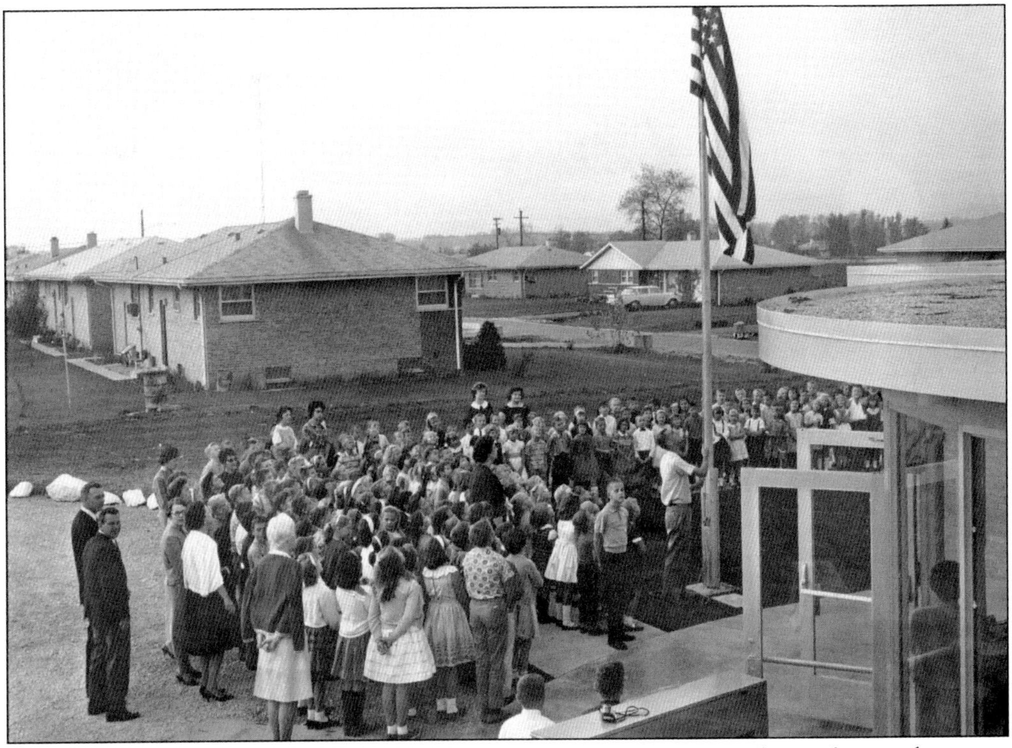

The PTA was formed in the 1930s and was always an active support unit for teachers and parents. Here, the PTA dedicate this flag to Oscar Weilinga Jr., the school custodian's son who lost his life in a plane crash over Tacoma in 1963. Today, a flag that covered the coffin of a young soldier who gave his life for his country flies above the Worth Ridge School.

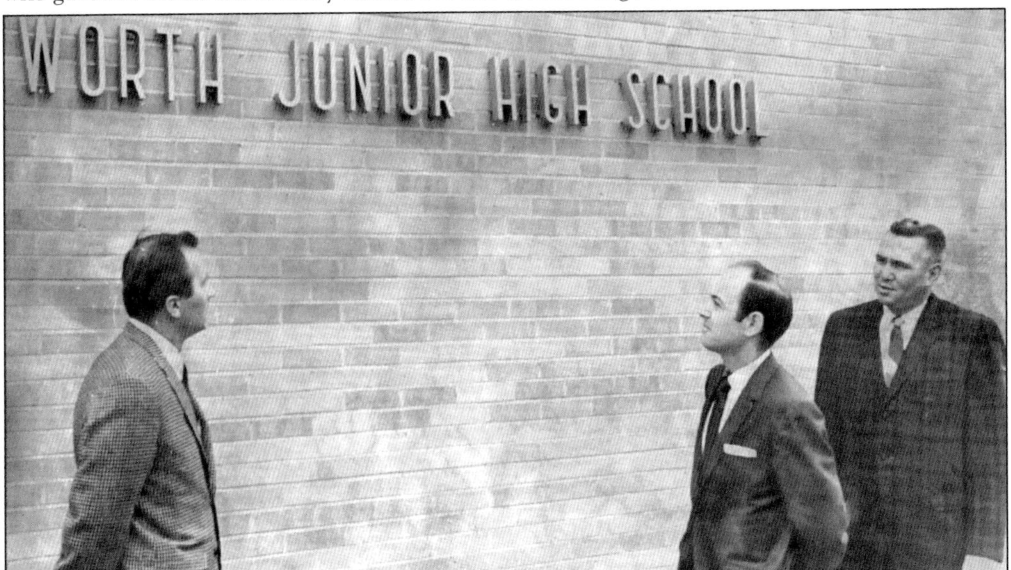

Worth Junior High School was opened in 1969. Visiting the outside of the building are, from left to right, Dennis Bronicki, Don Hacker, and Tom Kortz, all teachers scheduled to work in the new structure.

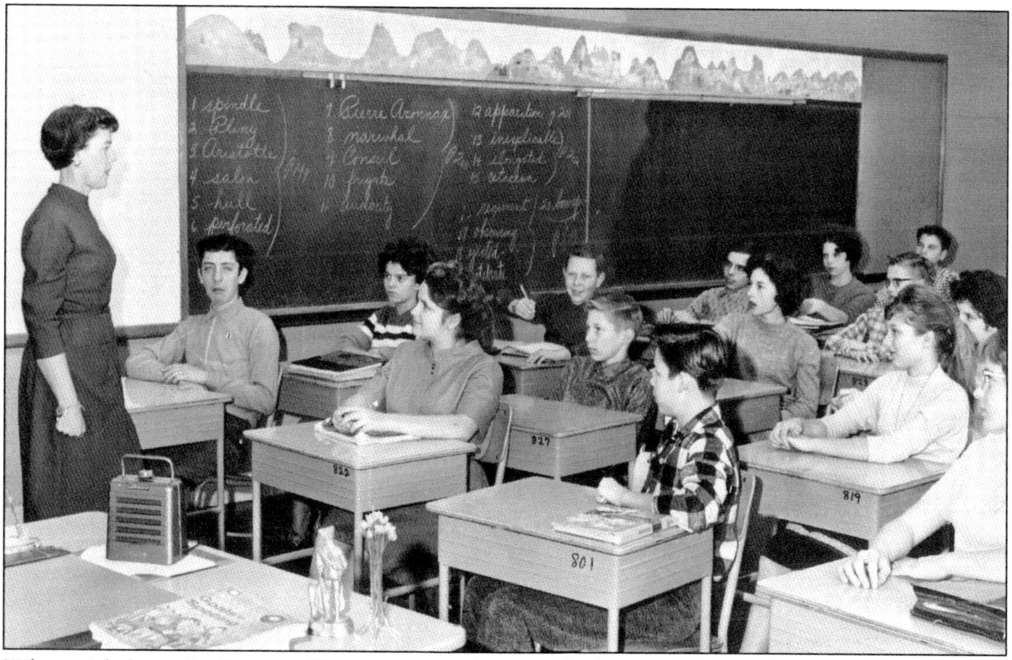

When eighth-grader Juanona Brewster came down with rheumatic fever, her physician prescribed a minimum of six weeks of bed rest. Supt. Rosemary Lucas answered a call for help by providing a service from Illinois Bell Telephone that enabled the student to attend class while listening by phone from her bed. Leah Rose Templin, Juanona's teacher, is seen teaching her class with the sick child listening in. Templin was the granddaughter of Edward P. Bishop, owner of Bishop's store in town. Her family has been in Worth since 1881. She married Vern Templin, who became village president.

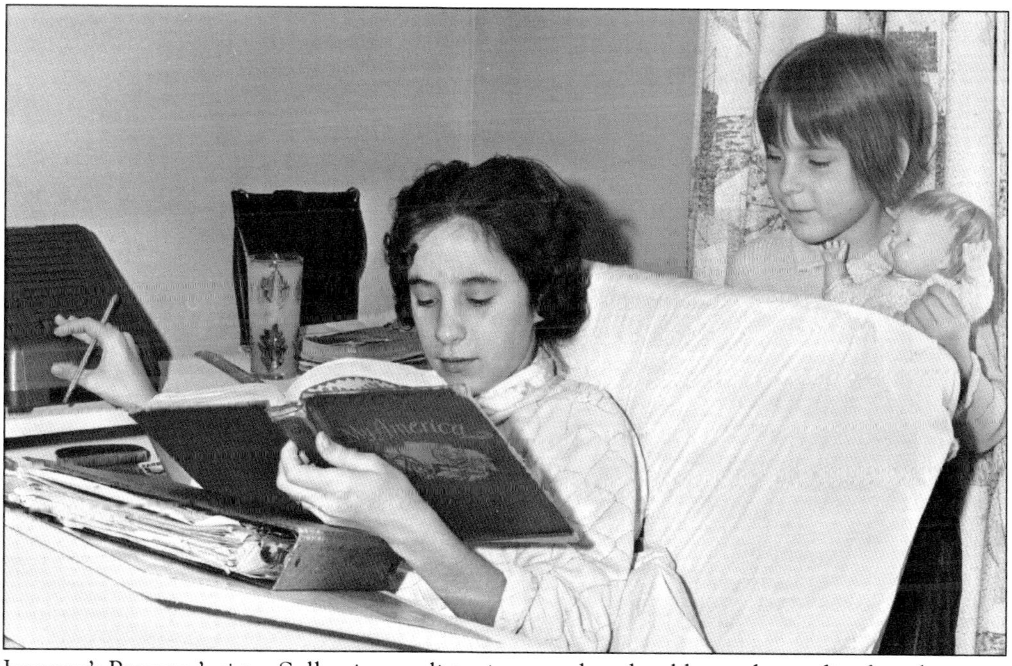

Juanona's Brewster's sister Sullen is seen listening over her shoulder as she studies from home.

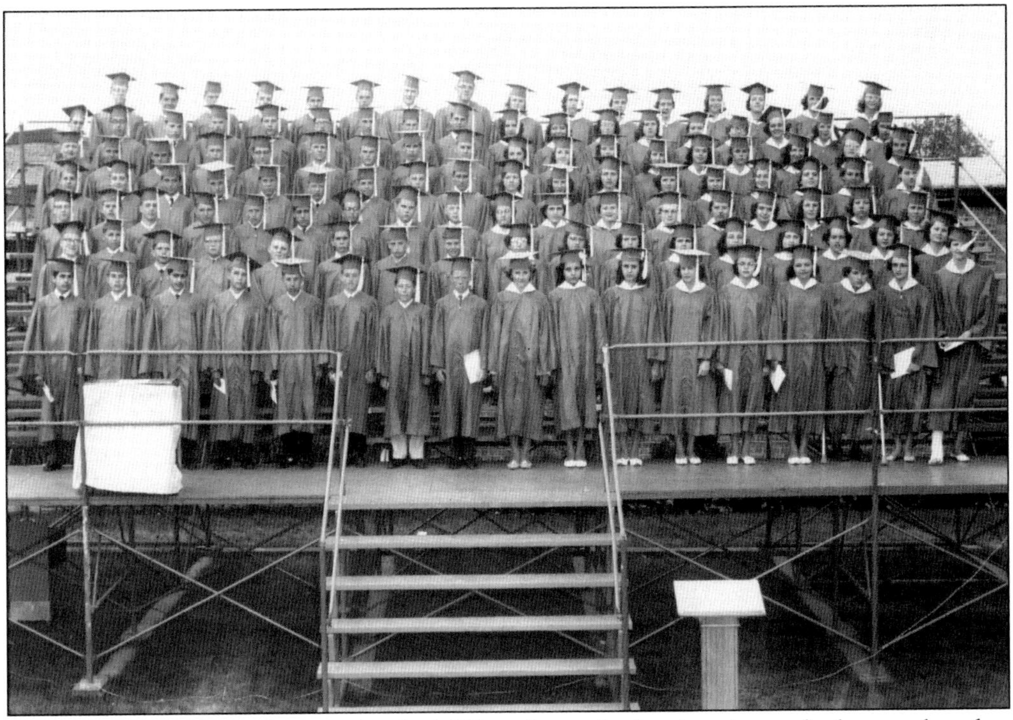

On June 8, 1961, the graduating class had 122 students. At the time, it was the largest class that had graduated from the elementary school, which was indication that the town was growing in population. A solution was needed for over-populated schools.

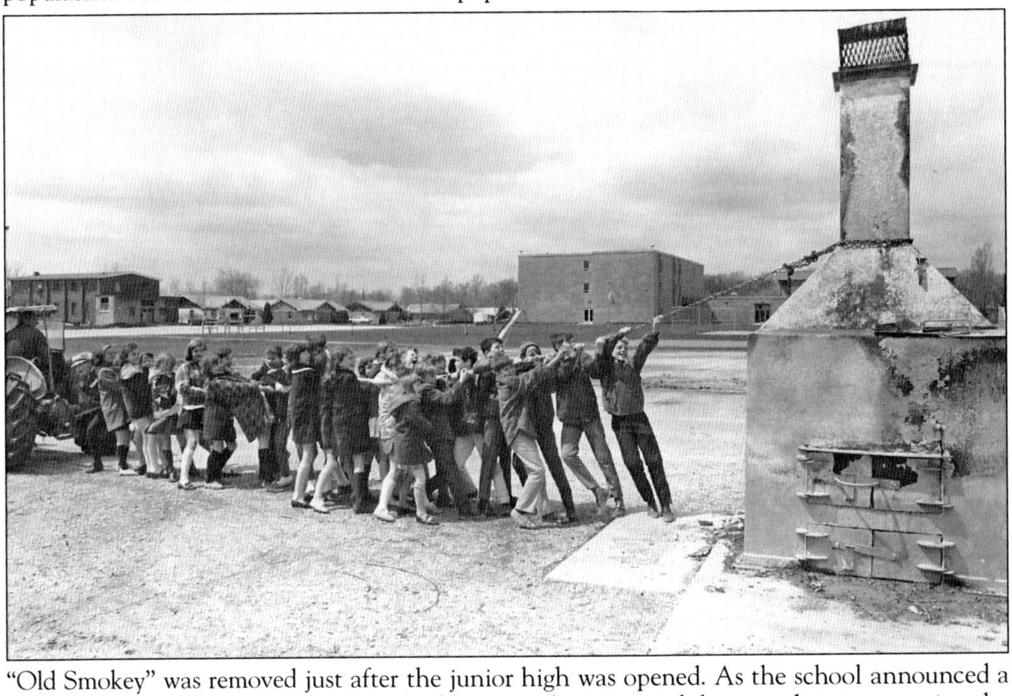

"Old Smokey" was removed just after the junior high was opened. As the school announced a new plan for handling refuse from the buildings, students assisted the custodian in removing the incinerator. The new junior high can be seen in the background.

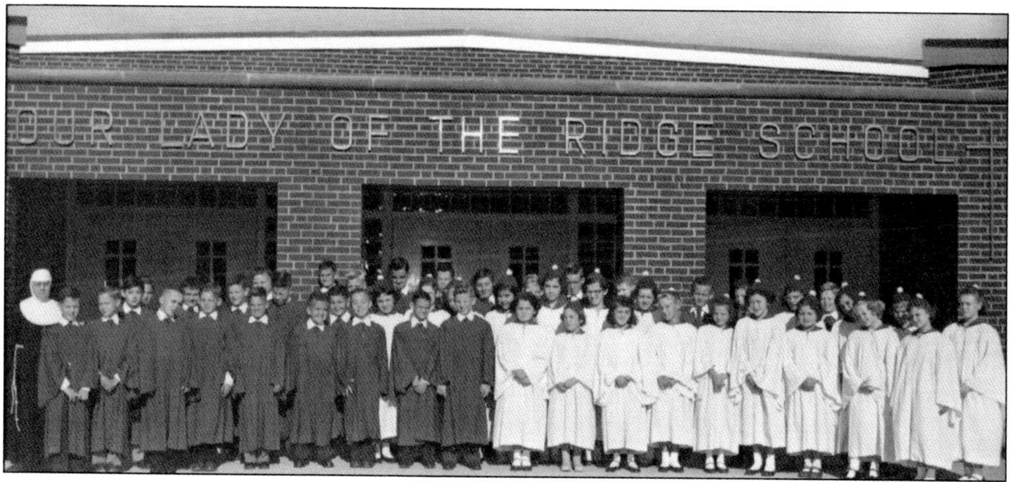

Our Lady of the Ridge School was founded by Rev. William Gentleman in 1948. As the congregation grew, a school building was constructed at 108th Street and Ridgeland Avenue, attracting students from not only Worth but Chicago Ridge and Alsip. Seen here is the first graduating class at the new building in 1958.

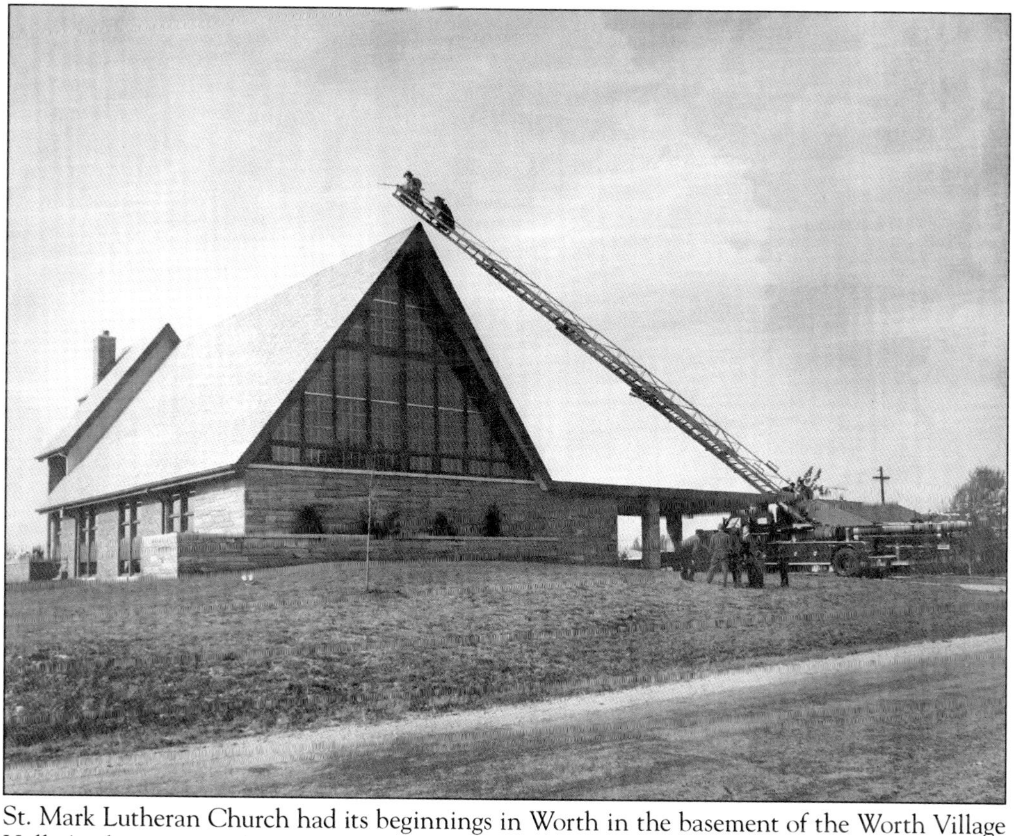

St. Mark Lutheran Church had its beginnings in Worth in the basement of the Worth Village Hall. As the congregation grew, a new structure was erected at Seventy-sixth Avenue and 111th Street. The building committee was led by Robert Ferrin and Ed Plahm. The first service in the new building was conducted on May 12, 1957.

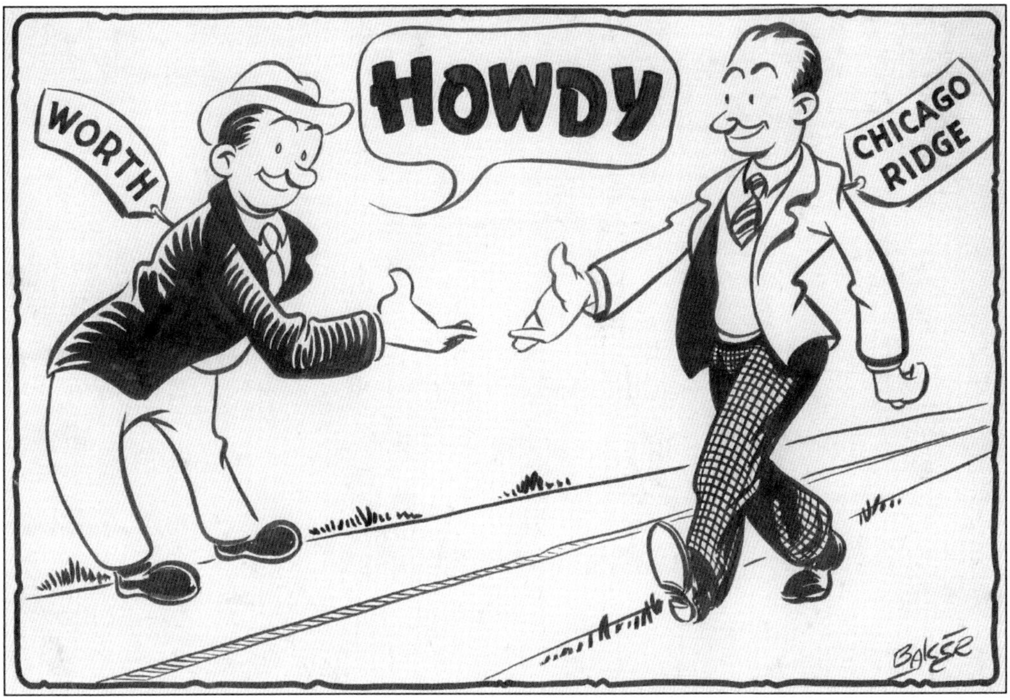

The *Worth Record* was located along 111th Street in the old Featherstone building. The *Record* was started by John and Agnes Daniels and was published from 1954 until 1963. The *Record* reported on news from Worth, Chicago Ridge, and Alsip.

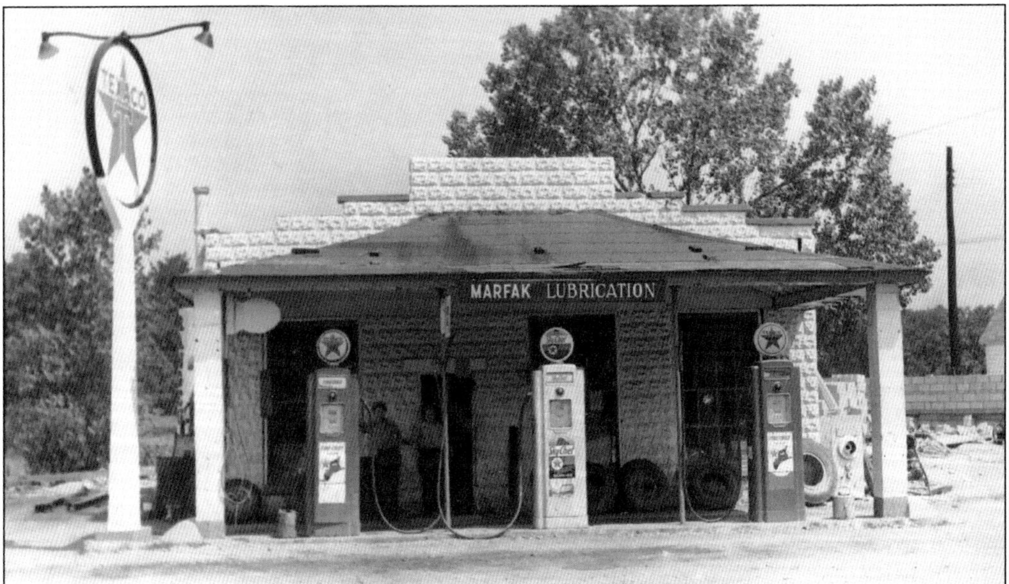

Ed Lode leased the Worth Texaco Service Station at 111th Street and Harlem Avenue from Louis Lange in 1939. Herb Foyle, William Haberichte, and Harry Kerkstra operated the station. In 1946, Lode purchased the location and started the Lode Petroleum Company, which he operated along with the Worth Texaco Service Station. The building remained until the mid-1980s, when the Veteran's Memorial was constructed on its site.

Four

The Friendly Village

"Welcome to Worth—the Friendly Village." The signs at the entrance of the village of Worth echo this sentiment that many have known, and it was finally coined in 1957 by local politician Bill Schneider. Worth has always been a town where money never seemed to get in the way of progress. Mayor Russert recalled in an interview that living on a shoestring budget never seemed to be an issue. He remembered a time where the entire village board worked on the weekend to fill potholes. It was not uncommon to see families that were involved in the Boy Scouts helping out with the Lions Club, Women's Auxiliary, Worth Achievers, Worth Father's Group, Worth Jaycees, or one of the 25 other organizations that existed during this time period. Volunteering and participating in community events was a civic, and often a generational, duty.

These benevolent societies and clubs were always eager to pitch in when help was needed. The majority of the police department was mostly voluntary until the 1960s, and so was the fire department until 1992. Many basic duties in town were simply done on a handshake.

The town had its chance to celebrate its "friendliness" at the annual Worth Days celebration. At the end of every summer, 111th Street was transformed with picnics and parades during the weekend celebration. All organizations in town would have a chance to proudly display their membership, their float-making skills, and their service to the community as they made their way west to the judges' stand. The parade continues on today, as does the spirit of camaraderie, during this weekend celebration. The parade was originally started by Bill Conway in 1947. He led the parade for 16 years. Picnics would be held after the parade at Diesing's Grove, Gale Moore Park, and eventually the American Legion. As more became involved in the celebration, it grew to include a Worth Days Commission, formed in 1956 by John Daniels and chairmen and representatives from the Lions Club, American Legion, and fire and police departments. They would plan a two- to three-day festival that eventually included a dance, entertainment, carnival rides, parade, and fireworks. The parade has moved several times, from Diesing's Grove to Gale Moore Park, the American Legion, and Peaks Park.

This chapter will explore these organizations and the reasons why many generations and business owners have chosen to use the phrase "It's worth a trip to Worth."

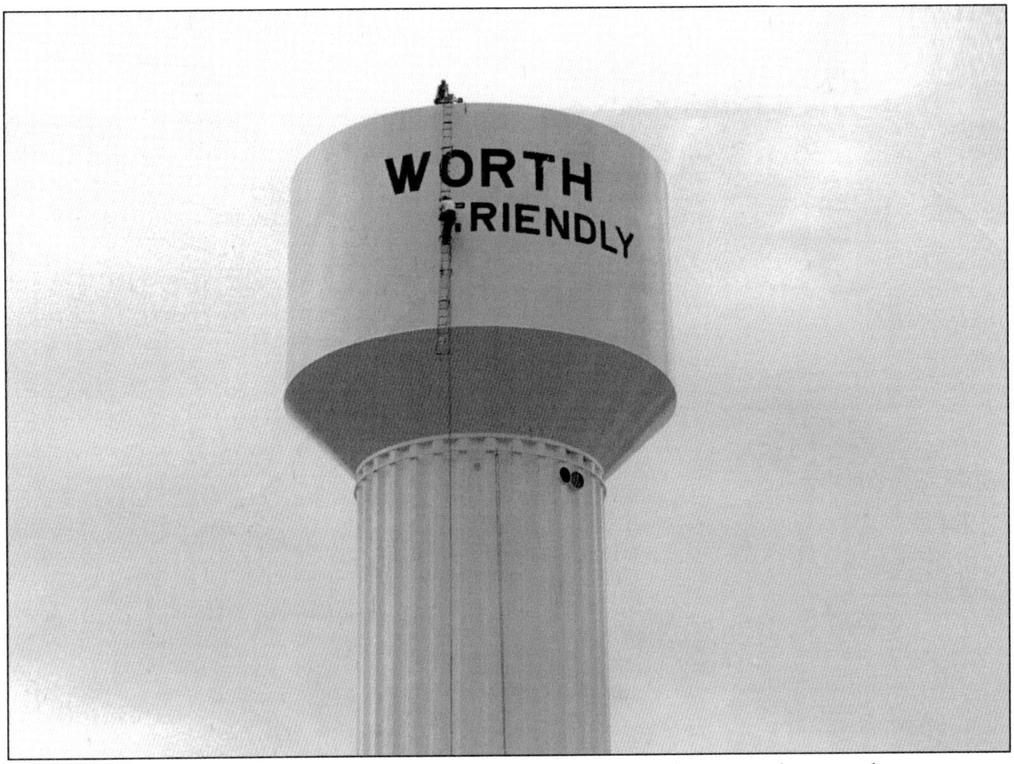

Worth got its place on the map with its nickname, "the Friendly Village," in 1966. Here, it is seen being applied to the water tower. The water tower is the beacon in the community and reminds everyone of the rich, benevolent history of Worth.

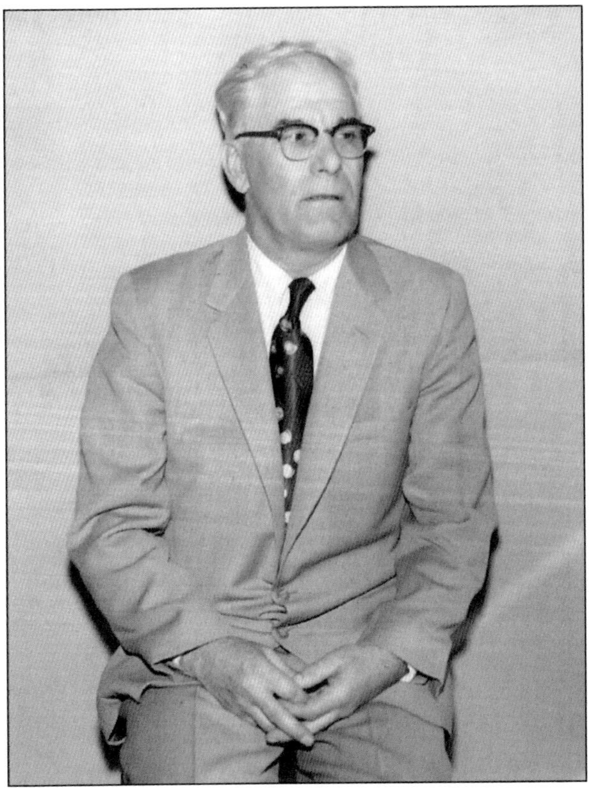

The man behind the nickname, "the Friendly Village," came up with it during his 1957 bid for election to the village board. Schneider visited every home in Worth during his campaign. After the election was over, he proclaimed that when he "visited homes in town, this Village had the friendliest people around." Although unsuccessful in his bid, Bill was appointed when a vacancy opened. He served on the village board and on the Worth Park District Board.

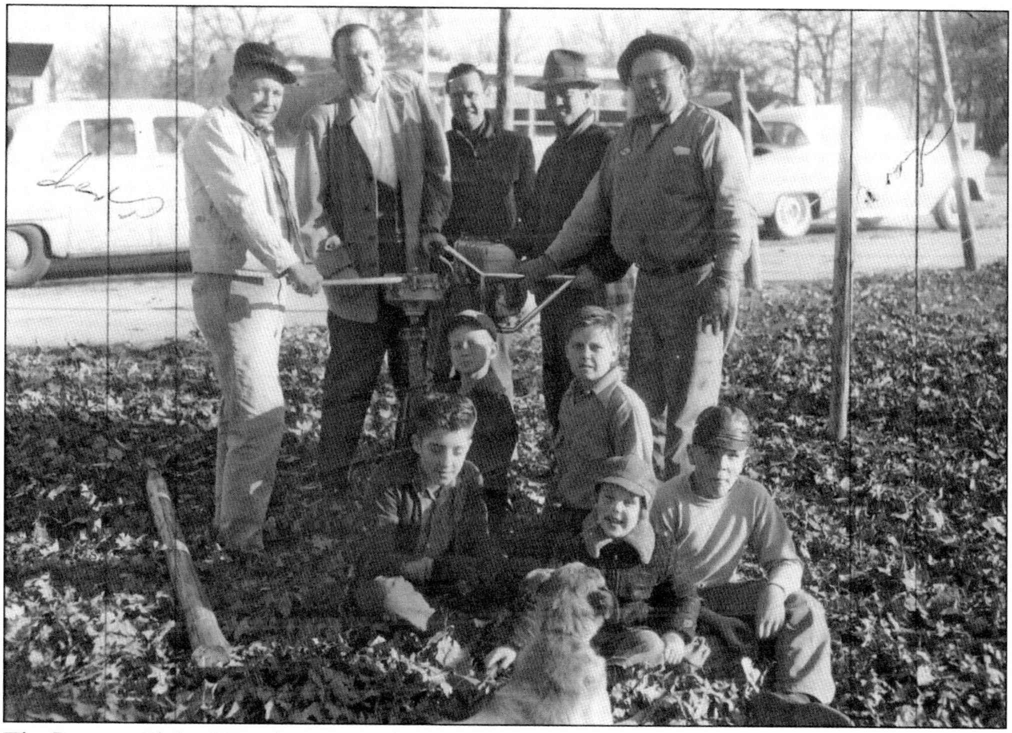

The Booster Club of Worth was Worth's first civic organization. Members had a hand in building the Plahm, Macauley, and Zuidema homes. Members purchased the first fire truck in 1925. In 1951, the organization was renamed the Worth Civic Association, headed by Ed Conrad, Lewis Macauley, William Mueller, and Karl Larsen. The Worth Civic Association gave way to the future Worth Homeowners Club. This club was instrumental in assisting with installing the first street sign program in Worth. The photograph shows unnamed members in the Worthwoods area.

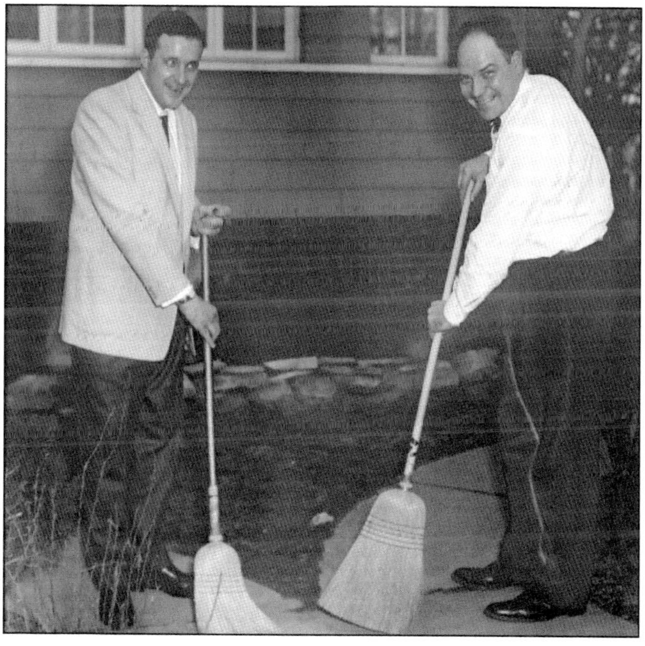

The Lions Club was officially chartered on January 6, 1954 This club has been the village's most benevolent service organization for nearly 60 years. Through the years, they have donated over $500,000 to community organizations. Seen here are charter members Dave Zuidima (left) and Vern Templin "cleaning up" the streets. The Lions Club assisted the civic association in many public works programs throughout town. There were over 50 active members.

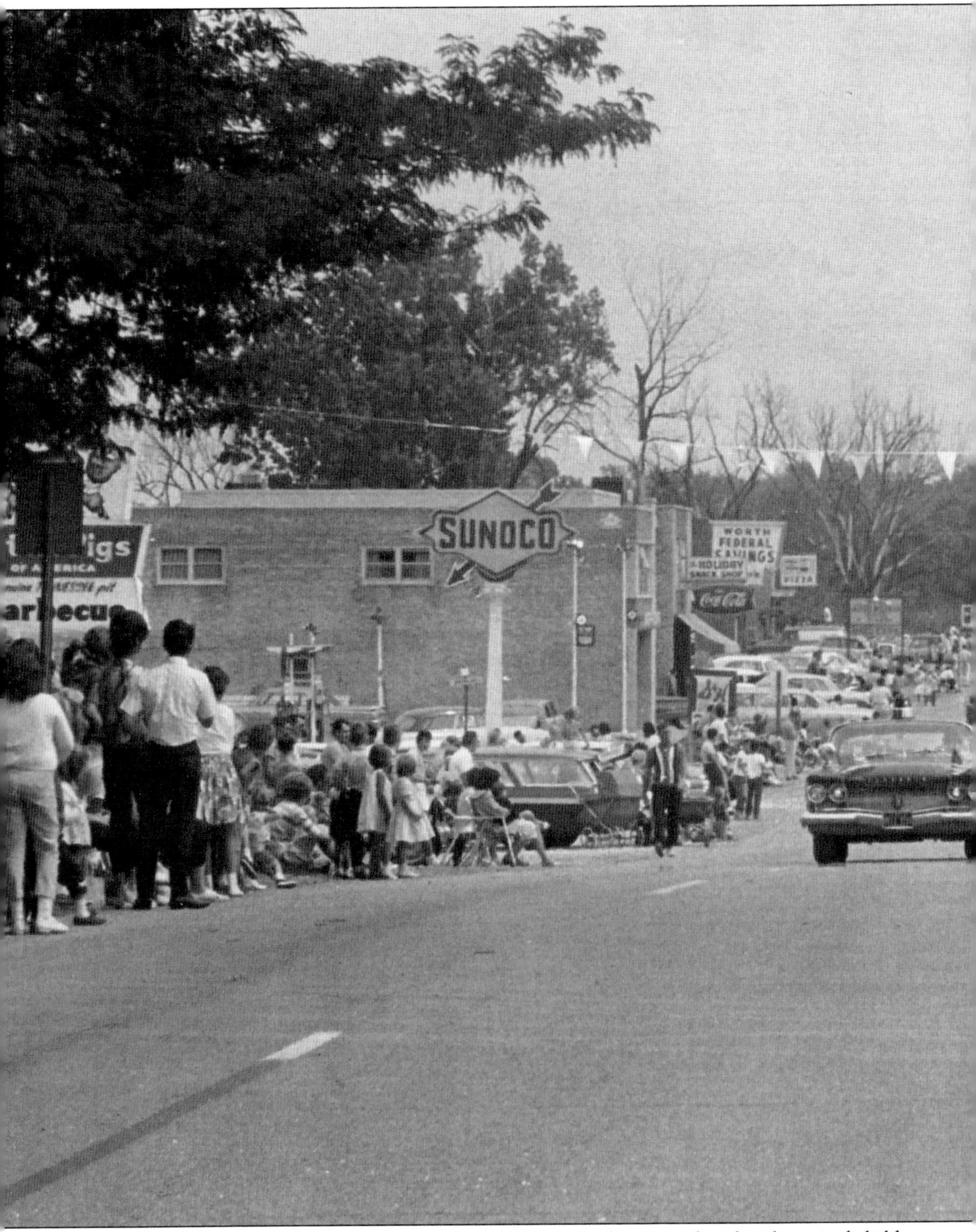

As the Worth Days Parade makes its way west, one can see the streets lined with excited children, eager to collect candy or a souvenir thrown from the floats. Residents utilize this time to put their best foot forward in this annual parade that celebrates the spirit of Worth. The background of

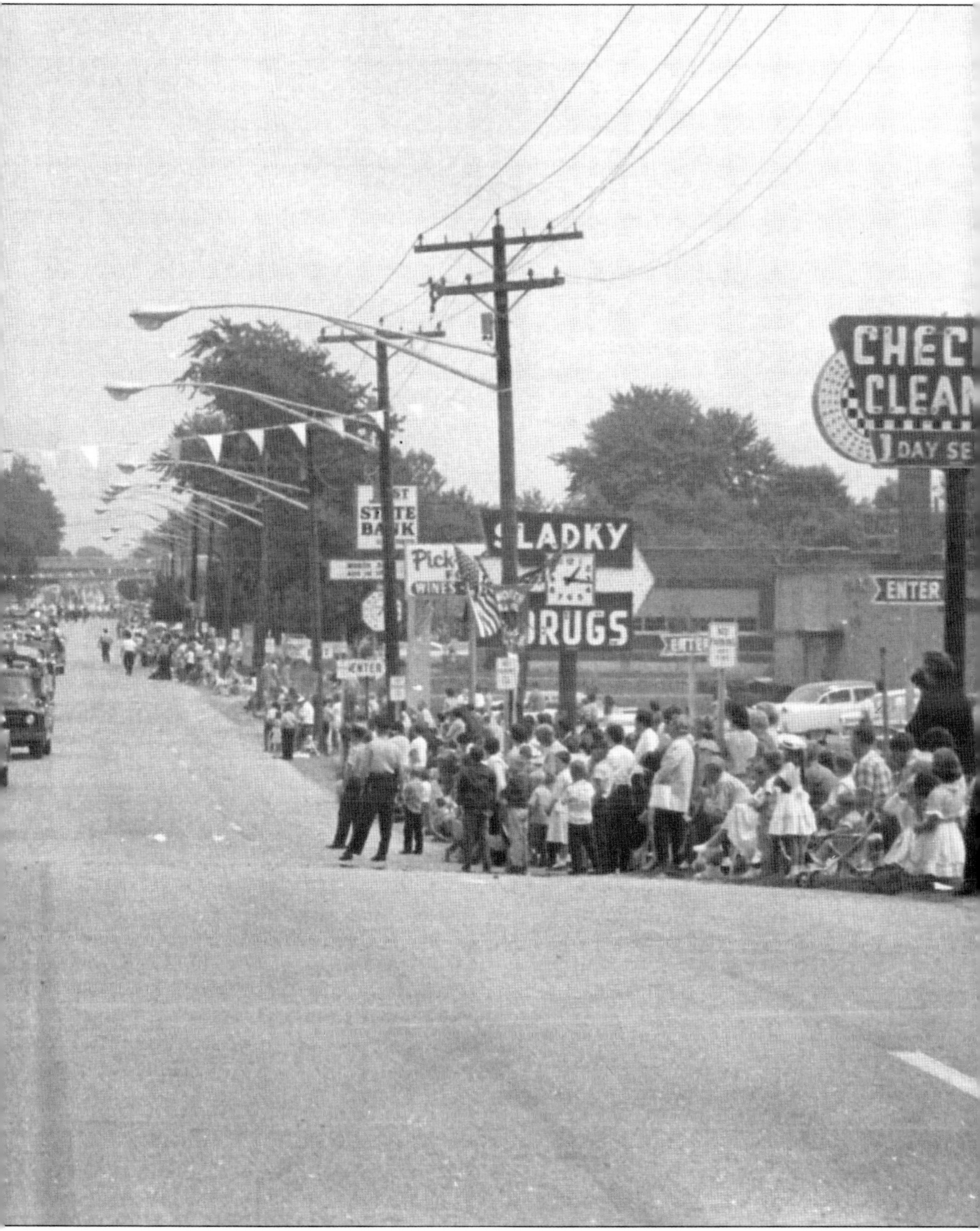

these grand photographs tell a tale of transition from the old wooden buildings to a modernization that was rapidly changing the face of Worth's main street.

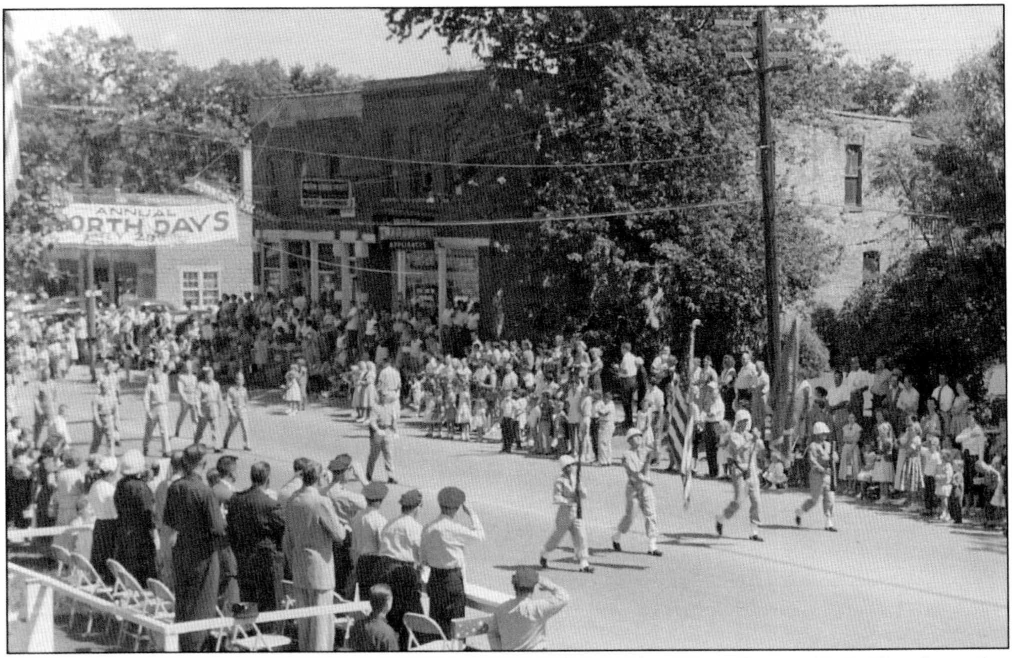

Veterans take the lead in 1956. The beginning of each parade was traditionally led by the color guard from the Marrs-Meyer American Legion Post No. 991. In 1956, they were joined by the VFW Post from Worth. It was not unusual to have over 50 entries of elaborate floats and entertainers in the parade.

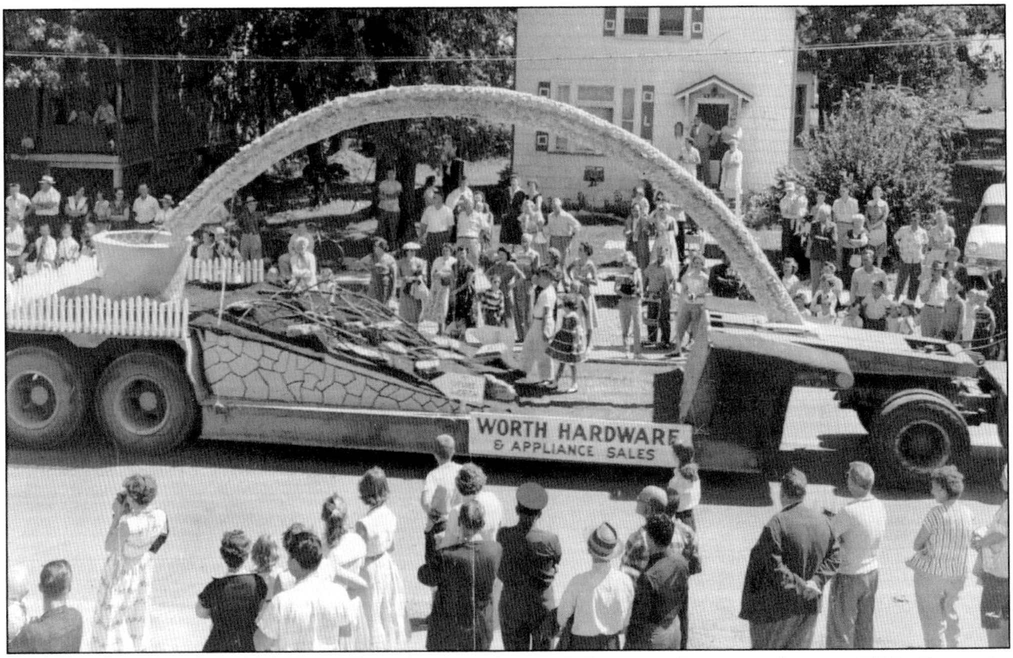

Worth Hardware was a staple in the community until the state began widening 111th Street in the early 1960s. Worth Hardware was in one of Worth's oldest buildings, Hildebrand Hall. Fred Hildebrand's son-in-law Bill Little took over the business in the 1940s and converted it into a hardware store, which he operated until 1950. The Holmbergs were the owners in 1956.

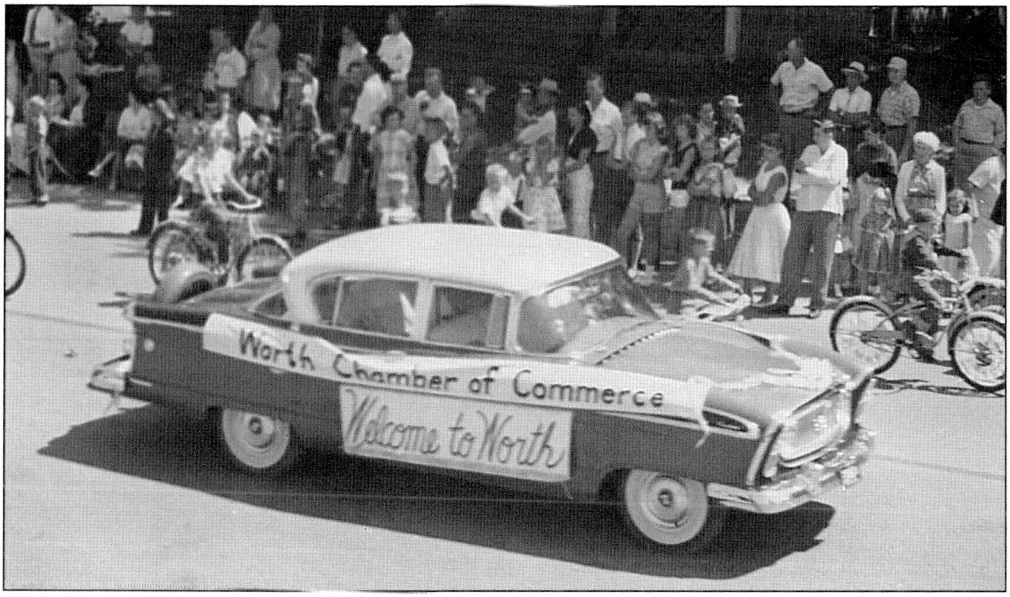

The Worth Chamber of Commerce was established with the help of Ed Kennelly, Aggie and John Daniels, and the Holmberg family. The chamber tried to assist local business owners in promoting their establishments. The chamber was involved with many special activities and events in the village, including Easter egg hunts, treasure days, and sidewalk sales. During 1955, there were 10 grocery stores, 3 gas stations, 3 barbershops, 9 clothing stores, a television repair shop, a drugstore, and 3 beauty shops.

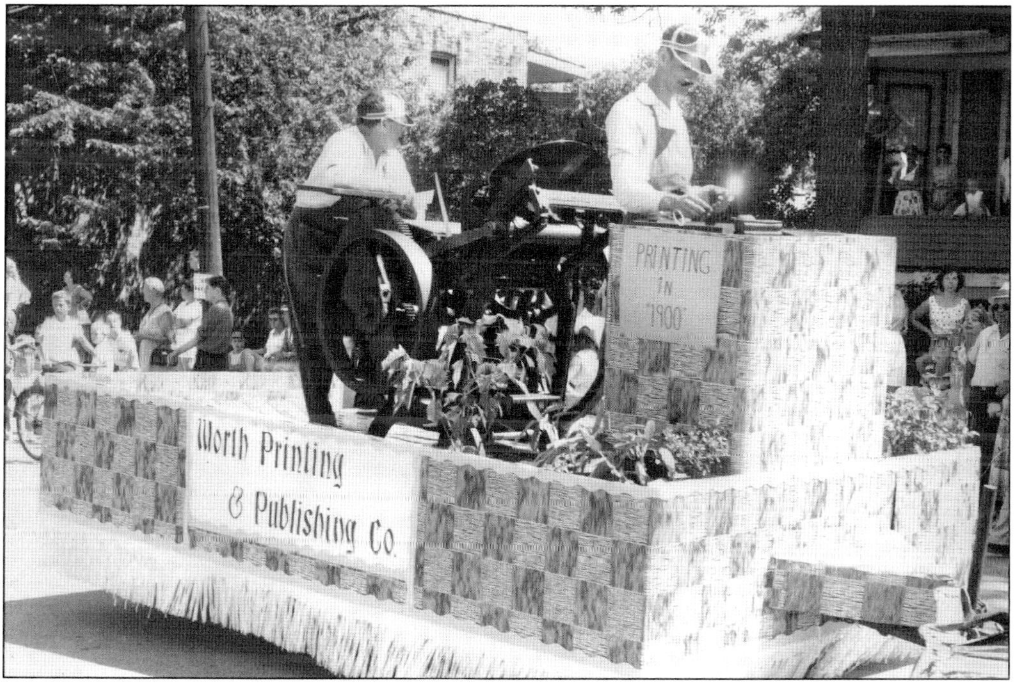

The experienced brothers Robert and Clyde Sasveld show off their old letterpress in the 1957 parade. The company was established in Worth in 1952. By calling GI8-778, people could get the news, invitations, and requests printed in no time.

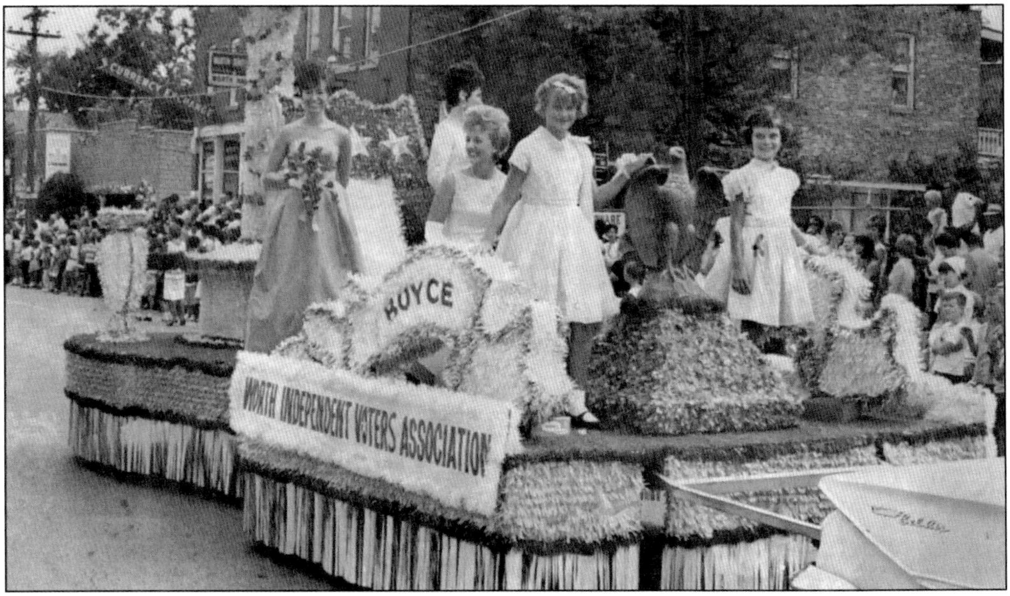

John Boyce was village president from 1965 to 1966. During his administration, he oversaw a new municipal water system, pumping system, and reservoir. Worth Hardware and Worth Currency Exchange can be seen in the background. The Kennelly family of Worth operated the currency exchange and credit union. The credit union opened on April 18, 1957, and was found in the old hardware building in town. The incorporators included Edward Holmberg, Edward Lode, Larry Wyma, Agnes Daniels, David Zuidema, Herb Foyle, and Henry Wiernga. The loan was approved in June 1957 for $290.

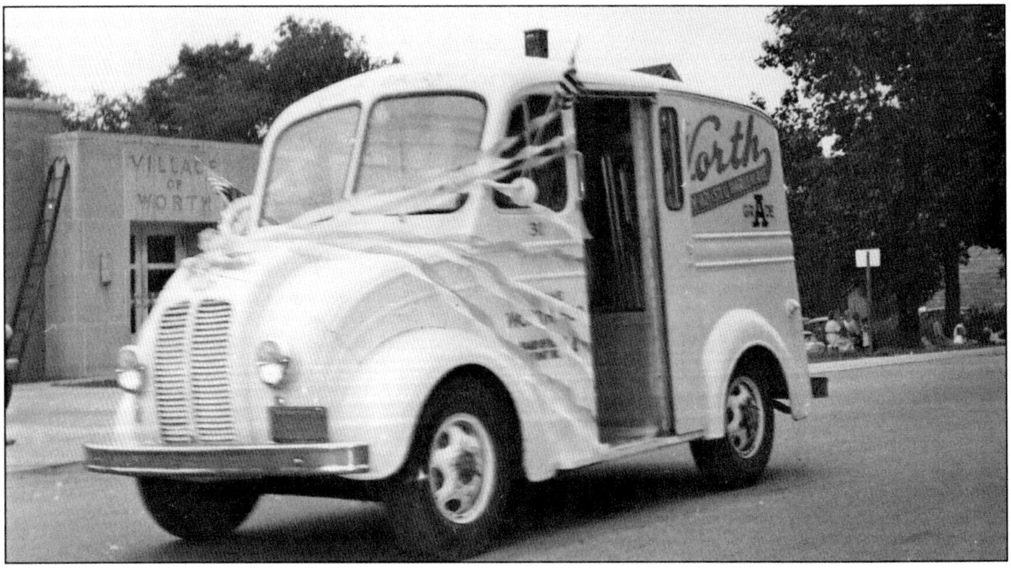

The Worth Dairy, with one of its trucks pictured here in 1956, was owned and operated by John Zuidima. It was located at 114th Street and Harlem Avenue. Zuidema began supplying milk in 1920 from his own cows. He delivered the milk with a horse and buggy. He expanded in 1943 when his sons Daniel and John were old enough to assist. The dairy was purchased by Borden and eventually closed. John was a member of the first volunteer fire department, Lions Club, and the Booster Club of Worth.

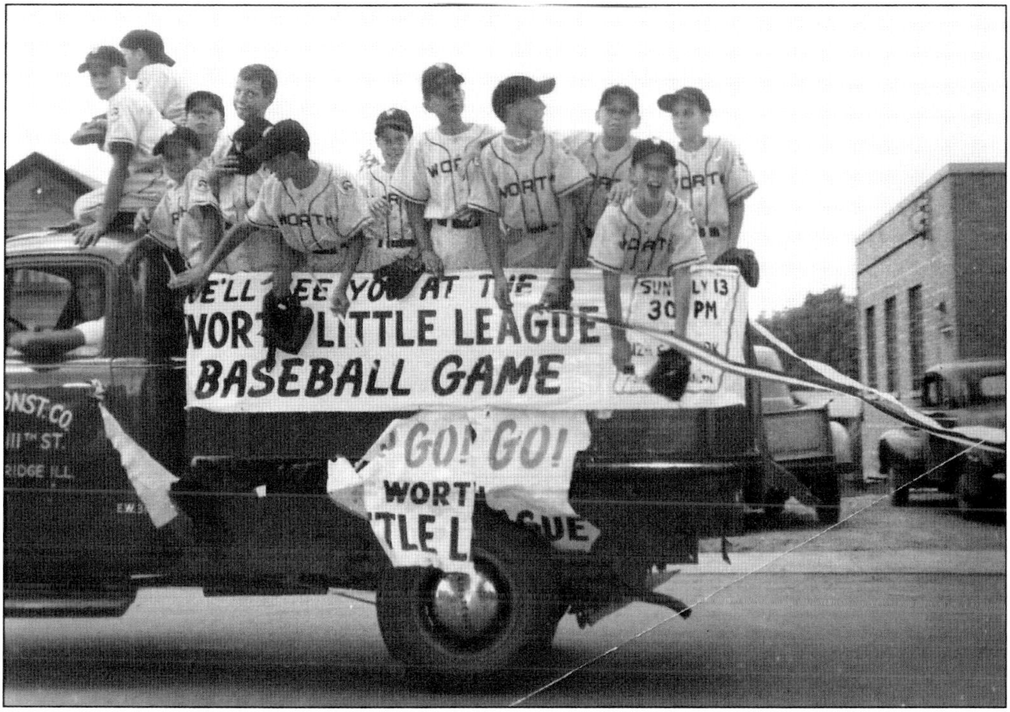

Members of the Worth Little League team are seen here in 1956. Homecoming games for the league were often held on the weekend of Worth Days. The Boys Club was established in 1954.

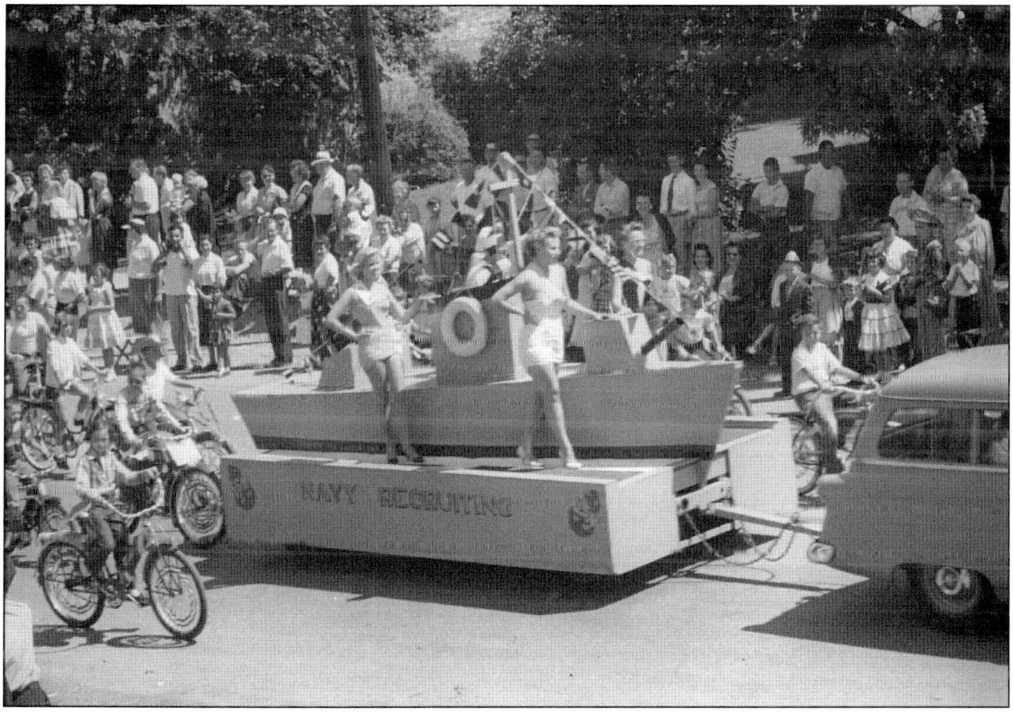

Even in peacetime, the Navy was always looking for new members to "see the world." Worth had a high number of veterans due to the post–World War II housing incentives that were given.

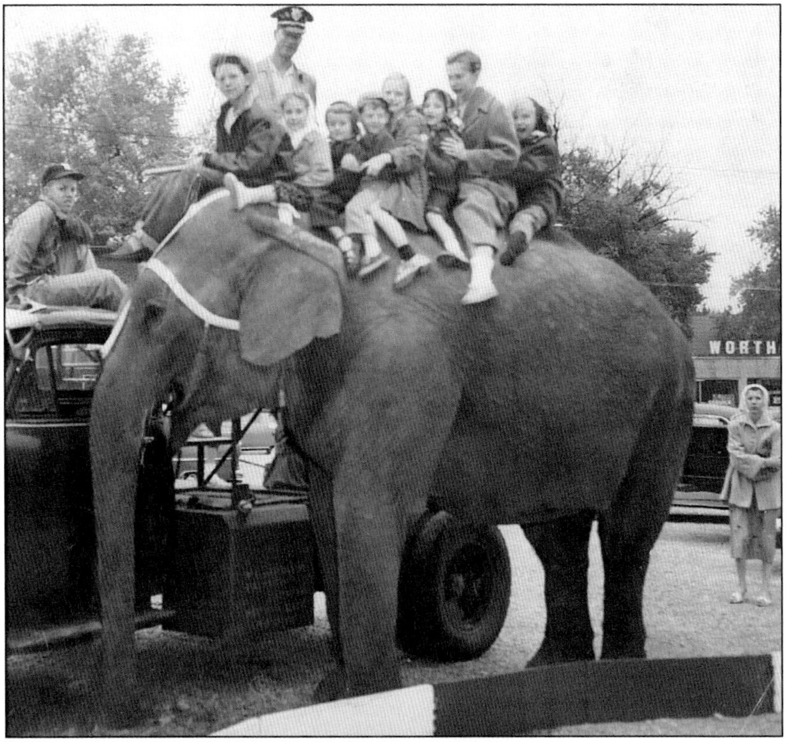

The lines were always long for the elephant rides across from the village hall. A patrolman watches over the jumbo guest brought in from the Ringling Bros. Circus that was being held the following weekend in a nearby town. The police department played an active role in organizing Worth Days.

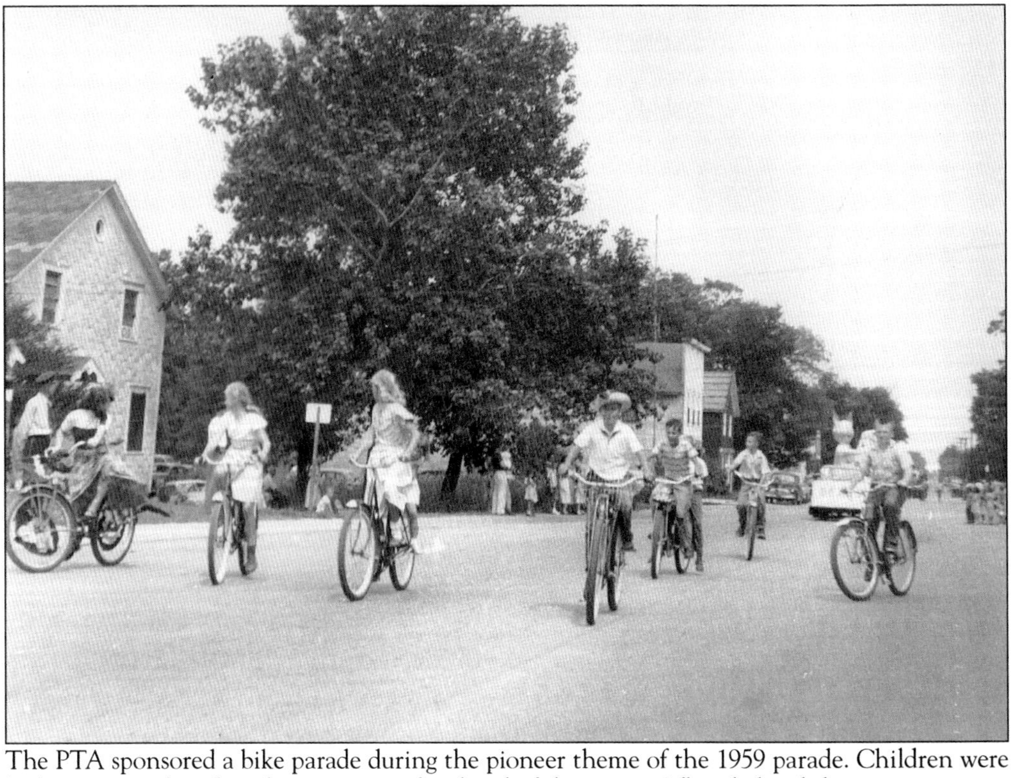

The PTA sponsored a bike parade during the pioneer theme of the 1959 parade. Children were looking to see that they do not get too far ahead of the parents' float behind them.

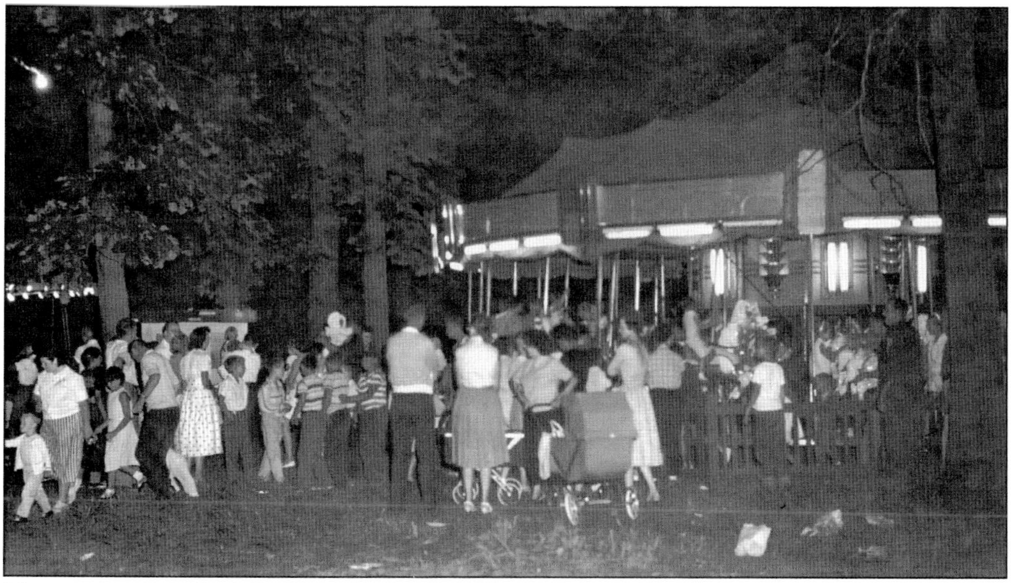

The year 1960 marked the first time the festival went on for three days. It was held at the Wagner Park, now known as Gale Moore Park after a school board member. Tickets for rides were $1 for eight rides.

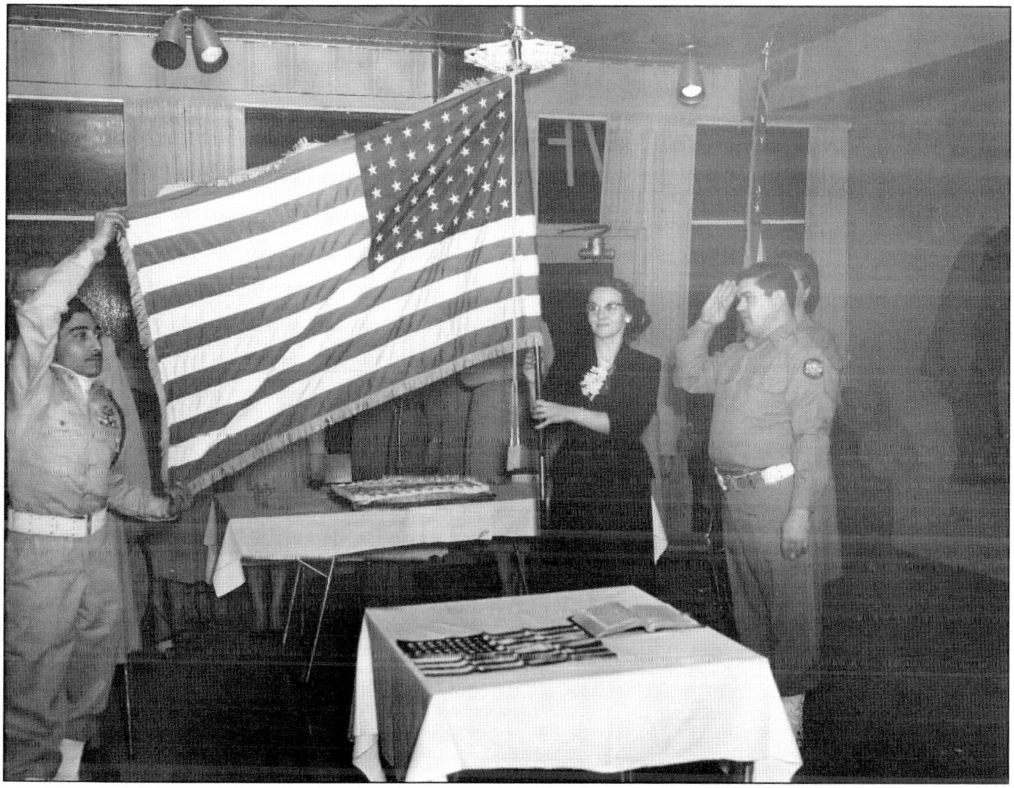

The Worth VFW was located on Harlem Avenue and 113th Street. The organization was involved in some civic organizations but only lasted two years in town. While active, they helped to plan Worth Days and assisted local veterans. Many members went on to join the American Legion.

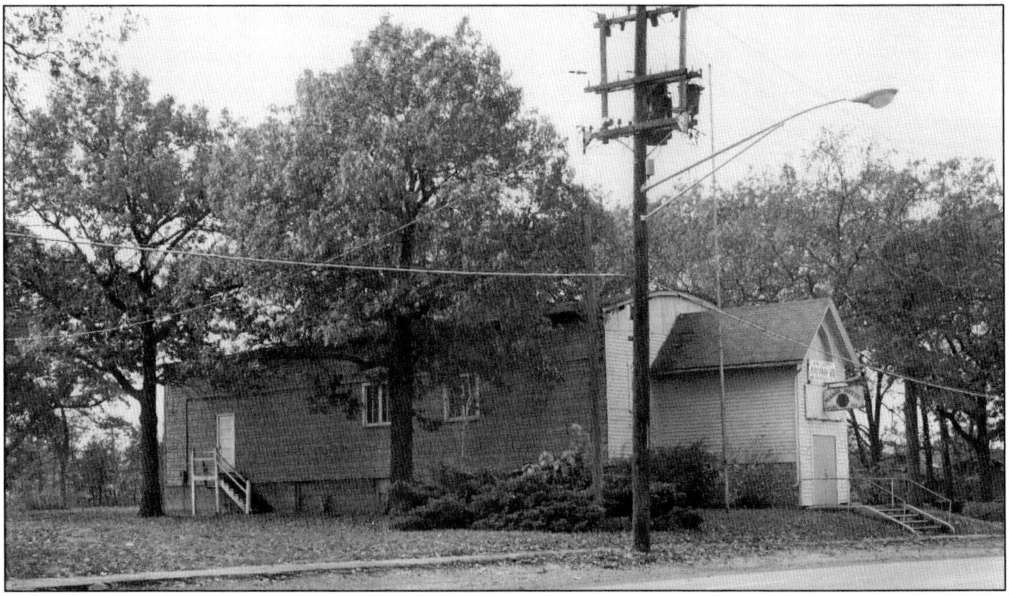

The American Legion Post No. 991 took an active role in Worth Days and other community events in town. First chartered on July 15, 1946, the post was named after Cpl. Raymond Marrs and Pvt. Walter Meyer. Both men were from Worth and gave their lives in the service of their county. This building was originally the Methodist church, but the legion purchased it after a fire. The building was rehabbed and utilized until the mid-1960s.

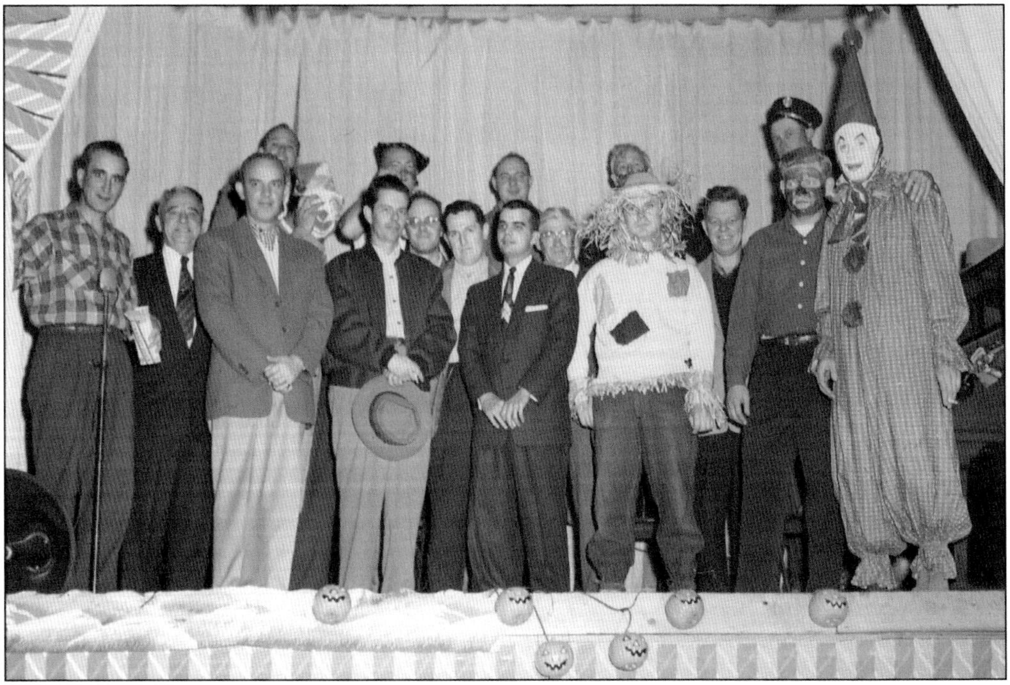

The American Legion's first commander was William "Bill" Little of Worth. He received much help from Jack Burgert of Palos Heights. The legion is responsible for many activities in town, including dances, food drives, Thanksgiving and St. Patrick's Day dinners, and the famous Poppy Day. Picture here is the 1957 board at the annual Halloween masquerade.

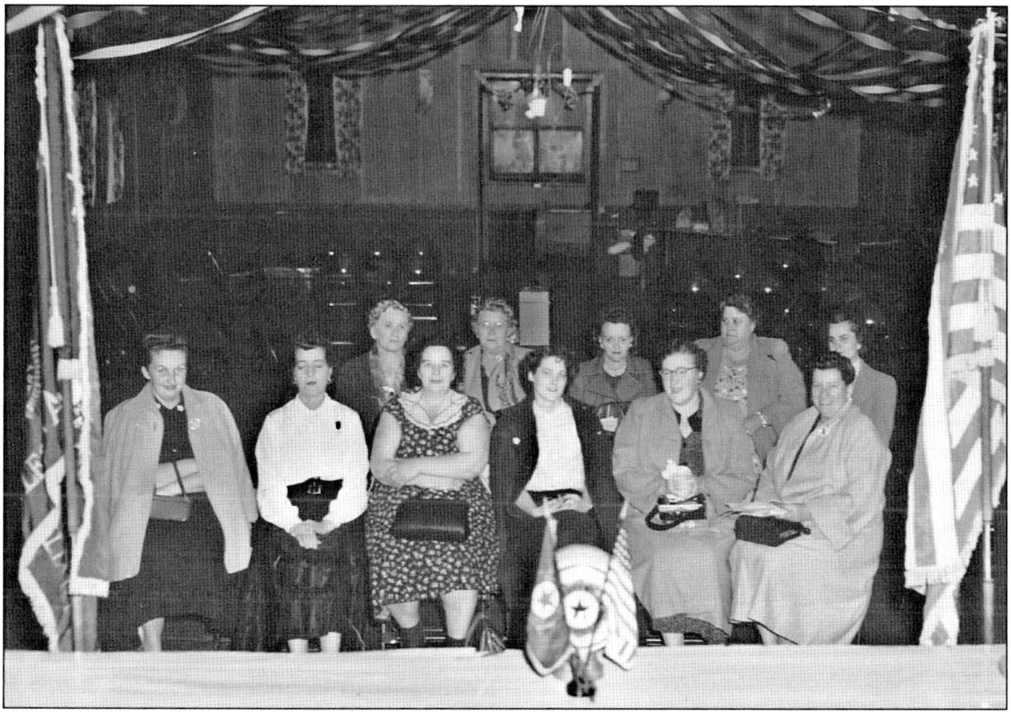

The American Legion Women's Auxiliary was chartered on January 25, 1947. Its aim and objectives are to support the American Legion and help veterans and their families. They visit veterans at nursing homes and hospitals with gifts several times a year. In addition, they prepare and distribute food baskets to needy families for Thanksgiving and Christmas. The first president was Mary Marrs. The second president was Vivian Meyer. Both of their husbands were the namesake of the American Legion.

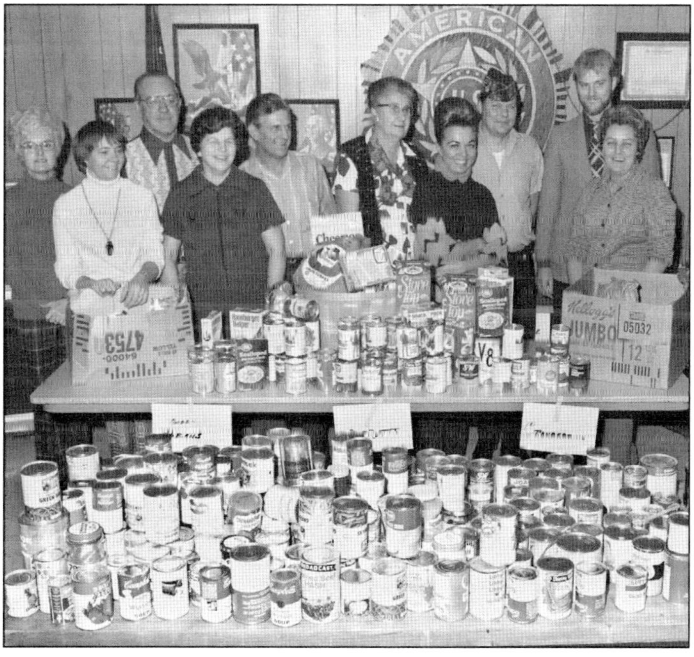

In 1954, Hazel Little formed a group that was associated with the auxiliary called the Community Service and Welfare Committee. Sis Lucas, in the center of the photograph, assisted with this program for 37 years. Sis would often keep items in her basement for any family that was in need of items. This committee would enlist the help of the Lions Club, police, Boy and Girl Scouts, and the Methodist church to host the annual "Ton of Food" drive. Baskets are created and distributed to needy families in town from the items that were collected.

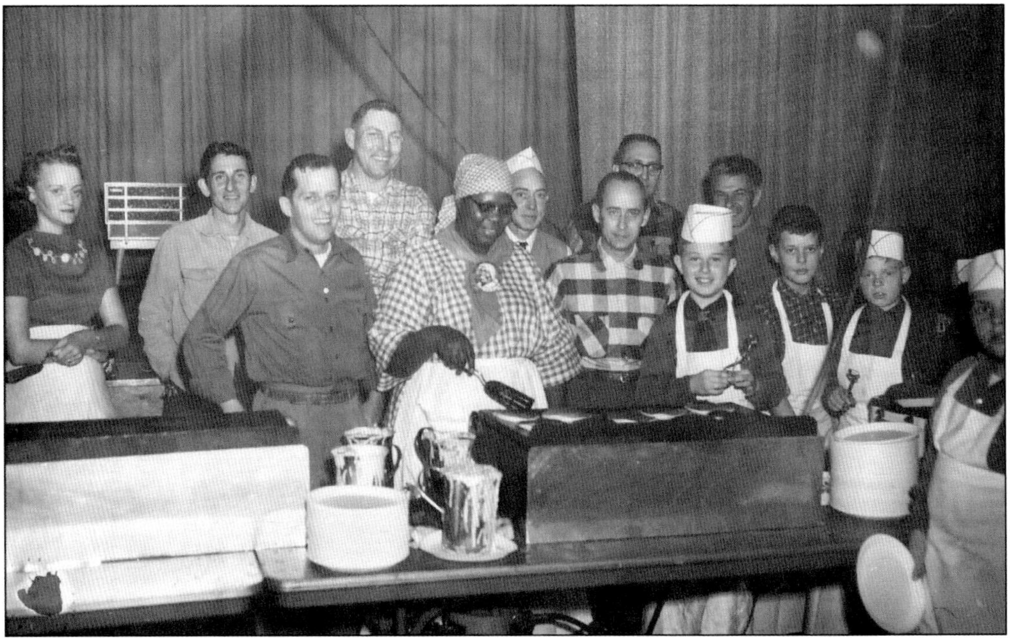

The Boy Scouts established themselves in Worth as early as 1938. The boys had some help from "Aunt Jemima" at their 1956 pancake breakfast. Tickets were sold for $1 for adults and 50¢ for children. Breakfast was held in the basement of the Methodist church. Pictured here are, from left to right, (first row) unidentified, "Aunt Jemima," unidentified, Ken Durkie, Bob Gilbert, Ed Wilson, and Jack Plahm; (second row) Ann Lode, Rich Klein, Gale Moore, Paul Cantwell, Buz Hayden, and John Schiera Sr.

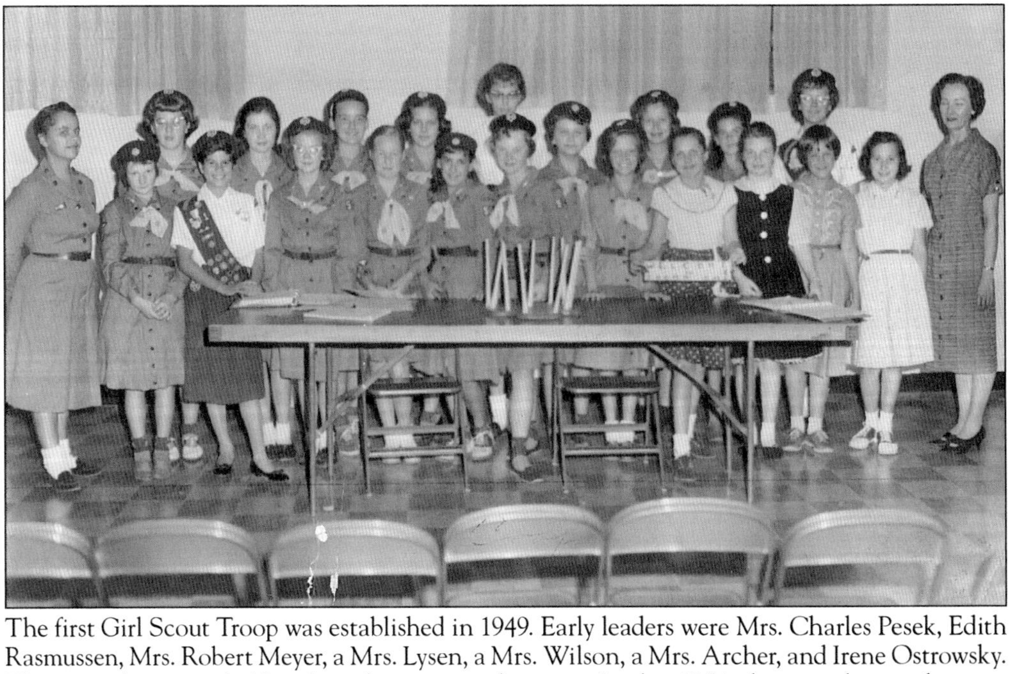

The first Girl Scout Troop was established in 1949. Early leaders were Mrs. Charles Pesek, Edith Rasmussen, Mrs. Robert Meyer, a Mrs. Lysen, a Mrs. Wilson, a Mrs. Archer, and Irene Ostrowsky. The group began with 19 girls and grew over the years. In this 1954 photograph, members are seen after a bridging ceremony.

The Campfire Girls were introduced to Worth in 1958 by Mildred St. Denis. Their sponsor was Ed Lode, who owned the Sinclair station on 111th Street and Harlem Avenue, and John Dembosz, who owned Roan Heating and Air Conditioning. Meetings were held at the Methodist church until the mid-1970s. Pictured here are Denise Tassone, Sandy Isaacson, and Debbie St. Denis along with local Girl Scouts. The girls are decorating the Christmas tree at the Worth Public Library.

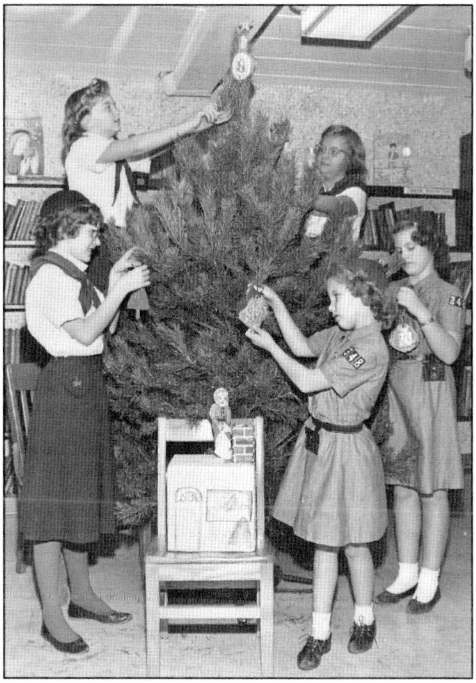

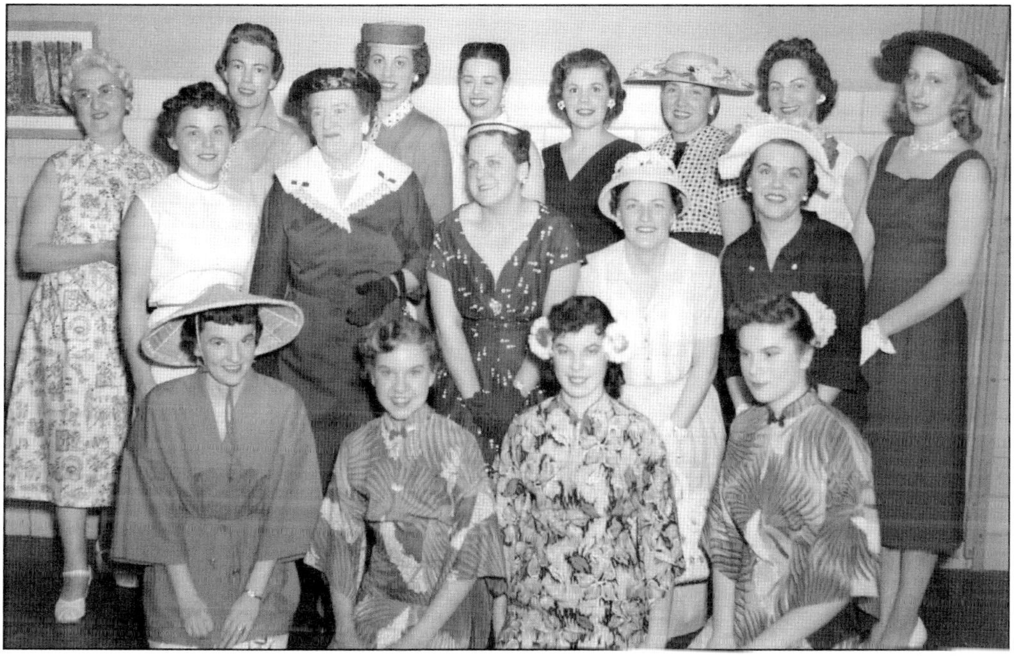

The 1957 members of the Forest Women's Club model fashions from Shirl's Shoes and the Sprite Shop of Worth and the House of Mary and Irene's Hats of Oak Lawn in their annual style show. Models pictured are, from left to right, (first row) Gwen Dobslaw, Darlene Rutkas, Arlene Sherman, and Gloria Sherman; (second row) Marie Singer, Rose Fairburn, Rose Dusold, Doris Sickles, and Patricia Singer; (third row) Mattie Karolich, Evelyn Hotho, Doris White, Jeanne Brunner, Grace Presbitero, Toni Karolich, Jean Sherman, and LaVerne Gorecki. The club assisted in many charity events in town and provided social opportunities for women in Worth.

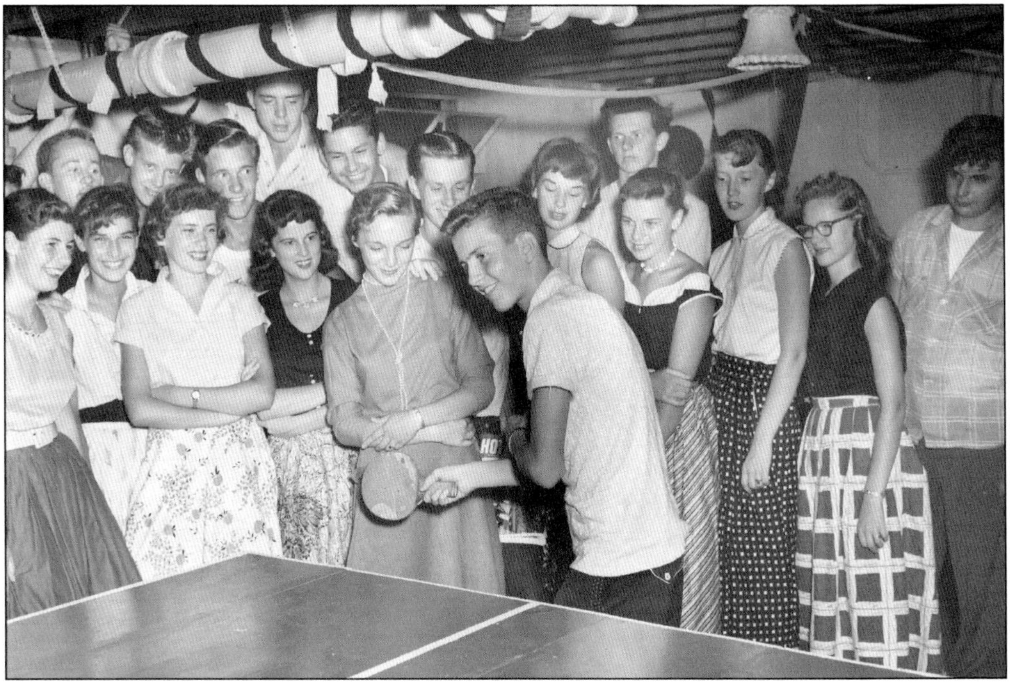

The Worth Keen Teen Club had their beginnings in the basement of the American Legion Hall in 1952. By 1957, there were 276 members. They held Friday night dances, splash parties, formal dances, roller-skating parties, and, in this instance, a ping-pong tournament.

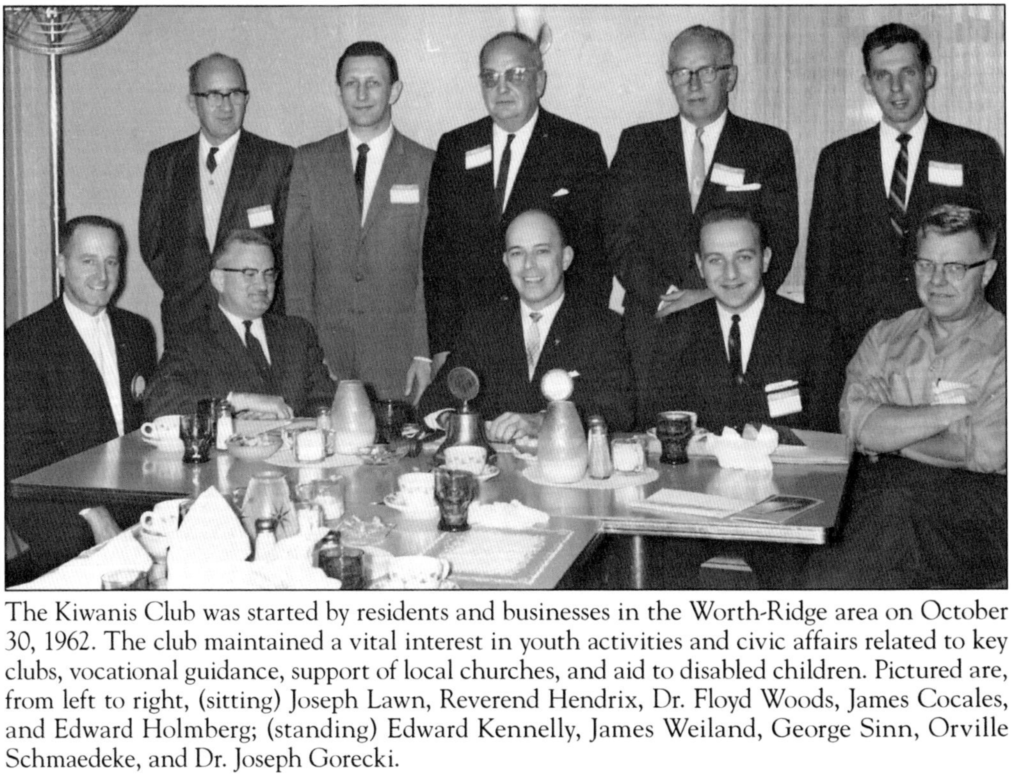

The Kiwanis Club was started by residents and businesses in the Worth-Ridge area on October 30, 1962. The club maintained a vital interest in youth activities and civic affairs related to key clubs, vocational guidance, support of local churches, and aid to disabled children. Pictured are, from left to right, (sitting) Joseph Lawn, Reverend Hendrix, Dr. Floyd Woods, James Cocales, and Edward Holmberg; (standing) Edward Kennelly, James Weiland, George Sinn, Orville Schmaedeke, and Dr. Joseph Gorecki.

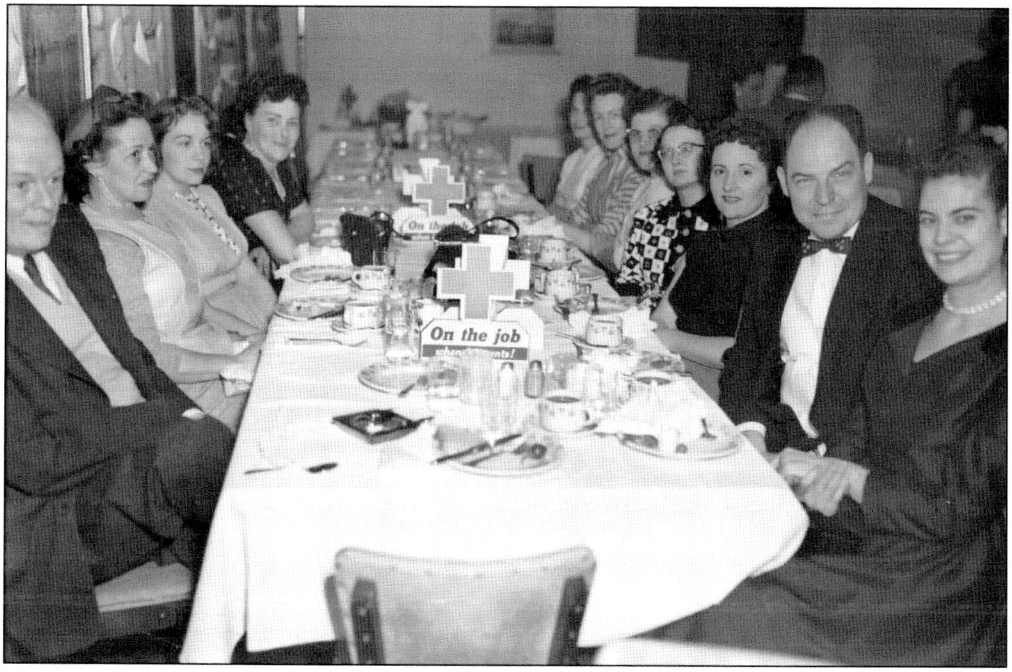

The American Red Cross had a local group in Worth. The group held an annual fundraiser that assisted the national organization in aiding those in need. The group in Worth held frequent blood drives and educated the public with first aid and safety training. The group also assisted the civil defense program on the southwest side.

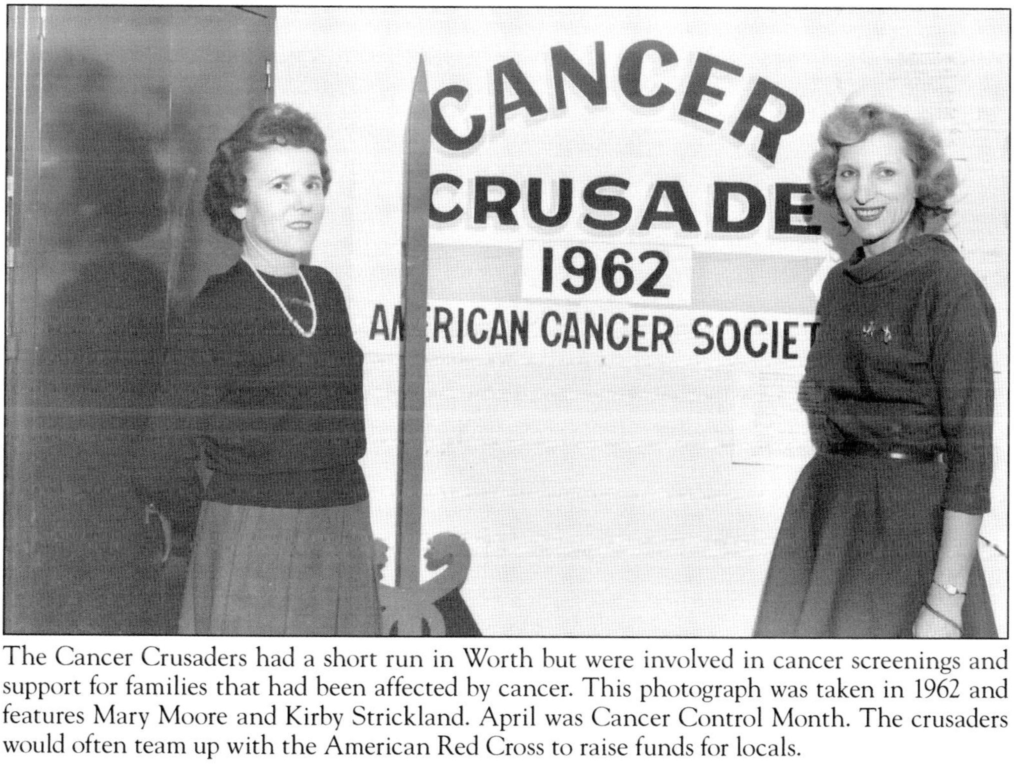

The Cancer Crusaders had a short run in Worth but were involved in cancer screenings and support for families that had been affected by cancer. This photograph was taken in 1962 and features Mary Moore and Kirby Strickland. April was Cancer Control Month. The crusaders would often team up with the American Red Cross to raise funds for locals.

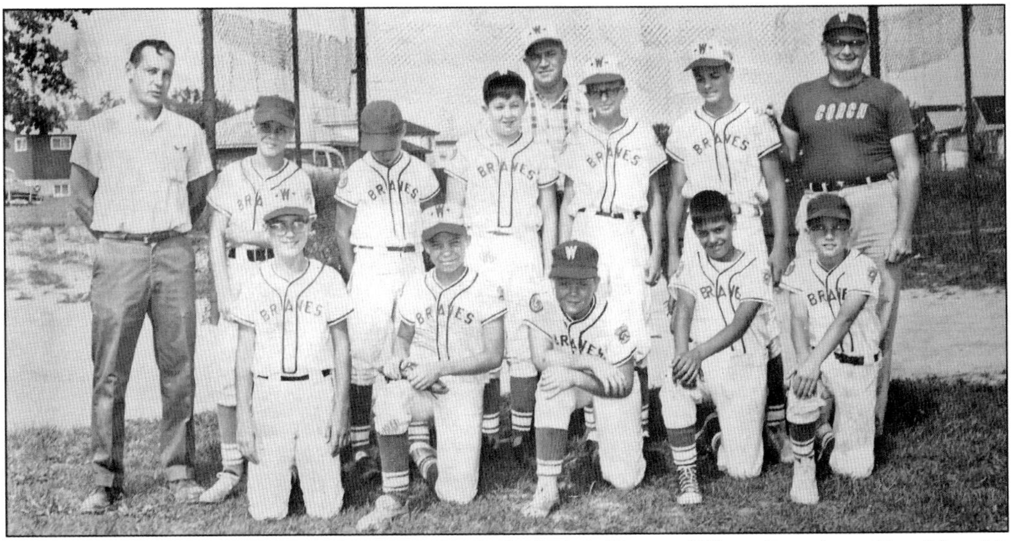

The Worth Boys Club originated in 1942. With the help of former White Sox player Don Hanski, Francis McDonough, and Herb Stewart, the first Little League Sox and Cubs teams began. This 1965 team was made up of, from left to right, (first row) Jerry Oracki, Billy Plahm, Carl Vanderwaude, Steve Mele, and Ray Lilja; (second row) coach George Demetral, John Urbaniak, Greg Crosley, Bill Crosley, Carl Sick, Larry Lilja, and coach Harold Sick; (third row) unidentified coach.

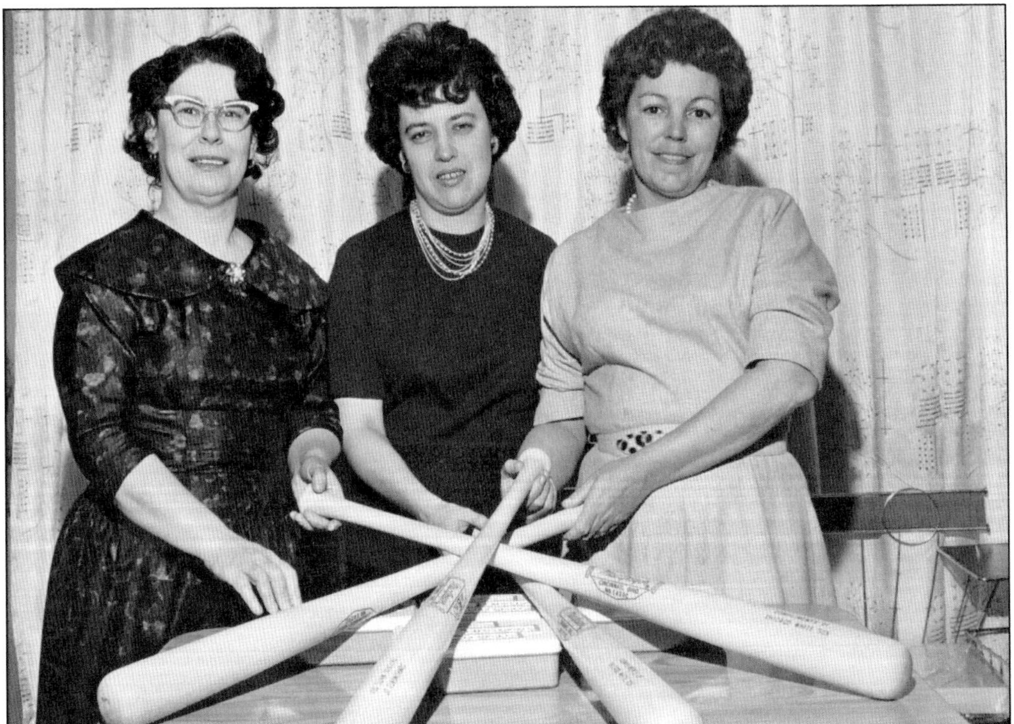

Behind every good man is a good woman. The Worth Mothers' Club was responsible for fundraising and providing snacks and support to the boys and coaches. Victoria Lukasiewicz, Mrs. Charles Barker, and Mrs. Bert Jaderberg show off their latest fundraising purchases to the *Worth Record* newspaper in May 1965.

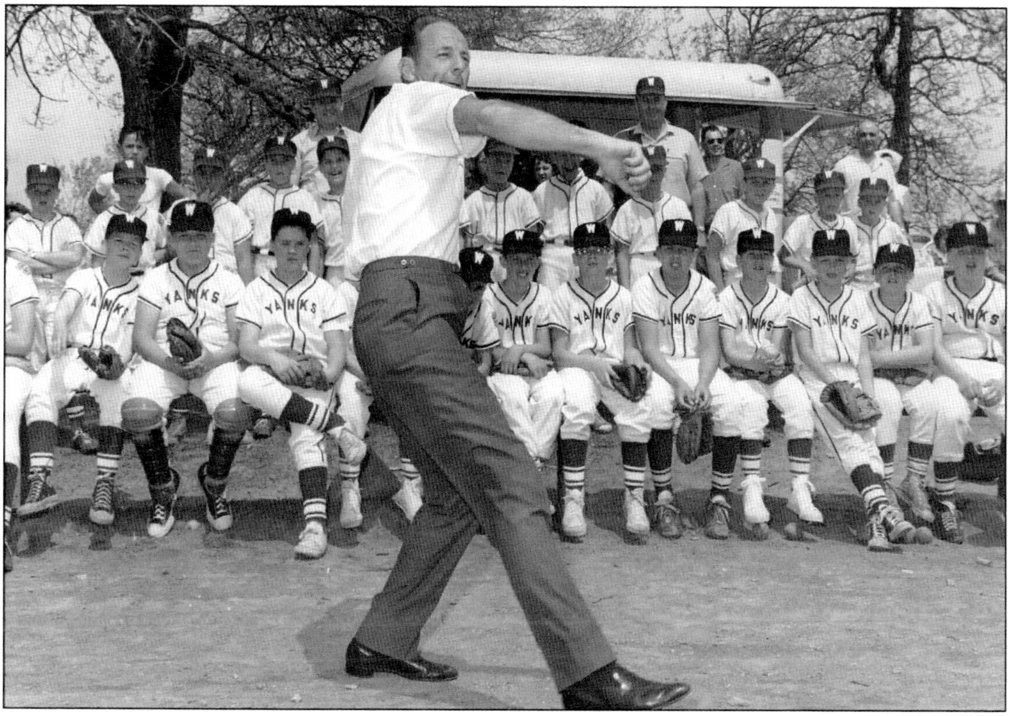

Throwing out the first pitch for the 1965 Little League season is coach Dave Wagner. Games were played on the Wilson-Wagner property, located at 108th Street and Depot Avenue. The property was purchased by the Worth Park District in 1970.

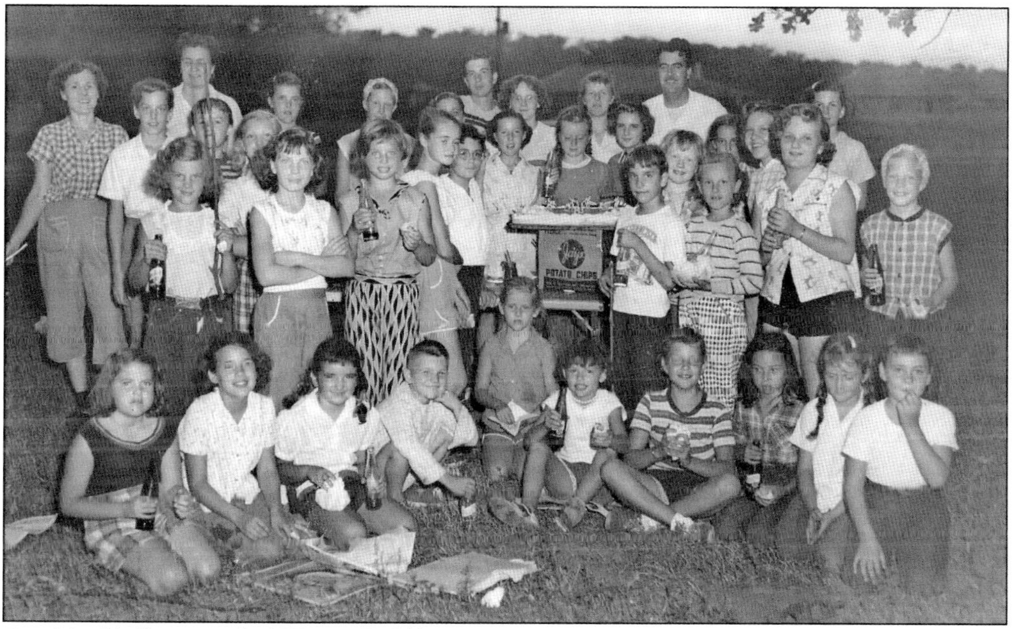

A girls' softball team called Wagner Field home in 1956 every Monday and Wednesday. Adult leaders of the group were Mrs. Kenneth Lucas and Mrs. Dan Moore. The girls are seen here celebrating the end of their season on the last Wednesday in August 1956. This group was sponsored by the Youth Council of Worth.

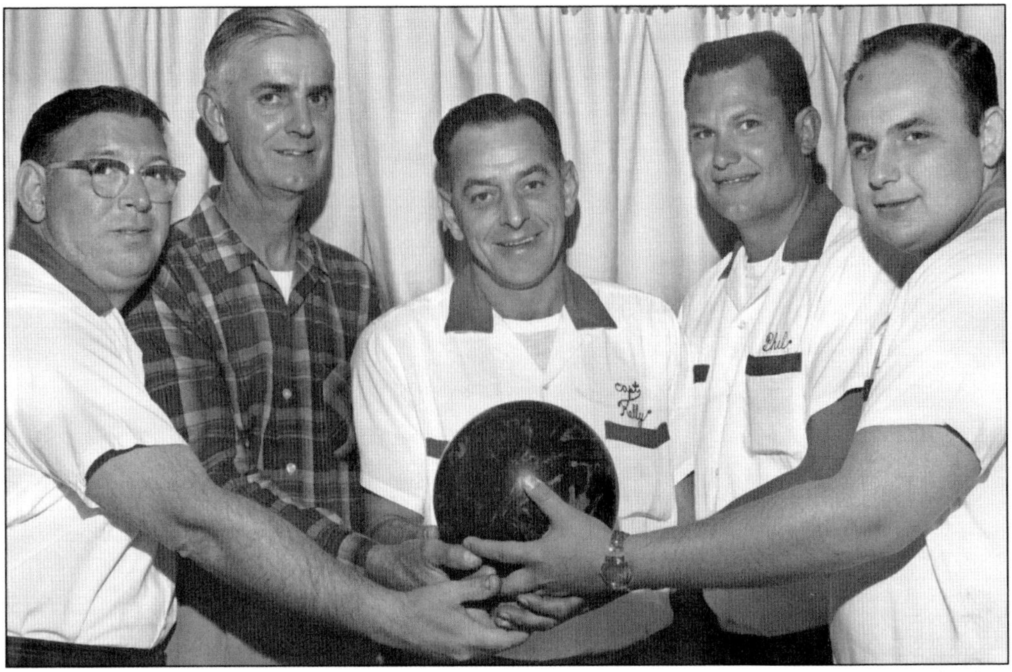

The Men's Bowling League was popular from 1955 through the 1960s. From left to right, Joe Parisi, Ray Foyle, Kelly Corso, Phil Shilling, and Bill Kowalski show their camaraderie as they make their way to the finals in May 1963.

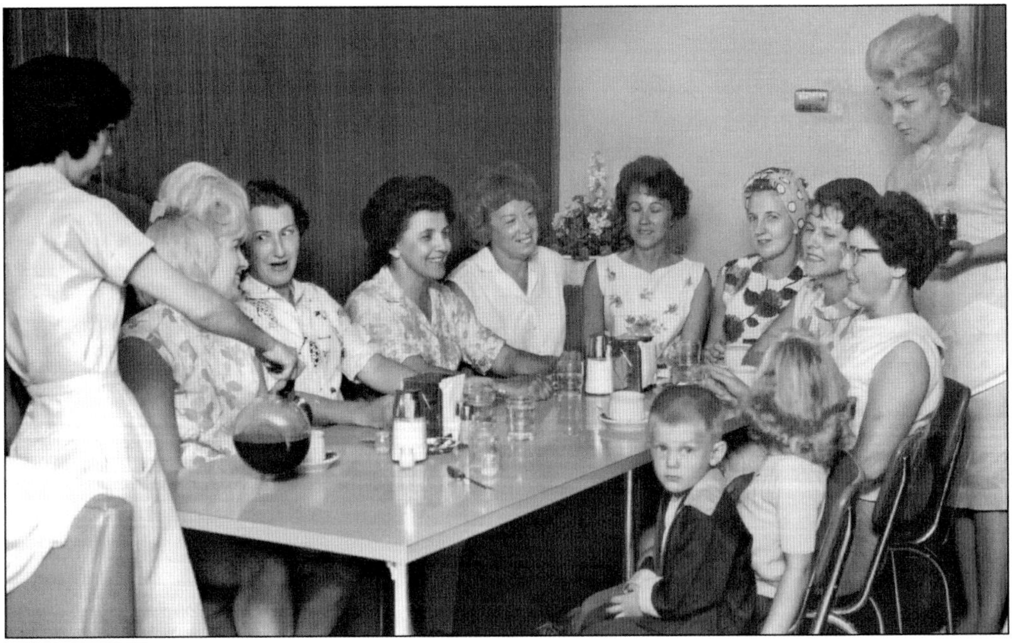

The Worth Snack Shop was opened on September 15, 1949, by Pete Taourmas. The second owner, Harry Nakos, remolded and employed seven other employees in addition to his wife. Being served at the Worth Snack Shop are, from left to right, Mary Kay Lift, Jean Pence, Helen Stack, Maxine Kulka, Beverly Schmidt, Claudene Schwertfeger, Marion Gaspar, Jean Holdcroft, and Debra and Paul Gaspar. All were members of the Women of Worth (WOW).

The Women of Worth always had a strong hand in building behind the scenes. The club had its beginning in 1949 as the Worth Women's Club. They worked closely with the Salvation Army for tag days, where organizations stood on street corners to collect donations. As years went by, the organization provided hours of activities for youth in the community prior to the establishment of the Worth Park District. WOW members Jan Nelson and Ellie Schoenfelder show off their latest fundraiser for Worth Days. The "Game of Worth" featured all the local businesses in town at the time. Proceeds went to the Worth Days Commission.

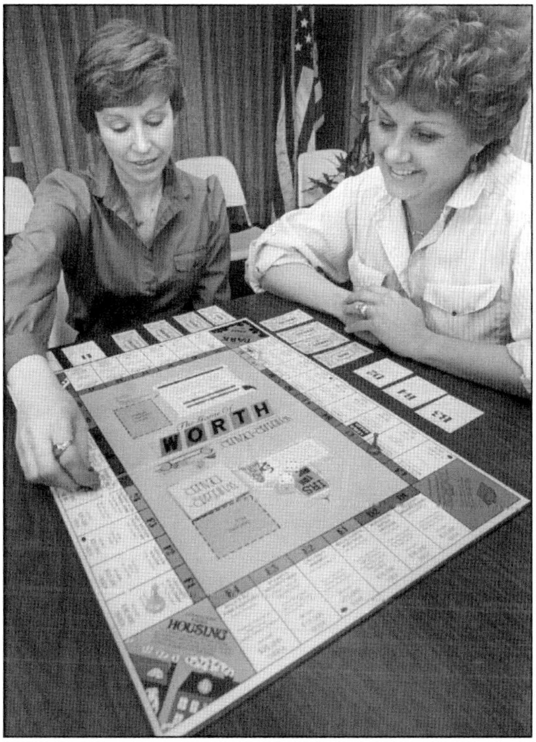

The Women of Worth sponsored a Worth Day queen contest. Pictured here are, from left to right, Frank Homerding, Andrea Daniels, and Dan Kumingo, president. The Women of Worth held many events prior to the creation of the Worth Park District that would provide recreational activities for residents.

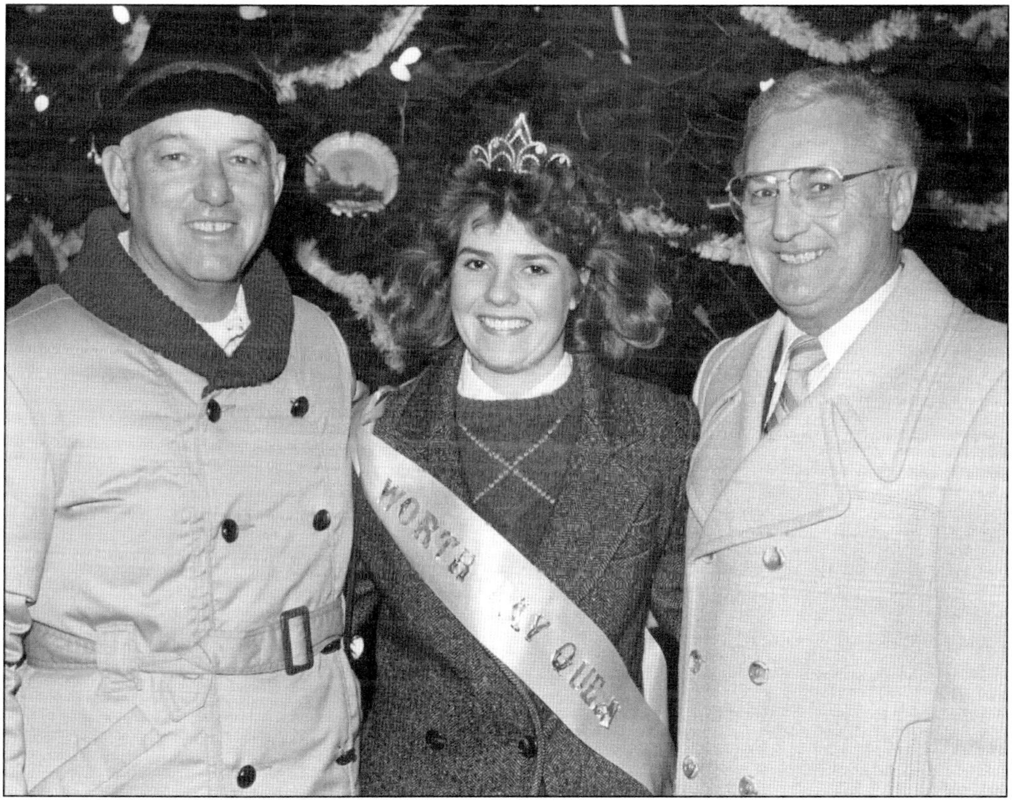

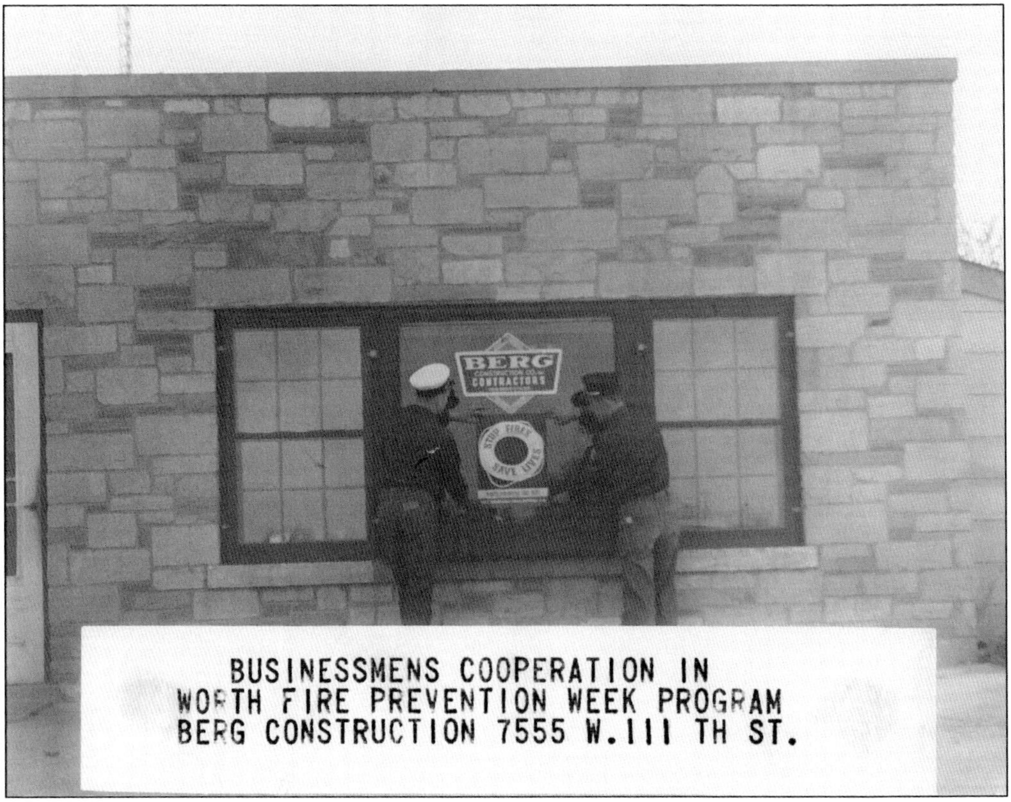

Working the pit in the early days of Worth, Frank Russert, village president from 1945 to 1949, recalled living in a home along 111th Street by the operating sand and gravel pit, known as Berg's Pit. Sam Berg owned the company from 1939 to 1970 and sold it to Harry Carlson in the 1970s. Pre-pioneer settlement land surveys and maps indicate a strong Native American presence on this land. The sand and gravel from this pit paved many of the roads in the southern suburbs of Chicago and provided many local jobs.

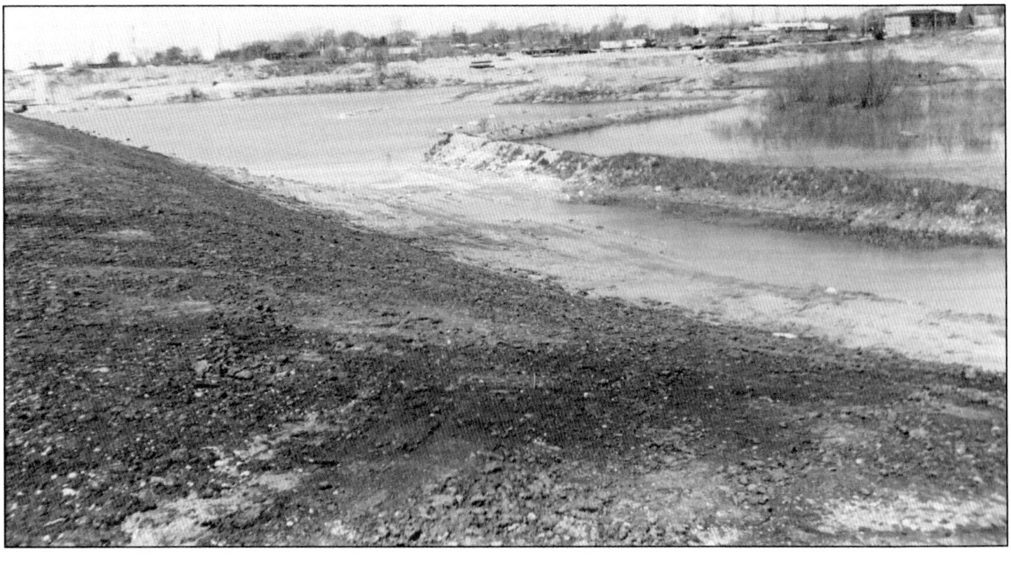

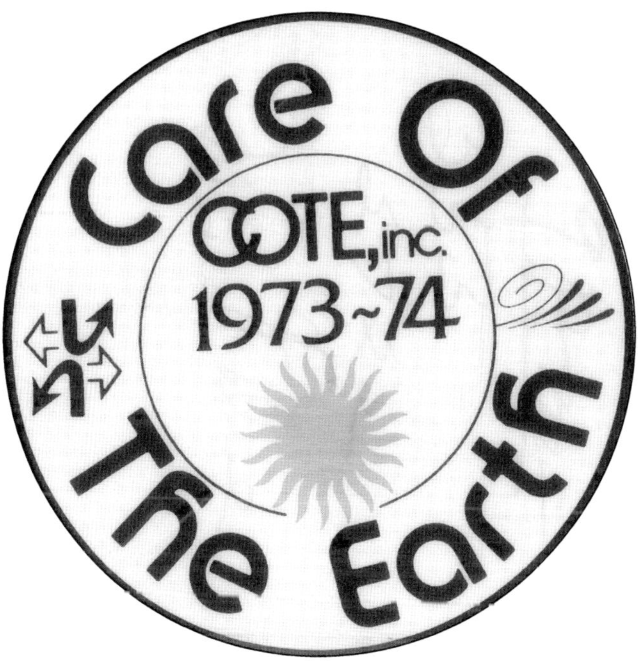

In 1970, Harry Carlson was going to utilize the pit as a garbage dump, a popular solution to waste management at the time. As a reaction to the proposal, a citizens group called Care of the Earth (COTE) was formed to find an alternative to dumping in this precious resource. Members often had fundraisers in order to support their research and print materials for their cause. The group was successful in their bid to provide a temporary solution to the dumping issue; a new group exists and is working with the Worth's Life Safety Commission to resolve the issue, which the village continues to struggle with in 2012.

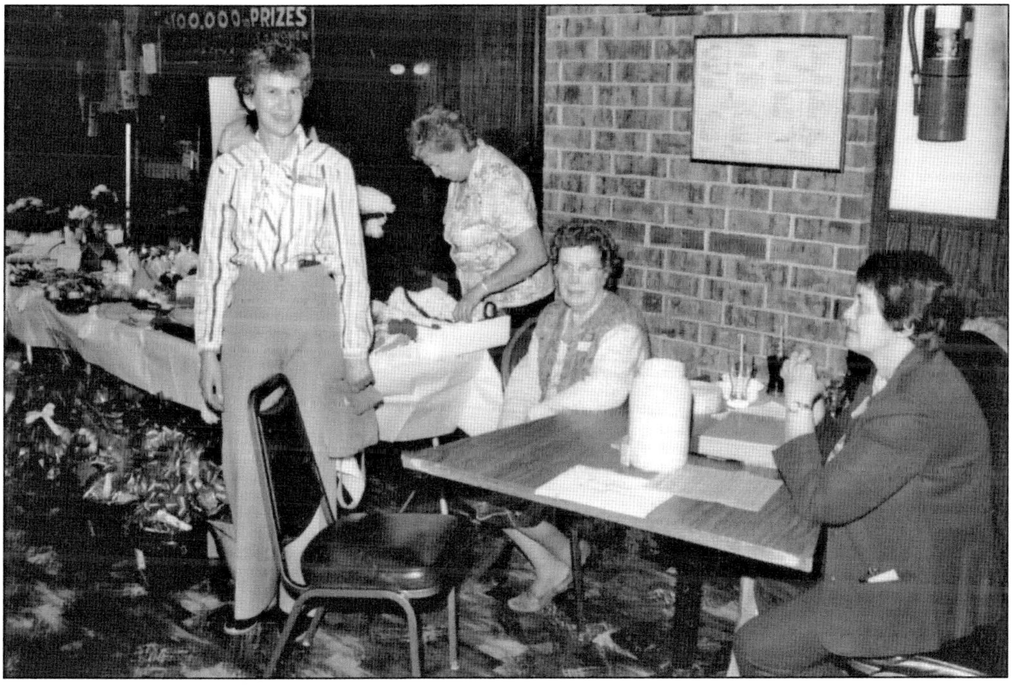

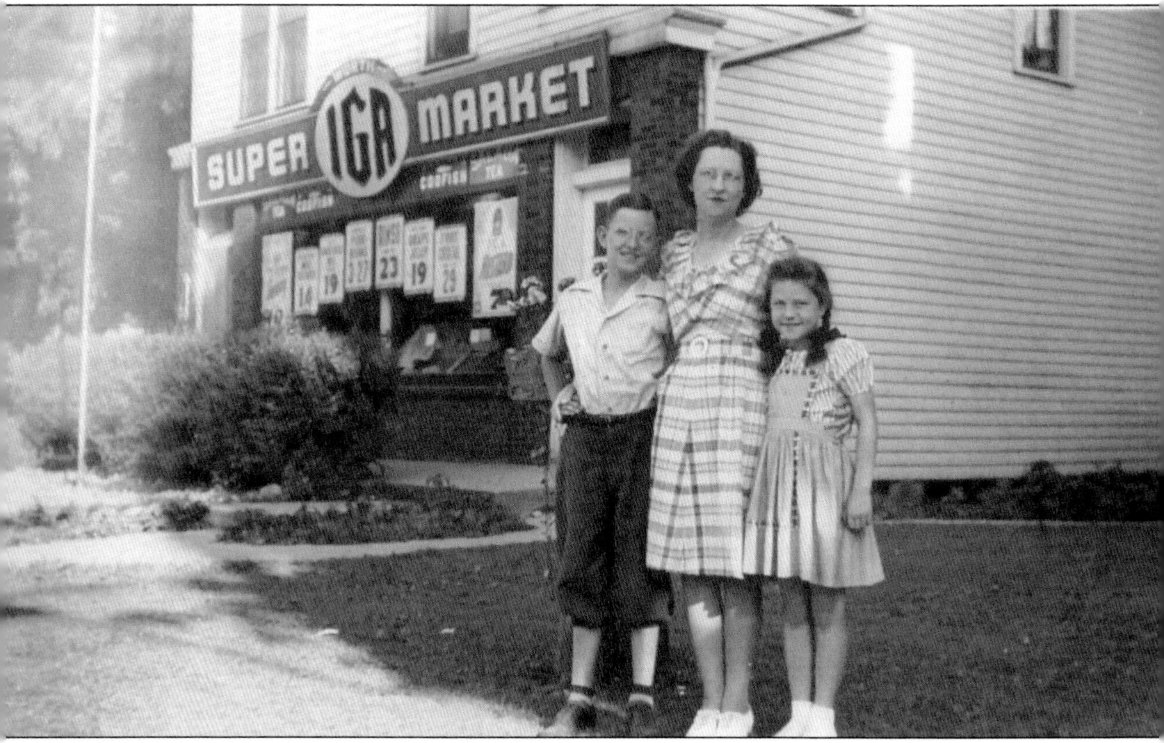

In 1942, the Crandall family was still active in the village. Gladys Crandall Rolfe, with children Robert and Barbara, assisted her husband, Frank Rolfe, in the IGA grocery store. The building was erected in 1904 by Harry Ferrin.

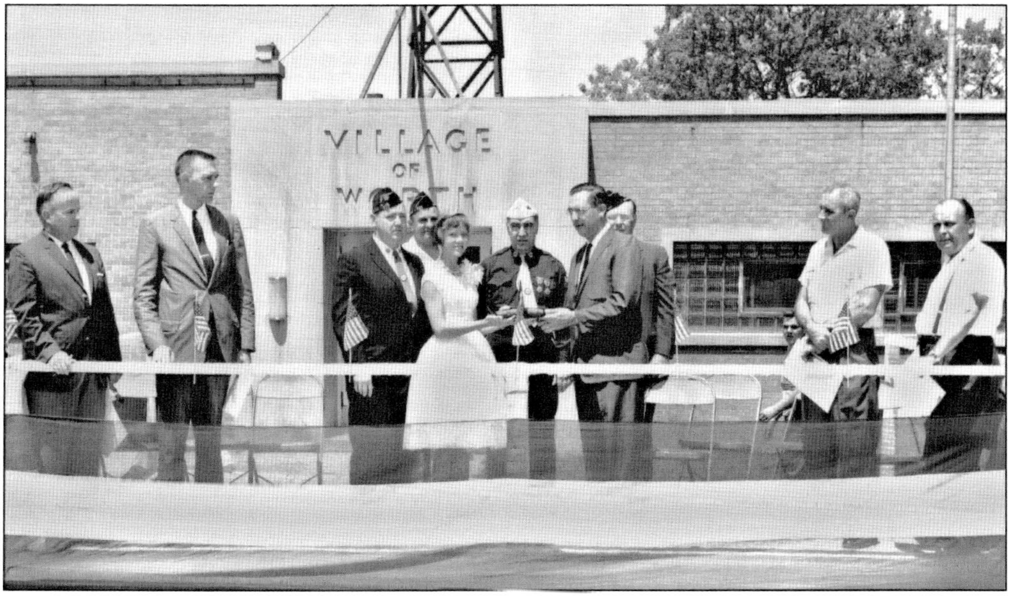

On July 9, 1961, the Village of Worth adopted a new "Worth flag." Christine Pischl, a student of Worth Elementary School, submitted the winning sketch to the American Legion after the call for a designated emblem was announced. Pictured are, from left to right, Palos Heights mayor Erral Smith, Carton Ihde from Palos Hills, Jerome Oracki, Jack Baldwin, Christine Pischl, unidentified commander of the American Legion, Worth village president James McCloskey, unidentified village official, Chicago mayor Art Coysen, and trustee Walter Tibutis of Alsip.

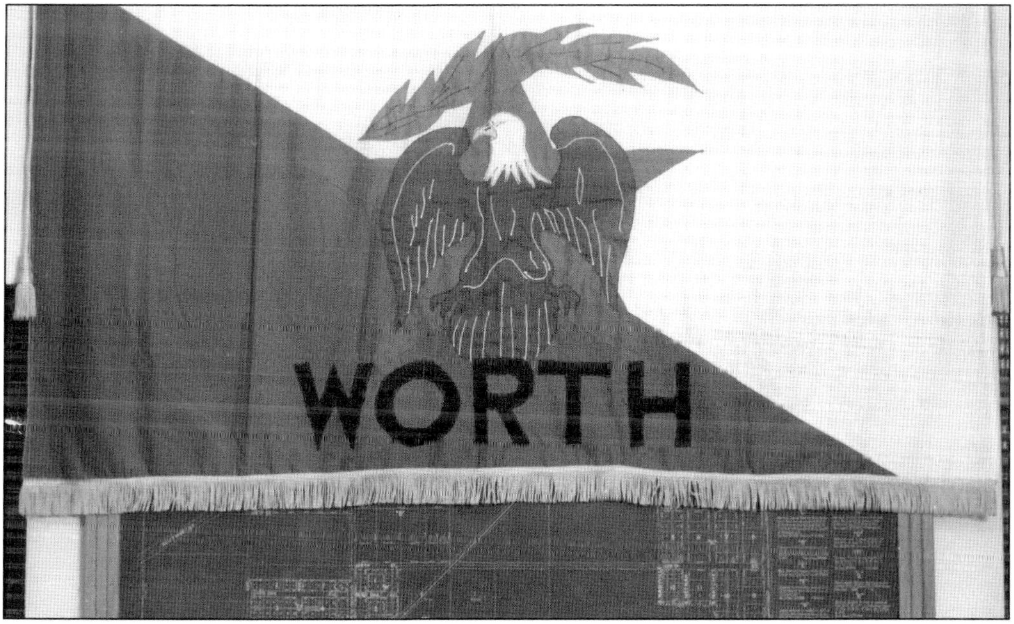

The green-and-white flag is displayed proudly at the village hall for all to see. The green represents the rich land of Worth while the white represents purity. The star means the coming together of people from different walks of life into one center and also stands for the federal government, which so many have given their lives in defending. The eagle is a symbol of great strength and stable principles. The olive branch denotes peace.

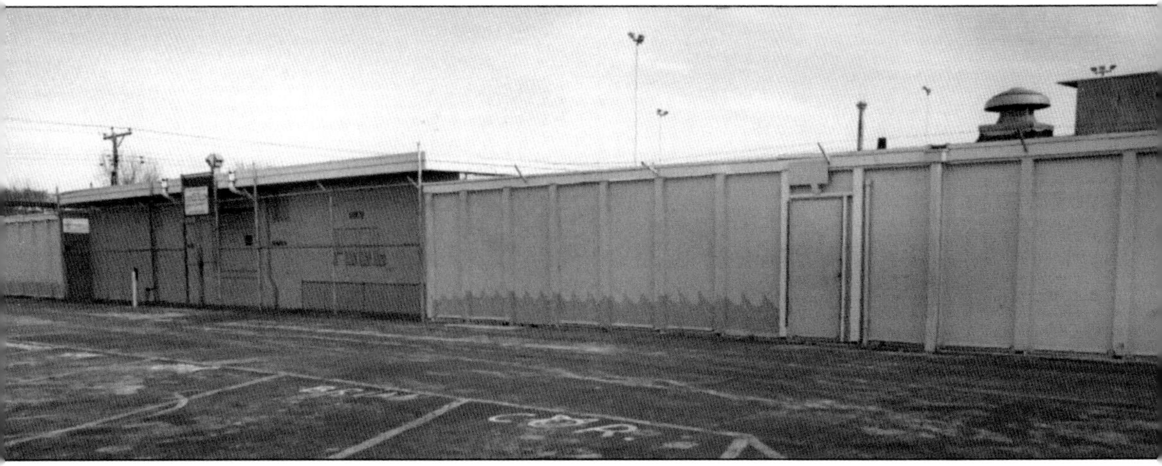

In 1949, John and Aggie Daniels convinced a group of citizens to form the Worth Pool Association. The name of the pool was Waterhaven. Shares were sold for $125, and membership was not limited to Worth residents. The Worth Park District attempted to preserve the pool, but due to the constant need of repairs and funding, it was sold to the Chicago Ridge Park District in 1986. The pool was permanently closed in the early 1990s.

Five

Parks and Recreation

It truly took a village to create the village of Worth. Through the years, many social clubs were formed to assist in varying projects and causes that trended during the teenage years of the village. In 1965, the village approved a referendum to create the Worth Park District. While many were seemingly excited for the district to form, the referendum only passed by a slim 26 votes. The creation of the district brought many community groups together and offered the town a central location for recreational activities to occur. Groups could use the public buildings acquired by the district for meetings and events that were previously held in backyards, basements, or garages.

The parks in the Worth Park District were named after significant residents in the village, except for Smile and Penny Parks. Penny Park was named after a promise that residents would only pay "pennies on the dollar" if they agreed to the purchase of some property for the park. Smile Park was so named after the school held a naming contest.

The mission of the Worth Park District is to offer residents opportunities to enjoy life through quality programs, service, and facilities. This chapter explores the namesake and history of the Worth Park District and village recreation opportunities for residents.

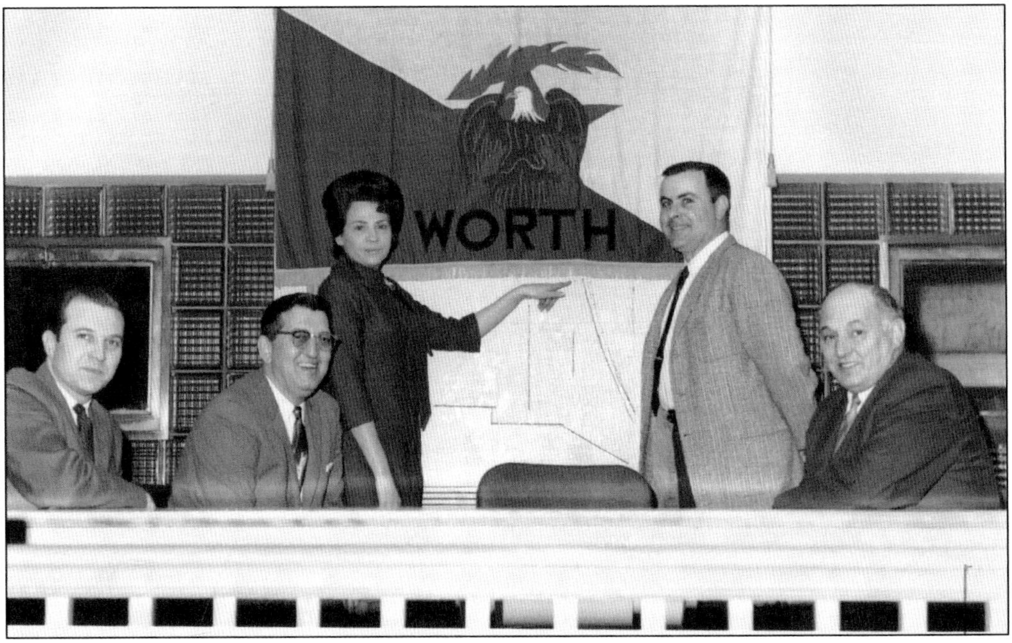

The Worth-Palos Park District was formed by a referendum in 1965 and consisted of a five-member board of commissioners. Pictured here are members of the first park board, from left to right, Robert Pinson, James long, Betty Micetic, Donald Christine, and Frank Stahlak. Meetings were held at the village hall.

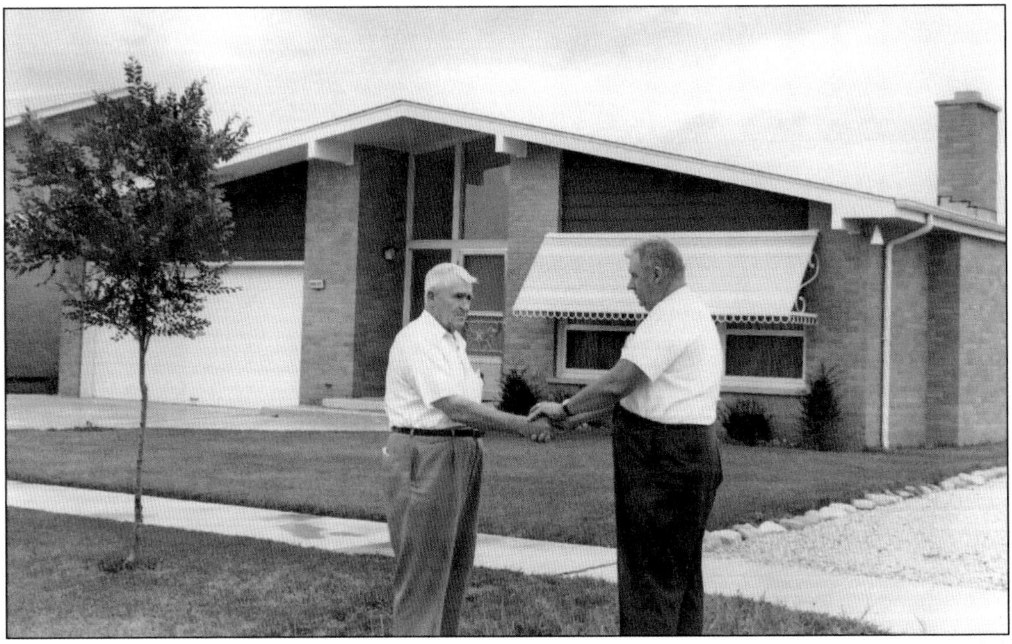

Peaks Park was originally owned by the Village of Worth after developer Wayne Peak (right) donated five acres of land around the neighborhood of his development. After the establishment of the park, the property was transferred to the district in 1966. In this photograph, developer Wayne Peak is shaking the hand of his father, Lloyd, after the last home in the development was completed and given to Lloyd.

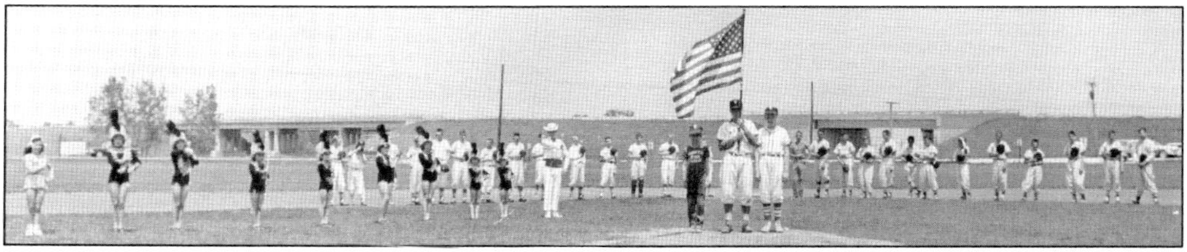

The opening game for the Worth Boys Club took place in Peaks Park in the spring of 1966. This field was the second home field location for the team. Interstate 294 can be seen to the rear of the field. The interstate cut almost through the middle of town.

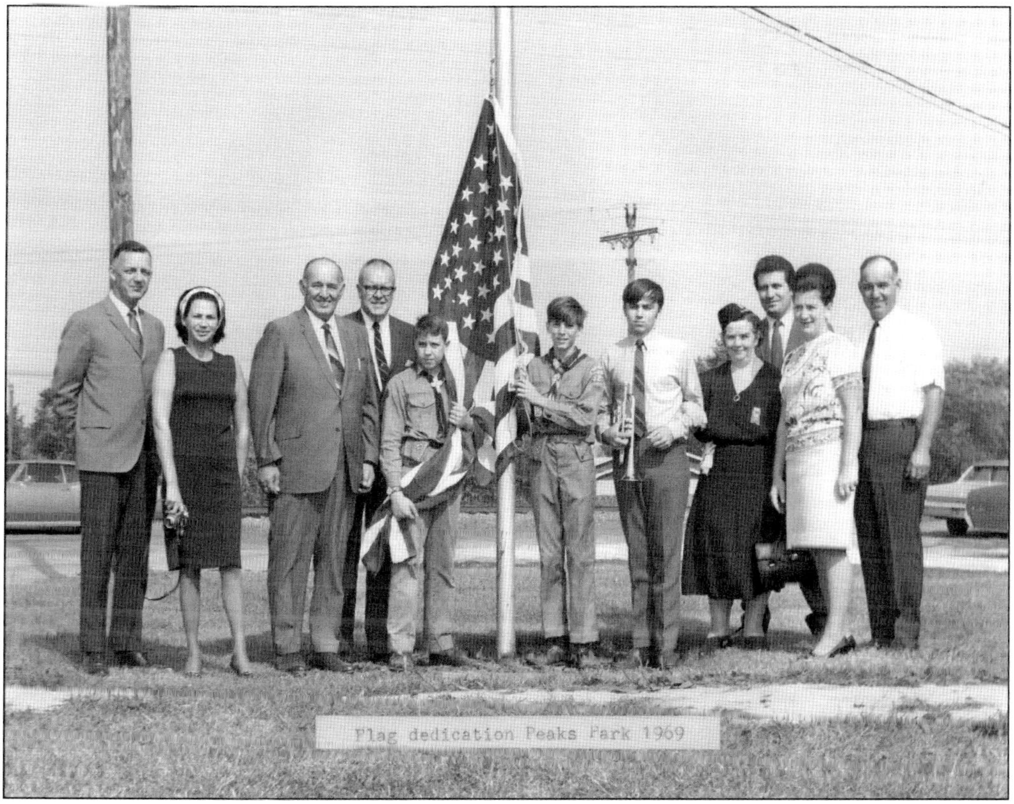

A flagpole was dedicated at Peaks Park in 1969. A flag that was flown over the US Capitol was presented by Congressman Derwinski as Boy Scouts John Schmidt and Dean Edwards raise the flag. Bill Boyars played the bugle. The adults taking part in the ceremony were, from left to right, Pres. Walt Kerkstra, Betty Micetic, Frank Stahlak, Congressman Edward Derwinski, John Schmidt, Dean Edwards, Bill Boyars, unidentified, district president Bob Cadell, Kay Whalen, and Frank Homerding. Ray Foyle donated the pole, and the Girl Scouts planted a blue spruce.

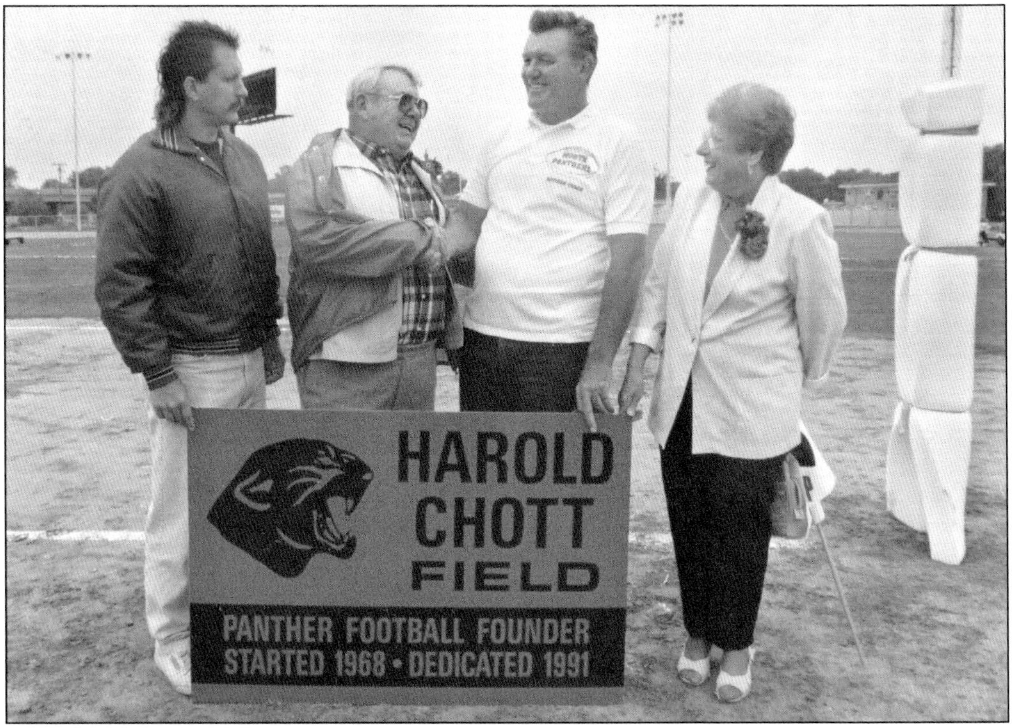

The fields located in Peaks Park were dedicated to resident Harold Chott in 1990. Coach Chott founded the Worth-Ridge Panthers, a youth football club. From left to right are Rudy Bajorek, Harold Chott, Bob O'Conner, and Pauline Chott.

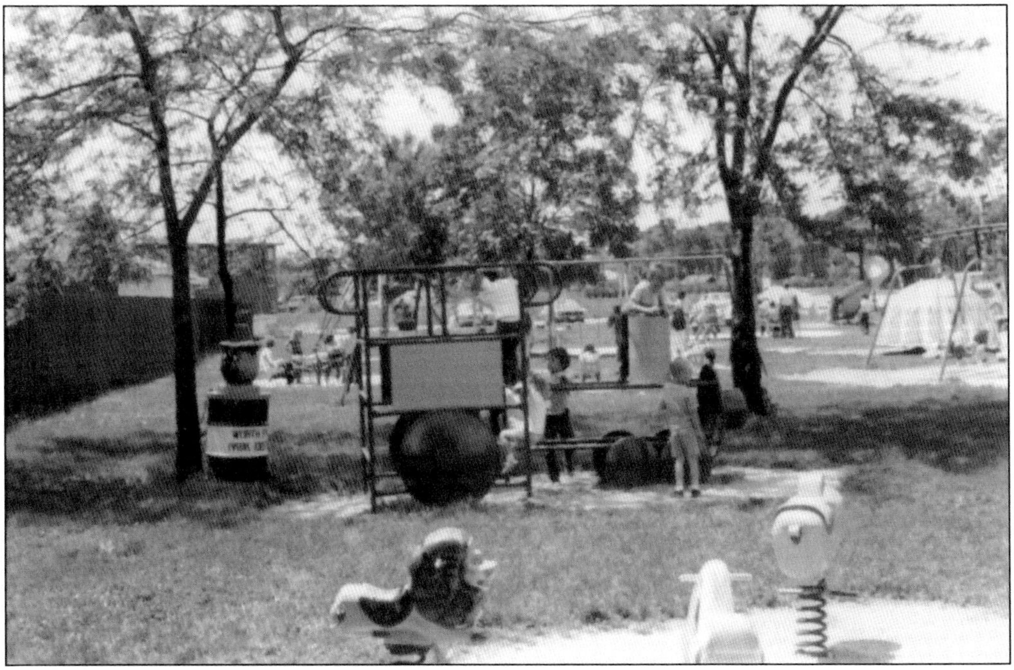

New playground equipment was installed and brought a new "locomotive" to Worth. This train made many families happy in the early 1970s at Peaks Park.

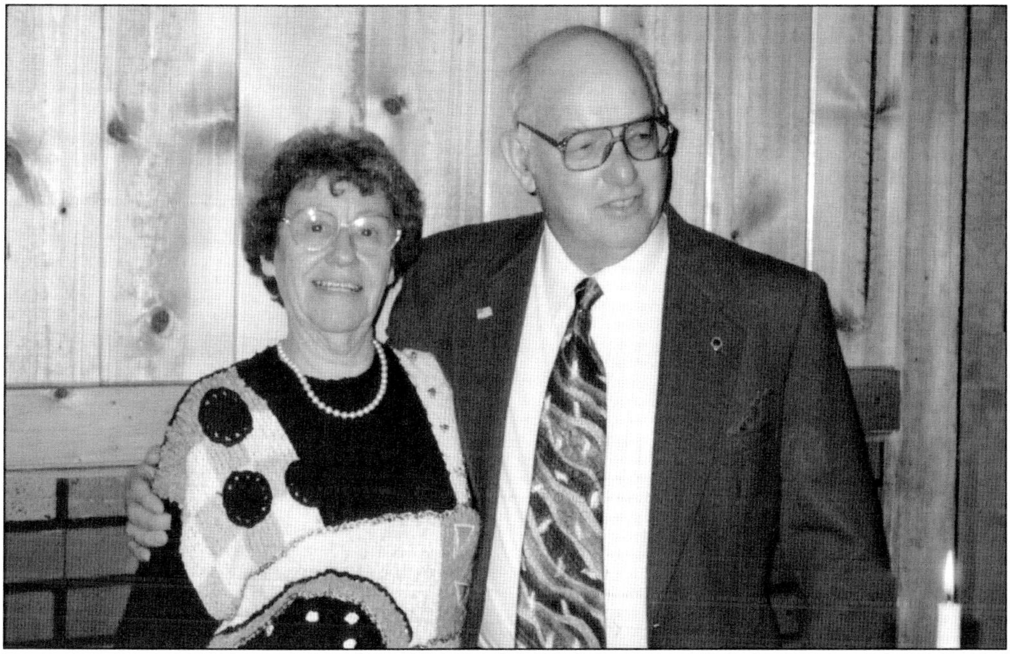

In 1992, the recreation building at Peaks Park was dedicated to Helen Goy. Helen worked for the park district for 39 years as secretary treasurer. Prior to the construction of the building, the park district operated out of Helen's home. The building was constructed in 1968. Pictured here is a photograph of Helen Goy with longtime commissioner Frank Homerding.

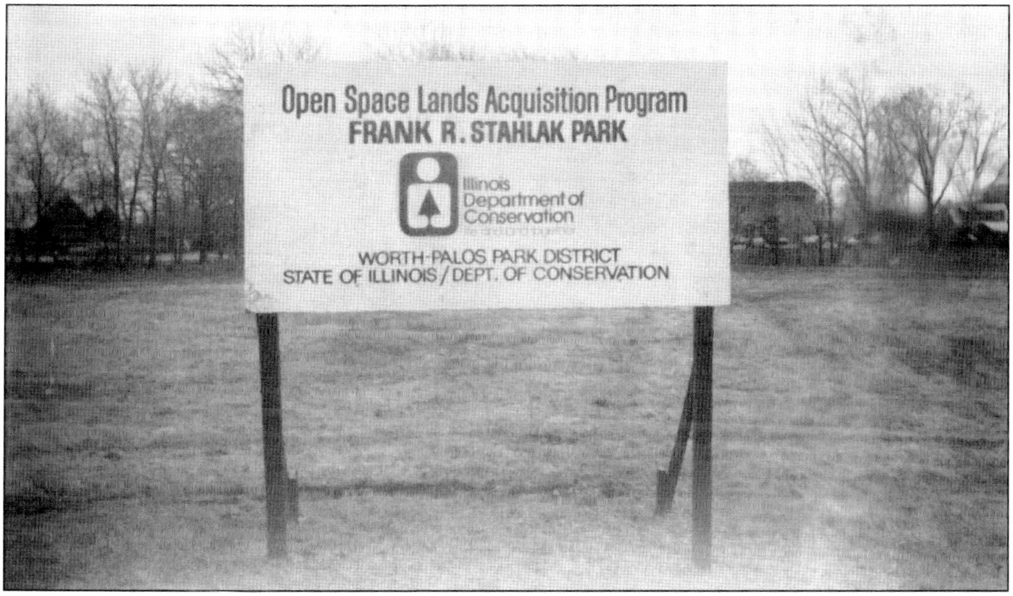

Frank Stahlak was a community activist and sat on the original Worth Park District Board of Commissioners. The park located at 112th Street and Natchez Avenue was named in his honor, as Frank was the first president of the district on May 3, 1965. Stahlak Park was purchased with Open Space Land Acquisition and Development (OSLAD) money in 1975. It was developed in 1979 with help from the Worth Ridge School. A 220-yard track, playground, and small ball field were installed with a physical fitness course built inside the track.

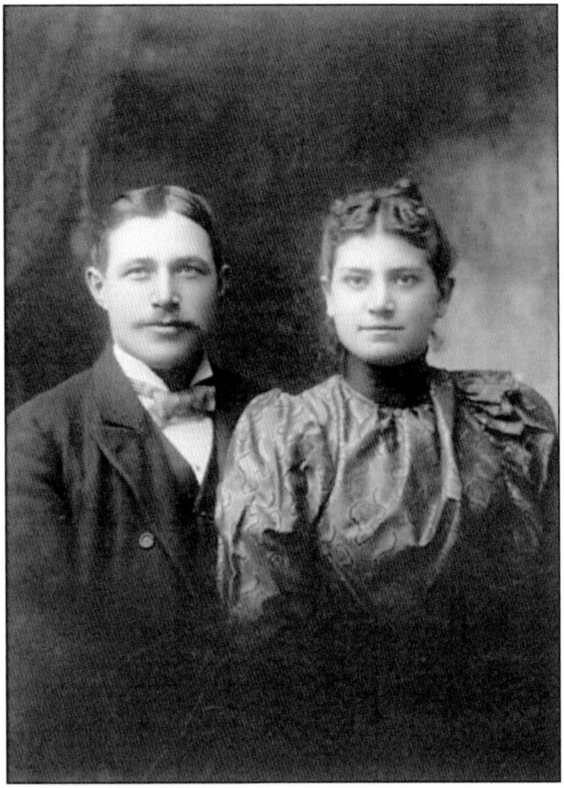

The original name of the surrounding area was named "Hildebrandt's Pond," after Fred and Emma (Preller) Hildebrandt's 163-acre farm. Known in the village for dense trees, coyotes, and an ice-skating pond near the northwest end of the city limits, pioneers would often enjoy ice-skating and horseback riding on the south end of their property. The Hildebrandts owned the Worth Hotel located at 111th Street and Depot Avenue. The name Worthwoods Park came in 1967 after the village officially transferred the half-acre property to the Worth Park District. A tennis court was added in the spring of 1975.

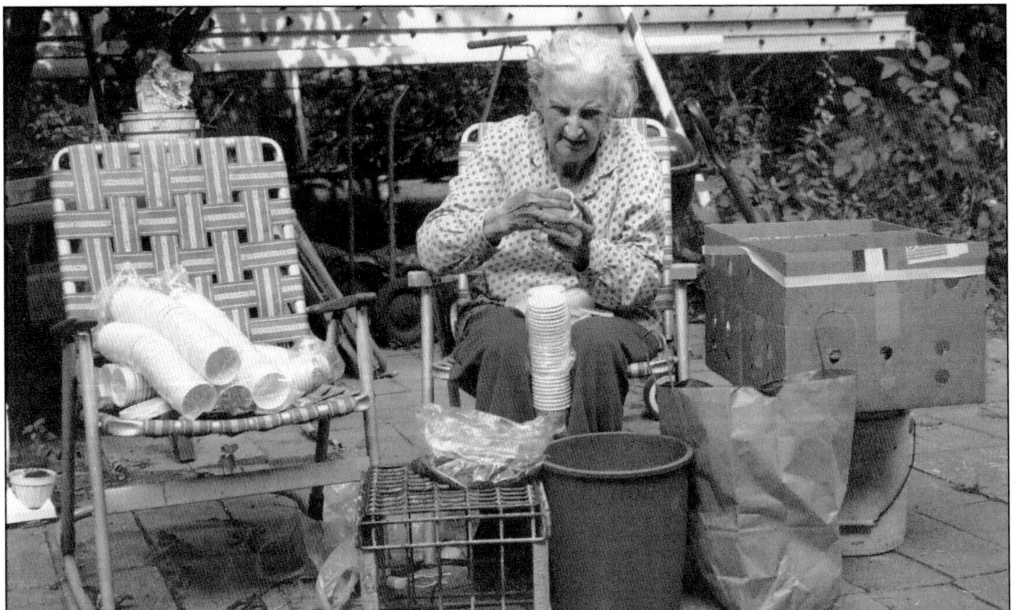

Ruth Cantwell, social activist in Worth, was known for her dedication to environmental issues in the village. She was nicknamed the "Ladybug Lady;" Ruth imported millions of ladybugs into the village to help with an aphid problem. A tree is dedicated in her honor and is located at Worthwoods Park.

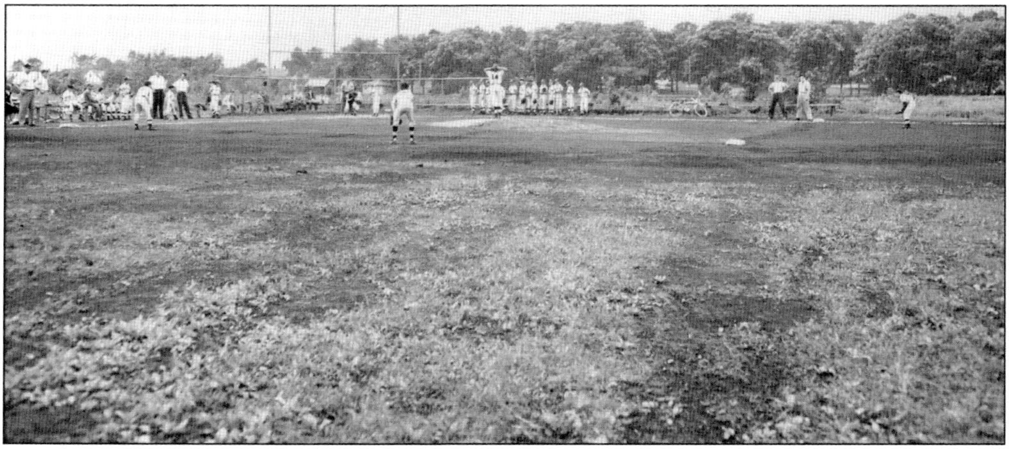

Originally known as the Wilson-Wagner property, this park was purchased in 1970 after a long court battle. The Wilson-Wagner property was originally a lettuce and cabbage farm on the north end and is a beautiful, wooded, five-acre tract of land. The property was host to the annual Worth Days event for several years in the mid-1960s and eventually converted to a baseball field. In January 1975, the Worth-Palos Park District agreed to a land exchange with the Illinois Department of Transportation. The Norfolk & Western Railroad was planning to build a railroad overpass at 111th Street and Harlem Avenue, which would require the purchase of some of the property. The transportation department took 40 feet of land on a temporary basis and 20 feet of land on a permanent basis along the north and west tracks. In exchange, the park was given 1,249 square feet to replace the property taken. The transportation department also agreed to move a baseball diamond and field at 111th Street and Harlem Avenue to the north end of the park at the cost of $5,065.

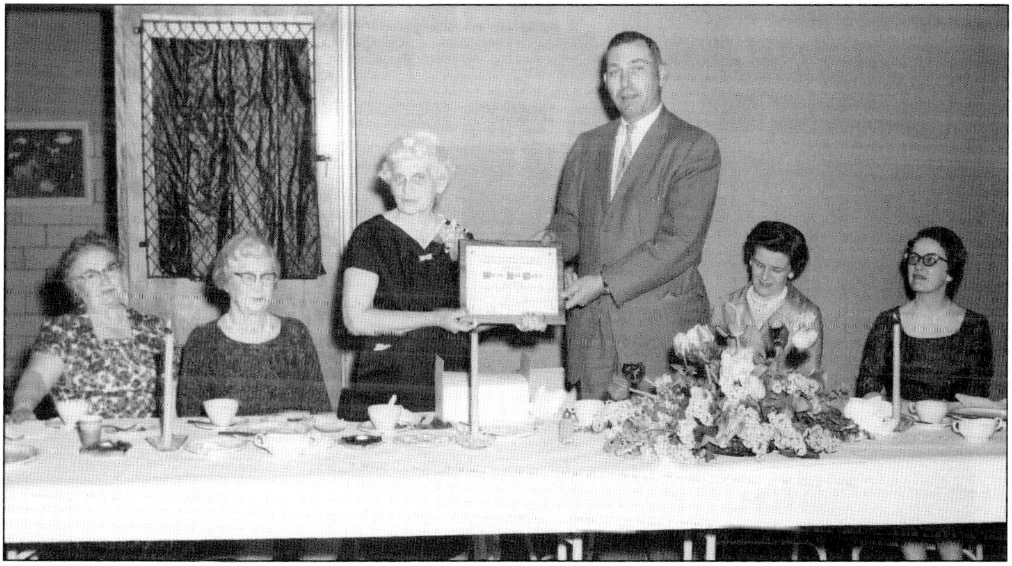

Gale Moore served for three terms on the District No. 127 School Board. He was the chairman for the Citizens Advisory Committee, which promoted a successful tax rate increase referendum. Moore participated in the Worth Boys Club as treasurer for the organization and was a devoted citizen. His untimely death occurred on March 27, 1968. From left to right are Marguerite McGovern, Ethel Goddard, Florence Jurlow, school board president Gale Moore, Clara Moore, and Rosemary Lucas, superintendent of schools.

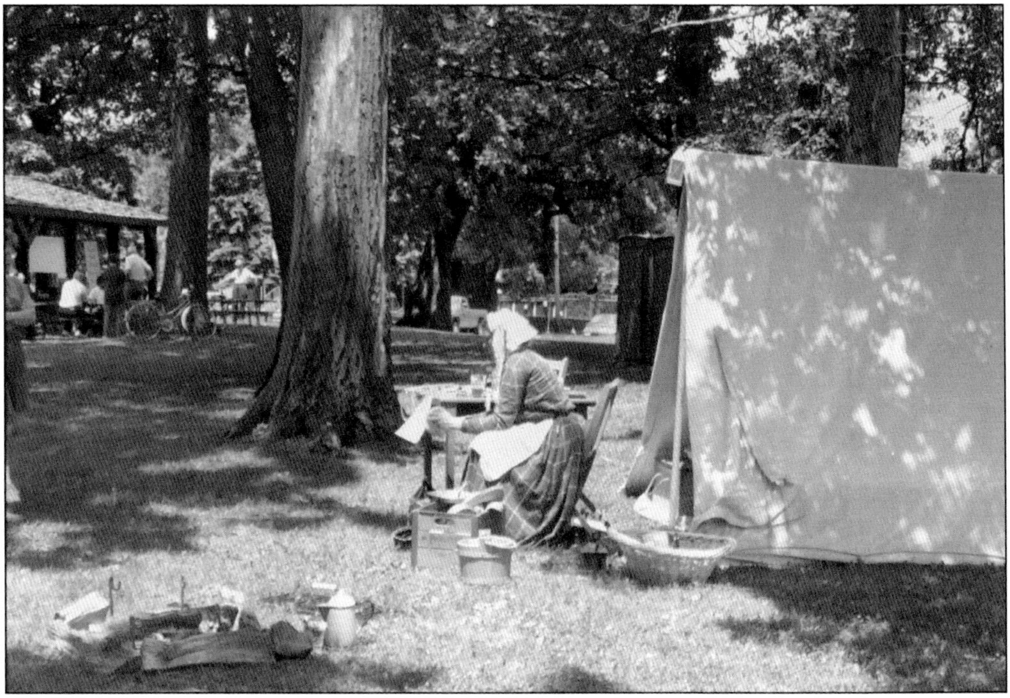

A pavilion was added in the spring of 1975, complete with electricity, parking, and benches. The park was the permanent site of the Civil War Days, organized by the Worth Park District Historical Museum in the 1990s, and continues to be a favorite picnic spot for residents and nonresidents alike.

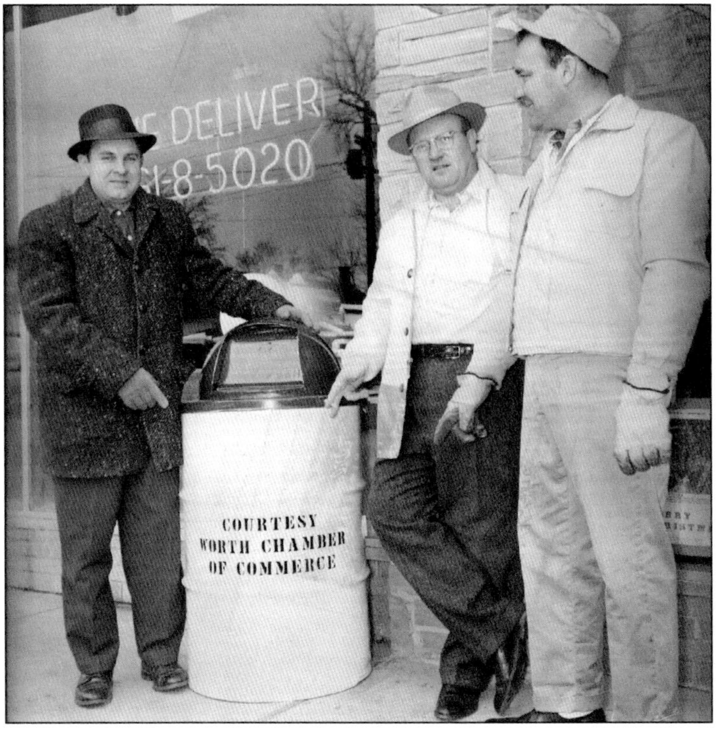

Baldwin Park is a small park located at 109th Street and Nashville Avenue. The property was purchased and donated by trustee Jack Baldwin in honor of his son, Officer Jack Baldwin Jr., who died of leukemia in 1977. Jack was a trustee in 1965 and active in many organizations in town, including the chamber of commerce. In this photograph are, from left to right, Jack Baldwin, Red Moore, and Bud Zuidema.

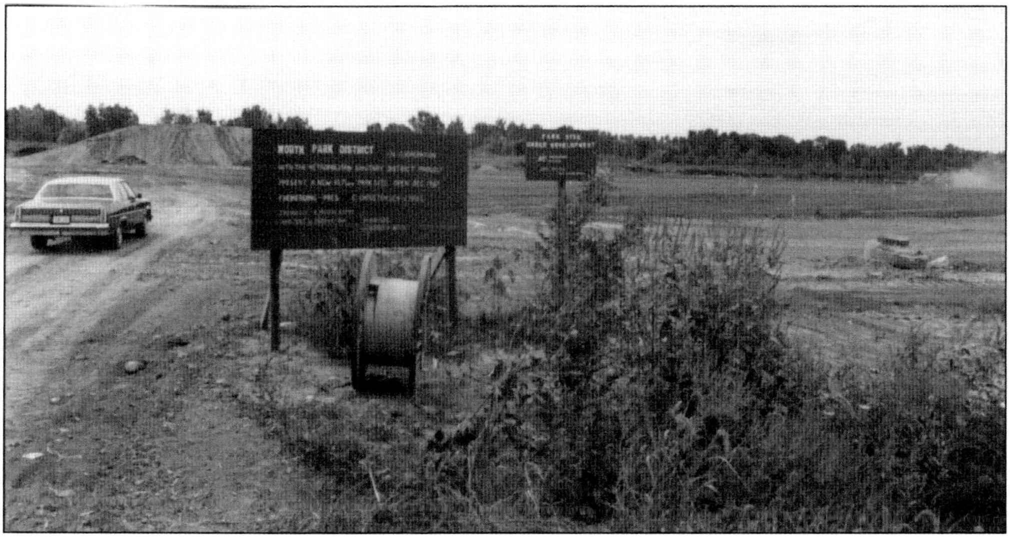

The Worth-Palos Park District acquired 5.75 acres of land in March 1976. Commissioner Frank Homerding cited the support of the Worth Boys Club for making it possible. The park district planned to develop the land into baseball and football fields, a sled hill, tennis courts, and a new play area. The land was originally leased by the Metropolitan Sanitary District (MSD) to the Harlem Avenue Petroleum Warehousing Company.

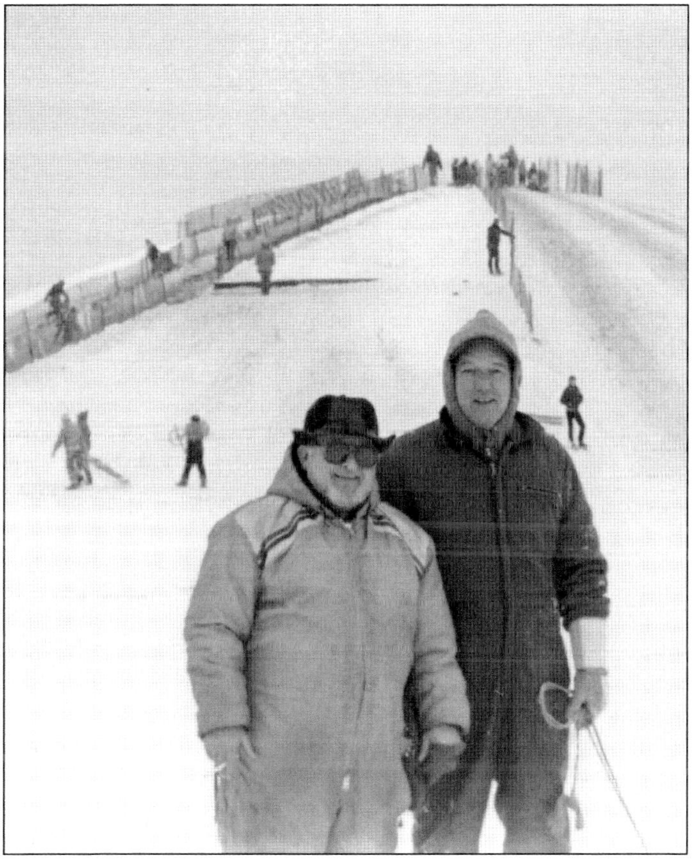

On April 10, 1982, Worth Park District signed a lease with the Metropolitan Water Reclamation District (MWRD) for a 13-acre parcel of land for a period of 39 years. With the help of Butch Harper and park commissioner Frank Homerding, a large hill was constructed on the parcel and proved to be an extremely popular place for sledding in the winter. The park was named after Frank Homerding in 1983. Frank Homerding and his wife, Lou, were instrumental in the Worth Days Committee. Commissioner Kozlowski (left) is seen with Homerding after making a successful slide down the hill.

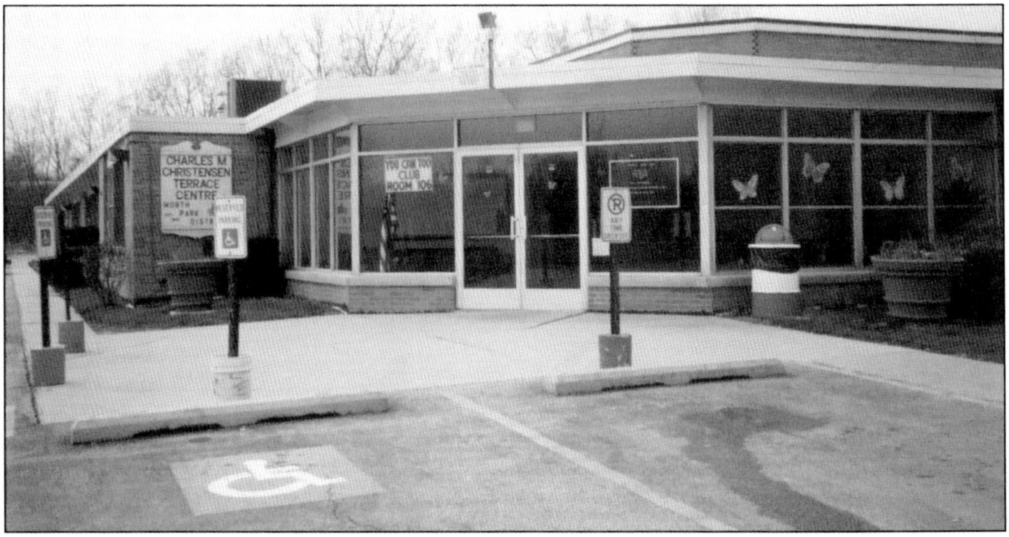

The old Worth Terrace School building was purchased by the Worth Park District in 1985 and was renamed the Charles M. Christensen Terrace Center in 1989 in honor of the trustee who had served 16 years on the board. The building includes the Karen L. Jones Memorial Indoor Park and Liz Lukacek Tot Lot Preschool. The acquisition allowed the Worth Park District to expand its program offerings, such as the Recreation After School program (RAS), which started in 1990, and Tot Lot Preschool. The Terrace Center is home to the Worth Historical Museum, which held its grand opening on April 23, 1995. Prior to owning this building, many park programs were held at the elementary school.

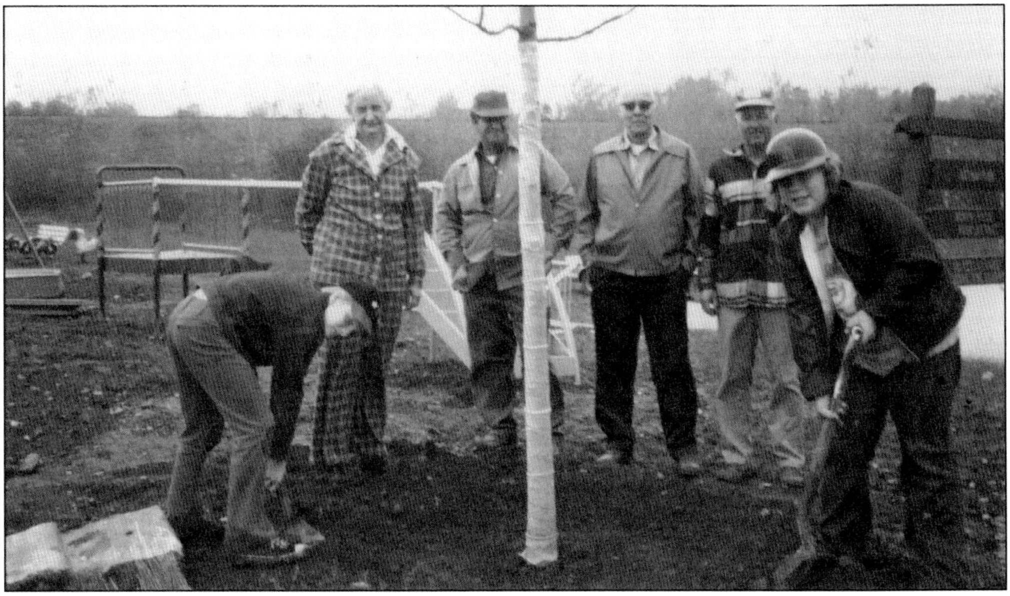

In January 1975, the board of commissioners approved a lease of property at 115th Street and Beloit Avenue from the Sag Warehouse and Terminal. The parcel of land was 300 by 300 feet. An addition was to be built on the present garage, totaling $2,000 for a 40-by-14-foot addition. The recreation director, Tom O'Neil, put in the request for more storage space. Planting a tree on Arbor Day in 1975 are Ruth Cantwell, Bacil Hurr, commissioner Charles Christensen, and commissioner Frank Homerding, and two unidentified boys.

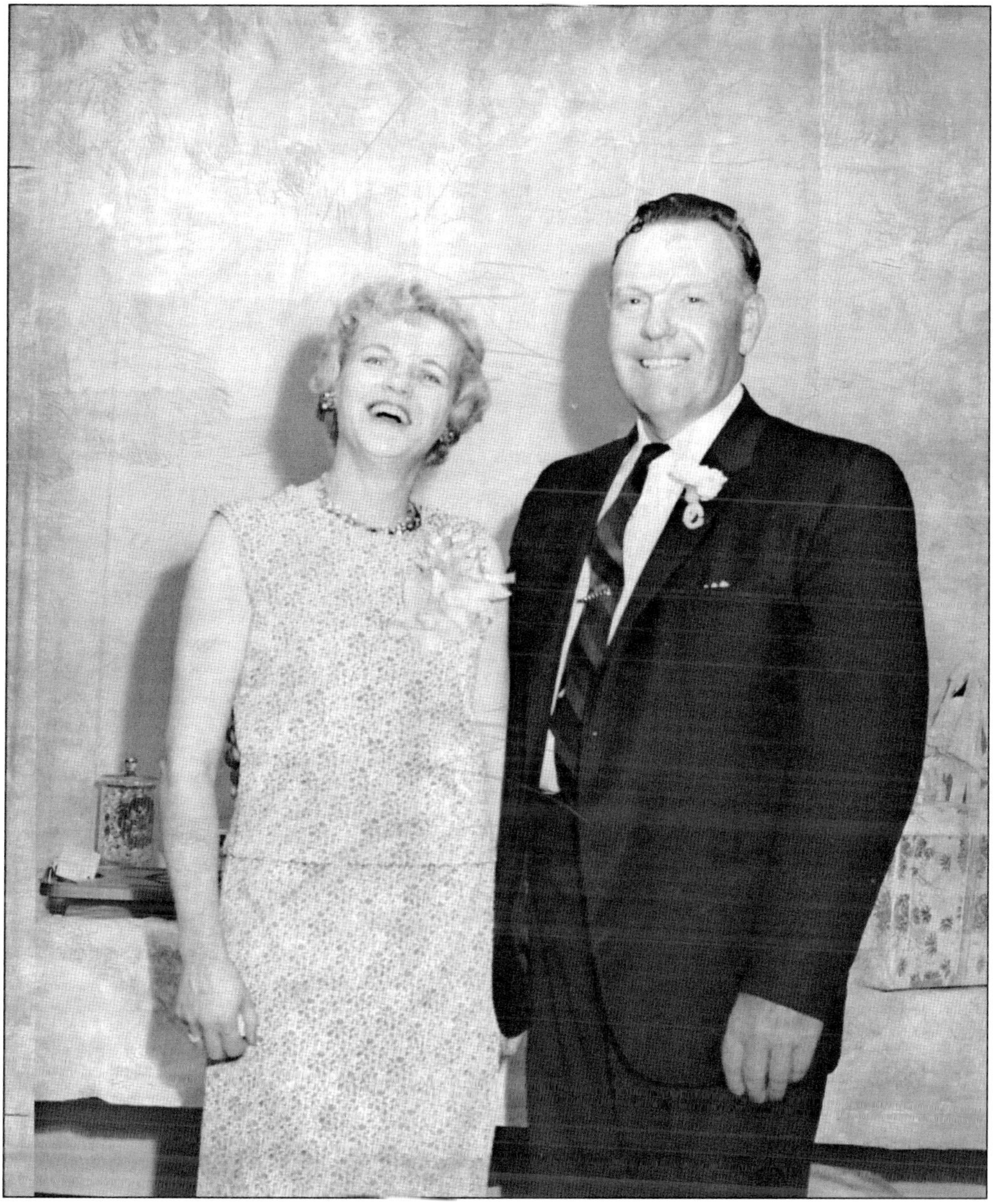

The park located at 115th Street and Beloit Avenue was named in the honor of Juanita Altman, a longtime village resident and trustee. Juanita descended from one of Worth's oldest families. Her great-grandfather John Crandall built the first house in 1858. Her grandfather Ben Crandall was a police magistrate, and her father, Dan Crandall, was Worth's first police chief. Altman Park is now owned by the Village of Worth under the name Betty Mattera Field. Pictured with Juanita is her husband, Jack, in 1964. Smile Park was dedicated in May 1975, after a contest to name the park was sponsored by the Worth-Palos Park District and Dr. Rosemary Lucas of the elementary school district No. 127. The "Podlasek property" was originally purchased in November 1974 and temporarily named Tot Lot. The cost of the property was $8,000 and is 85 by 135 feet. Scott McGrath won first prize and received a savings bond for the winning name change. He was given the honor of planting the Norway maple tree donated by landscaper Bacil Hurr.

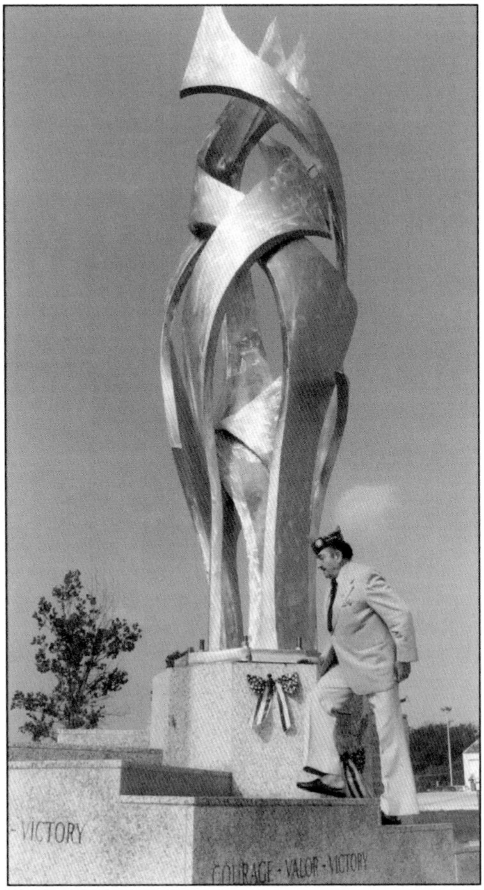

The Veteran's Memorial Park, located at 111th Street and Harlem Avenue, was dedicated on May 23, 1993. Instrumental in the dedication and design of the memorial was Alfred W. Grajek, a veteran of World War II and state commander for Chapter No. 84 of the Disabled American Veterans. The "Eternal Flame" monument was designed by Bruce Niemi of Gurnee, Illinois. The flame stands 18 feet tall, and the granite monument is 16 feet long, 8 feet wide, and 6 feet high. Grajek is seen inspecting the flame prior to the unveiling.

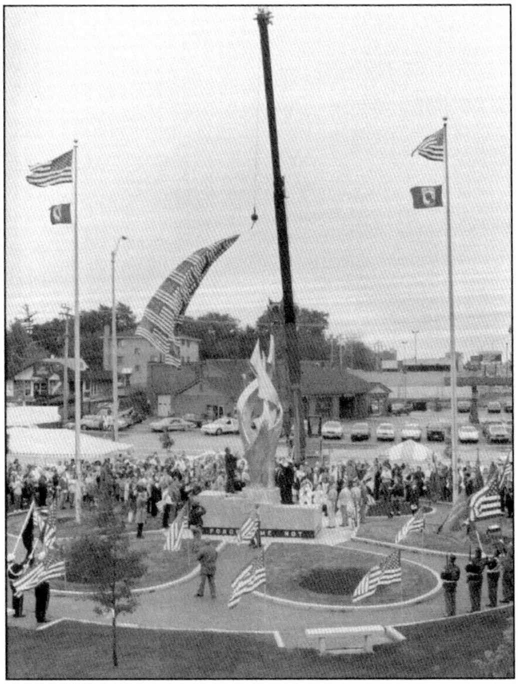

Through the Illinois state legislative process, 13,000 square feet of land was purchased on the corner of 111th Street and Harlem Avenue for $1. A committee was formed to raise the $200,000 necessary to complete the project. With the help of citizens, legislators, and community groups, the dedication occurred in 1993. Much of the labor was donated. The park district maintains the property.

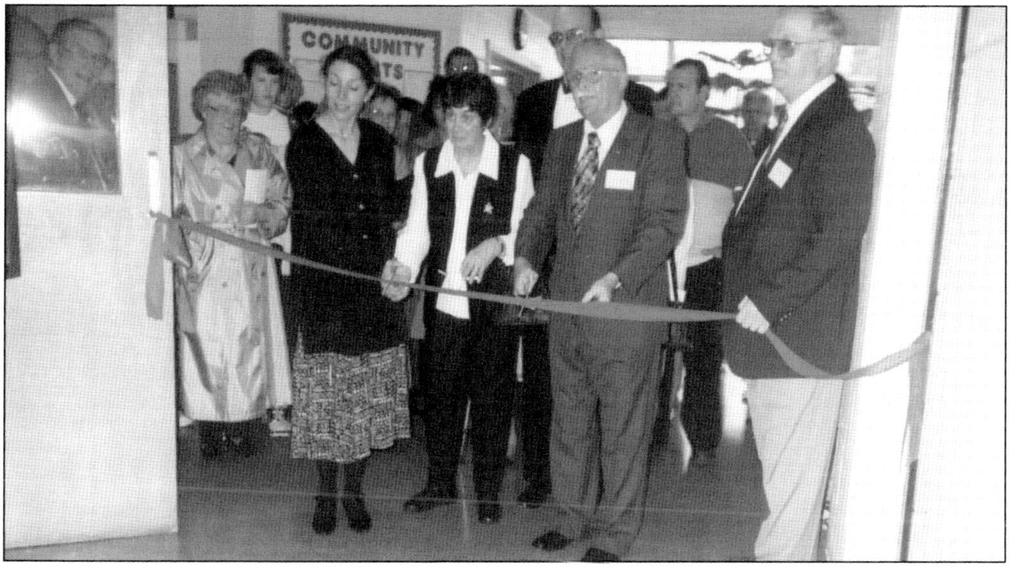

The Worth Park District dedicated a museum inside of the Worth Terrace Center on April 23, 1995. Cutting the ribbon are, from left to right, curator Tiina Benck Russ, Agnes Daniels, former park board commissioner Marvin Christianson, and commissioner Robert Fickes. Behind them is president of the park board Jim Kennelly. Tiina, Agnes, and Marvin were instrumental in the formation of the museum. The museum was opened in the former teachers' lounge when the building was a school.

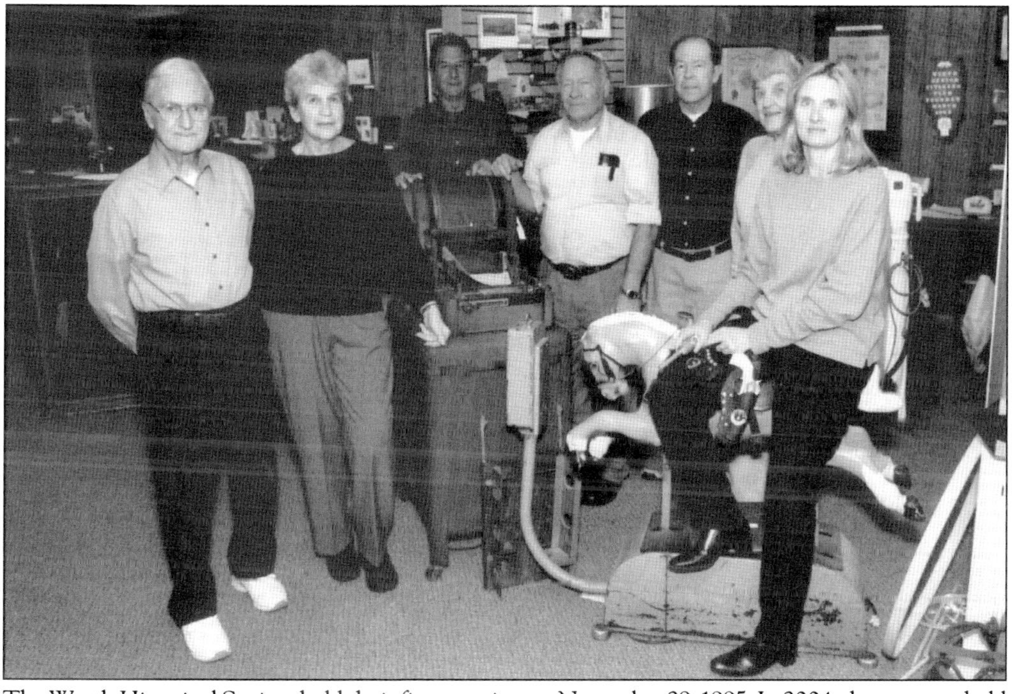

The Worth Historical Society held their first meeting on November 29, 1995. In 2004, the museum held a grand reopening in a larger location within the same building. Seen in 2006 in their new location were founding members, from left to right, former village president Dan Kumingo, Adele Benck, John Schiera, Bob Burns, Don Schmiege, Agnes Mrakovic, and curator Christine Brooks.

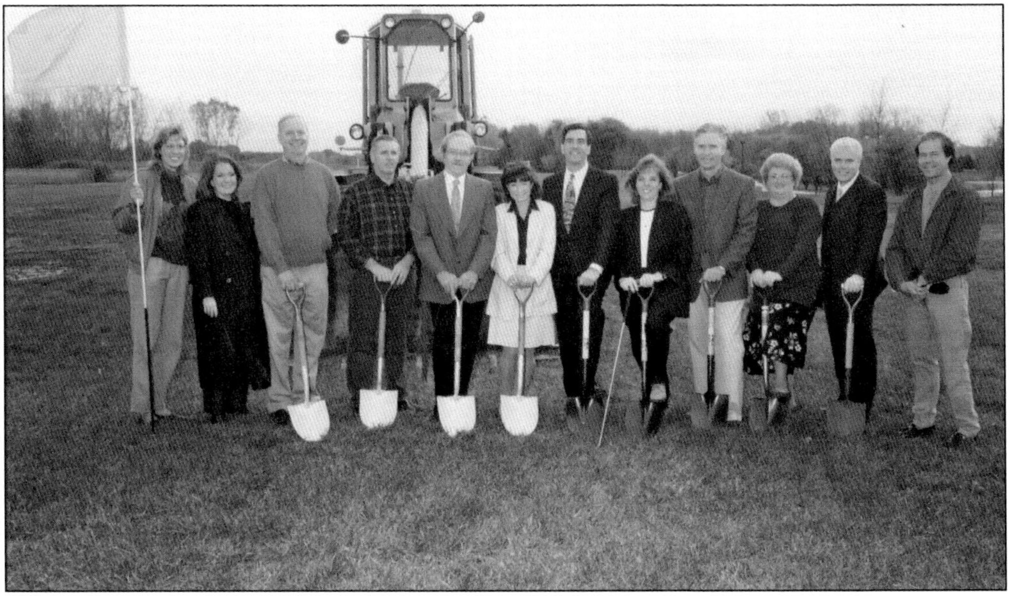

In 1996, the Village of Worth entered into an agreement with the MWRD to lease property along the Cal-Sag to build a golf course. Ground was officially broken for the Water's Edge Golf Club on October 26, 1996. Pictured are, from left to right, Bernie Bilder, MWRD commissioner Pat Young, Bob Douglas, John Kooyenga, trustee Frank Bonham, trustee Georgia Duffy, Mayor Jim Bilder, trustee Sharon Wiernga, Sen. Pat O'Malley, clerk Betty Mattera, trustee Mark Meany, and Todd Krzyskowski. The course was completed in 1998.

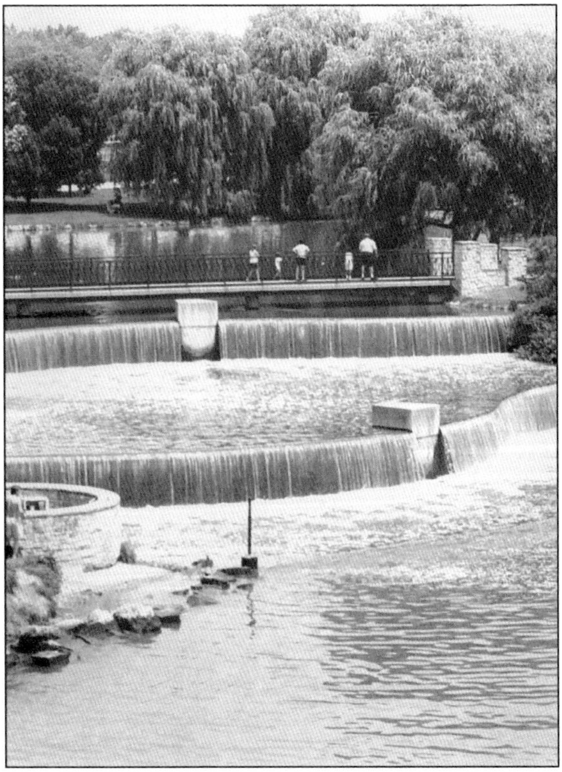

The Sidestream Elevated Pool Aeration Stations along the Calumet Channel opened in 1992. It provides aeration for the Cal-Sag and serves as a natural filter for the waterway. The area includes a multipurpose trail and benches.

BIBLIOGRAPHY

Christensen, Marvin. *History of Worth*. Worth Park District, 1995.

Daniels, Agnes and John. "A History of the Worth Volunteer Fired Department, 1925–1962." *Worth Record*, 1962.

Gallager, Joyce, Dave McNamara, and Elsie McNaughton. *A Town of Worth: Yesterday . . . Today*. Chicago, IL: St. Xavier College, December 1976.

"The Story of Worth: 50 Years As A Village." *Worth-Palos Reporter*, August 1964.

Worth Park District Historical Museum and Historical Society. "The History of Worth." Worth Park District, 1996.

———. "The History of Worth, 2nd ed." Worth Park District, 2006.